LEVEL
E

Teacher's Guide

Comprehension PLUS

Dr. Diane Lapp
Dr. James Flood

Modern Curriculum Press

Program Reviewers

Carmen Arzt
Reading Recovery/Resource Teacher
LaPuente, California

Meg Ballantyne
Literacy (Reading) Specialist
Commerce City, Colorado

Sharon Bonner
Literacy Resource Teacher
Glen Ridge, New Jersey

Alison Heath
Classroom Teacher
Houston, Texas

Carrie Jefferson
Teacher on Special Assignment
Antioch, California

Bonnie Nadick
Reading Specialist
Chicago, Illinois

Sr. Mary Jean Raymond
Teacher/Educational Consultant
Cleveland, Ohio

Bess Ann Sommers
Language Arts Consultant
Canton, Ohio

Fran Threewit
Reading Specialist
Kenwood, California

Celebrity Authors

Joyce Annette Barnes, "A Long Walk Home," Lesson 3
Joseph Bruchac, "My Greatest Teachers," Lesson 27
J. Lynett Gillette, "The Death of the Dinosaurs," Lesson 6
Ann Hodgman, "Pets I Have Known," Lesson 11
Norma Johnston, "Make New Friends," Lesson 23
Trinka Hakes Noble, "Bigfoot," Lesson 5
Betsy Sterman, "Onions to the Rescue," Lesson 20
Lou Ann Walker, "Erik Weihenmayer," Lesson 1

Program Development

Executive Editors: Leslie Feierstone-Barna, Magali Iglesias
Supervising Editor: Cindy Kane
Teacher's Guide Editor: Mary Bulkot
Design Development: MKR Design, New York, NY
Design: Scott Golem
Illustrations: T50: Don Larson/Mapping Specialists, LTD.

ISBN: 0-7652-2190-X
Printed in the United States of America

5 6 7 8 9 10   09 08 07 06 05

Modern Curriculum Press

Pearson Learning Group

1-800-321-3106
www.pearsonlearning.com

Contents

Teacher's Guide Lessons

Graphic Organizers Blackline Masters

Overview of COMPREHENSION PLUS

Comprehension Plus is a six-level comprehension program that provides explicit instruction and practice in major comprehension skills and strategies students need to derive meaning from written text. The Student's Editions and Teacher's Guides for grades 1–6 (Levels A–F) are designed to help students master the most frequently tested comprehension skills. *Comprehension Plus* provides another plus by giving students opportunities for application of comprehension skills in related study skill areas. For example, after students have developed skill in recognizing main idea and supporting details, they are given the opportunity to apply this skill to related study skills such as outlining, summarizing, paraphrasing, and using an encyclopedia.

Thorough Instruction

The basic lesson plan in *Comprehension Plus* provides another big plus. It is based on a simple, fundamental premise: Students can be taught the strategies that will help them comprehend written text. Recent studies have shown that in order to improve in a specific comprehension skill, students must be aware that the skill exists. They must also understand the dynamics involved in applying the skill in a meaningful context. Instruction directed to the students and accompanied by meaningful practice improves proficiency in comprehension.

The biggest plus in *Comprehension Plus* is that students are given much more than practice. They are given direct instruction in the strategy behind each comprehension skill as well as practice activities that allow them to apply the skill in a meaningful context.

Comprehensive Scope and Sequence

The focus skills that comprise the scope and sequence of *Comprehension Plus* are widely accepted as the most important comprehension skills students need to understand a variety of written texts. Students learn the skills that are tested on the following major standardized tests:

- Stanford Achievement Test (SAT-9)
- California Achievement Test (CAT-5)
- TerraNova
- California Test of Basic Skills (CTBS-5)
- Iowa Test of Basic Skills (ITBS-M)
- Metropolitan Achievement Test (MAT-7)
- National Assessment of Educational Progress

The Skills Index on page T9 of every Teacher's Guide provides a complete listing of every focus skill and maintenance skill and lists the lesson in which the skill can be found.

Range of Text Difficulty

All reading passages included in *Comprehension Plus* have been evaluated using either the Spache or Dale-Chall formula for determining text difficulty. The following chart provides the range for each level of the program.

Comprehension Plus Level	Grade Level	Range of Text Difficulty Formula	Range of Scores
A	1	Spache	1.0 – 1.6
B	2	Spache	1.8 – 2.6
C	3	Spache	2.8 – 3.6
D	4	Spache	3.8 – 4.6
E	5	Dale-Chall	4.8 – 5.6
F	6	Dale-Chall	5.8 – 6.6

Using the COMPREHENSION PLUS Teacher's Guide

The Teacher's Guide has everything you need to help students learn and practice the comprehension strategies, study skills, and word study skills they need to succeed. Carefully sequenced instruction, application of focus skills, maintenance skills, and assessment tests help students master the key comprehension skills and strategies necessary for them to understand written text.

Focus Skill
• The focus skill and instructional objective are clearly presented at the beginning of each lesson.

Teaching Tips
• Provide valuable information about the purpose for teaching each skill.
• Help you pinpoint students' understanding of each focus skill.

Reviewed and Maintained Skills
• Two or three comprehension skills, one phonics skill, and one writing skill are maintained within each lesson.

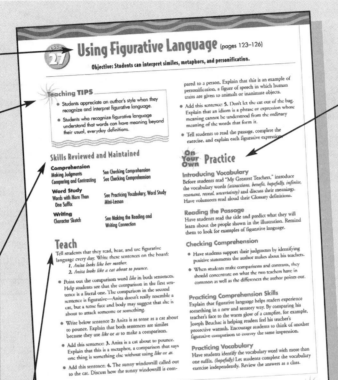

On Your Own Practice
Easy-to-use teaching tips help you assign and assess five practice opportunities:
• **Introducing Vocabulary**
Aids students' understanding of the passage by preteaching the key words.
• **Reading the Passage**
Prereading discussions help students get ready to read the passage and learn the focus skill.
• **Checking Comprehension**
Expands on the answers to the two comprehension questions in the Student Edition to help you determine if students understood the passage.
• **Practicing Comprehension Skills**
Provides tips to help students apply the focus skill.
• **Practicing Vocabulary**
Reviews key words in each passage and identifies the words that focus on the featured word study or phonics skill.

Teach
A quick, step-by-step mini-lesson for teaching the focus skill through interactive activities.
• The skill is presented or modeled for the student through a familiar, real-life example.
• Students get a first-hand opportunity to interact with the focus skill while completing the activity with the teacher.

On Your Own Apply
Helpful suggestions for reviewing and evaluating students' writing, as well as cross-references to related lessons in **Modern Curriculum Press's The Write Direction**, reinforce the reading-writing connection.

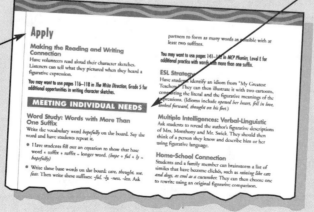

Meeting Individual Needs
Support your students' diverse needs with meaningful activities that interest all students. Each lesson includes
• an activity that reviews the phonics maintenance skill.
• an activity that makes the lesson more accessible to students acquiring English.
• an activity that addresses one or more of the Multiple Intelligences.
• a simple activity related to the focus skill for students to take home and share with family members.

Using the COMPREHENSION PLUS Student Edition

Student-friendly and designed to create meaningful reading experiences, each lesson in the Student Editions is designed to help students master a skill in context.

Easy as 1-2-3. Teach. Check for Understanding. Practice.

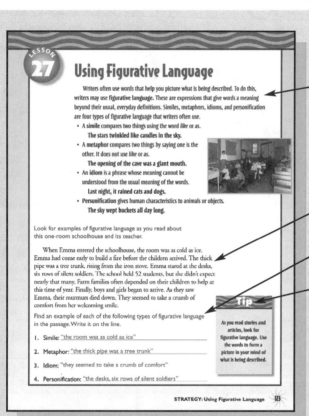

LESSON 27
Using Figurative Language

Writers often use words that help you picture what is being described. To do this, writers may use figurative language. These are expressions that give words a meaning beyond their usual, everyday definitions. Similes, metaphors, idioms, and personification are four types of figurative language that writers often use.

- A **simile** compares two things using the word *like* or *as*.
  The stars twinkled like candles in the sky.
- A **metaphor** compares two things by saying one is the other. It does not use *like* or *as*.
  The opening of the cave was a giant mouth.
- An **idiom** is a phrase whose meaning cannot be understood from the usual meaning of the words.
  Last night, it rained cats and dogs.
- **Personification** gives human characteristics to animals or objects.
  The sky wept buckets all day long.

Look for examples of figurative language as you read about this one-room schoolhouse and its teacher.

When Emma entered the schoolhouse, the room was as cold as ice. Emma had come early to build a fire before the children arrived. The thick pipe was a tree trunk, rising from the iron stove. Emma stared at the desks, six rows of silent soldiers. The school held 52 students, but she didn't expect nearly that many. Farm families often depended on their children to help at this time of year. Finally, boys and girls began to arrive. As they saw Emma, their murmurs died down. They seemed to take a crumb of comfort from her welcoming smile.

Find an example of each of the following types of figurative language in the passage. Write it on the line.

1. Simile: "the room was as cold as ice"
2. Metaphor: "the thick pipe was a tree trunk"
3. Idiom: "they seemed to take a crumb of comfort"
4. Personification: "the desks, six rows of silent soldiers"

Tip
As you read stories and articles, look for figurative language. Use the words to form a picture in your mind of what is being described.

STRATEGY: Using Figurative Language 123

Direct Instruction
Clear, student-friendly instruction introduces students to the focus skill.

Guided Practice
- Students are guided through a brief passage that clearly illustrates the skill.
- Students then have an opportunity to apply the learning through a short practice activity.

Tip
A helpful tip reinforces instruction and helps students remember how to recognize and use the skill.

On Your Own Reading Passage
- High-interest reading passages engage readers immediately.
- These are stories and articles your students will want to read, covering a wide variety of fictional and nonfictional genres.

Celebrity Authors
Several selections in each level have been written by well-known trade book authors, such as Joseph Bruchac, Trinka Hakes Noble, Ann Hodgman, Norma Johnston, Betsy Sterman, and more.

On Your Own
Read the following story. Notice where the author has used figurative language. Use the expressions to form pictures in your mind.

My Greatest Teachers 🍎
by Joseph Bruchac

School isn't easy. It doesn't matter if you're a shrimp with thick glasses, as I was, or a sports giant. There are times when you wish you were grown up and graduated. If you're lucky, in the midst of that sea of uncertainty, you will find teachers who draw out the best in you. Let me tell you about two of mine.

The first was Mrs. Monthony. When I first saw her, I fell in love with her. Her hair was as red as autumn leaves. Her face was warm as the glow of a campfire. I was the smallest kid in second grade, always chattering nonstop like a bluejay.

Mrs. Monthony opened her heart to me. When I held up my trusty pencil box in show-and-tell to describe how moving a certain panel would reveal a secret compartment, I looked at her hopefully. Would she be yawning in boredom like my classmates? Instead, she nodded her head and smiled. My voice slowed down, my nervousness was gone.

I saw Mrs. Monthony recently. Her hair had burned gray as ashes, but her eyes still sparkled like the first stars in the sky. "Hello, my precocious second grader," she said. "Remember that pencil box?"

The second memorable teacher was Charles Swick. His house was just up the road from my grandparents' general store, and I often took the Swicks their groceries. What I liked best about delivering to Mr. Swick, apart from the attractions of walls lined with bookshelves and the open books everywhere, was his voice. It was as clear and resonant as a copper bell. I looked forward to the day when I would walk into Mr. Swick's tenth-grade English class. When it came, it as even better than I expected. In our mental race, Mr. Swick was always waiting for me at the finish line.

"Mr. Bruchac," he would say, leaning over his desk like an owl looking down from a tree, "give us the benefit of your infinite wisdom on this poem." Then, no matter what I said, he would look at me with a sly smile and point out something I'd never thought of before. He truly thought on his feet—except that you never saw Mr. Swick standing without the aid of his crutches. He'd had polio as a child, wore heavy braces, and could barely move his legs. His subtle courage taught us as much as his wide knowledge.

To this day, whenever I speak well in public, I think how Mr. Swick would have approved. The measure of a person is never in his height, but in the heart.

126 Lesson 27

Checking Comprehension

1. What judgment does the author make about the teachers he describes? [Making Judgments/Critical]

   They were excellent teachers who brought out the best in their students.

2. What is one way Mrs. Monthony and Mr. Swick were alike? What is one way they were different? [Comparing and Contrasting/Inferential]

   Possible similarities: Both were caring teachers. Possible differences: Mrs. Monthony was more

   kindly and nurturing. She gave the author confidence. Mr. Swick was more challenging and inspired the author to work hard.

Practicing Comprehension Skills

Reread the second paragraph of the selection. Complete the similes. Then explain what each one means.

3. Mrs. Monthony's hair was as _____red_____ as _____autumn leaves_____

   The teacher's hair color is being compared to the red color of fall leaves.

4. Mrs. Monthony's face was as _____warm_____ as ___the glow of a campfire___.

   Her face was warm and welcoming, like a campfire.

5. The author was always _____chattering_____ like a _____bluejay_____.

   He spoke rapidly and noisily, like a bluejay.

Fill in a circle to complete each statement.

6. When the author says he was a "shrimp with thick glasses" in school,

   ○ he is using an idiom meaning he was good in sports.
   ○ he is using a simile comparing a shrimp to being nearsighted.
   ● he is using a metaphor to show how small and nearsighted he was.
   ○ he is using personification showing he was a sports giant.

7. The author compared Mr. Swick's clear, resonant voice to

   ○ a hooting owl.   ○ a public speaker's.   ○ his grandfather's.   ● a copper bell.

STRATEGY: Using Figurative Language 125

Checking Comprehension

• Open-ended questions help you evaluate students' understanding of the reading passage.
• Questions give students an opportunity to use higher-level thinking skills as they reflect on the passage as a whole.

Practicing Comprehension Skills

• Students practice and solidify their understanding of the focus skill through a variety of activities, including multiple choice, question and answer, written response, and graphic organizers.
• The variety of practice formats motivates students to master the skills.

Identify the type of figurative language in each of the following sentences. Then explain what each expression means.

8. He truly thought on his feet.

   Idiom. Possible answer: He came up with good answers on the spur of the moment.

9. He was in the midst of a sea of uncertainty.

   Metaphor. Possible answer: He was so unsure of himself that he felt he was drowning in doubts.

10. I held up my trusty pencil box.

   Personification. Possible answer: He felt his pencil box was something he could rely on.

11. Her eyes still sparkled like the first stars in the sky.

   Simile. Possible answer: Her eyes were as bright as stars.

Practicing Vocabulary

Write the word from the box that belongs in each group.

12. endless, unlimited, _____infinite_____

13. booming, resounding, _____resonant_____

14. doubt, indecision, _____uncertainty_____

15. expectantly, wishfully, _____hopefully_____

16. show, disclose, _____reveal_____

17. assistance, help, _____benefit_____

18. charms, fascinations, _____attractions_____

| attractions |
| benefit |
| hopefully |
| infinite |
| resonant |
| reveal |
| uncertainty |

MAKING THE Reading AND Writing CONNECTION

Writing a Character Sketch
On another sheet of paper, write a character sketch of a teacher who "draws out the best" in students. Use figurative language as you describe your teacher's physical appearance and personality. Support your comments with an example of something the teacher said or did.

126 Lesson 27

Practicing Vocabulary

• Students practice key words from the passage through a variety of exercise formats.
• A Glossary, containing these words and their definitions, is included at the end of the Student Edition.

Making the Reading and Writing Connection

• Connecting to the lesson topic and the focus skill, writing activities motivate students to apply their knowledge as they use a variety of writing forms.

Scope and Sequence

The following chart shows the Focus Skills with a ☆ symbol and the Maintenance Skills with a ★ symbol. A more detailed Skills Index is provided in the Teacher's Guide for each level.

LEVEL	A	B	C	D	E	F
COMPREHENSION						
Strategies and Skills						
Activating prior knowledge			★			
Analyzing		★	★			
Author's purpose	☆	☆	☆★	☆★	☆★	★
Author's viewpoint			☆	☆	☆	☆
Cause and effect	☆★	☆★	☆★	☆★	☆★	★
Classifying	☆★	☆★	★			
Comparing and contrasting	☆★	☆★	☆★	☆★	☆★	☆★
Context clues to determine meaning	☆	☆	☆★	☆	☆	☆
Details	☆★		★			
Drawing conclusions	☆★	☆★	☆★	☆★	☆★	★
Expressing opinions		★	★			
Fact and opinion		☆	☆★	☆	☆	☆
Fantasy and realism	☆	☆	☆			
Hypothesizing		★	★			
Main idea	☆★	☆★	☆★	☆★	☆★	☆★
Making generalizations		★	☆	☆★	☆	☆★
Making inferences			★			★
Making judgments about ideas and text		☆★	☆★	☆★	☆★	☆★
Outlining and Notetaking					☆	☆★
Paraphrasing		☆	☆	☆	☆	☆
Personal opinions			★			
Persuasive devices and propaganda					☆	☆
Point of view		☆	☆	☆	☆	☆
Predicting outcomes	☆★	☆★	☆★	☆★	☆★	☆
Problem and solution			★			
Sequence: order of events	☆★	☆	☆★	☆★	☆	☆
Sequence: steps in a process	★	☆	☆	☆	☆	☆
Summarizing	☆	☆★	☆★	☆★	☆★	☆★
Supporting details		☆★	☆	☆★	☆★	☆★
Synthesizing information			★			
Text structure: method			☆	☆	☆	☆
Visualizing	★	★	★			★
Story Structure						
Character	☆	☆★	☆★	☆★	★	☆
Plot	☆★	☆	☆★	☆	☆★	☆★
Setting	☆	☆	☆	☆	☆★	☆★
Theme		☆	☆	☆	☆★	☆
Word Study						
Alphabetizing	☆	☆				
Analogies						☆★
Antonyms		☆	☆	☆	☆	☆
Compound words		☆	★			
Connotation and denotation				☆	☆	☆
Figurative language: simile and metaphor			☆	☆		
Homonyms		☆			☆	
Synonyms		☆	☆	☆	☆	☆
Suffixes			★			

LEVEL	A	B	C	D	E	F
Using figurative language					☆	☆
RESEARCH AND STUDY SKILLS						
Charts and tables		☆	☆	☆	☆	☆
Dictionary		☆	☆★	☆	☆	☆
Encyclopedia		☆	☆	☆	☆	
Following directions	☆★					
Graphs	☆	☆	☆	☆	☆	☆
Library card catalog/the Internet					☆	☆
Maps		☆	☆	☆	☆	☆
Picture maps and clues	☆★					
WRITING						
Article			★			★
Bar graph	★					
Book report		★	★			
Campaign speech						★
Cause and effect sentences	★					
Character sketch	★	★	★			★
Compare and contrast paragraph			★	★		
Description		★	★			★
Description of a setting		★	★			
Descriptive paragraph			★		★	★
Dictionary page					★	
Directions			★		★	★
Eyewitness account						★
Fantasy		★	★	★	★	
Graph			★			
How-to paragraph			★	★		
Informative paragraph		★	★	★		
Journal entry		★	★	★		★
Label Book	★					
Letter		★	★		★	★
Log entry			★			
Myth					★	★
Movie review						★
Narrative paragraph			★	★	★	★
News report			★		★	
Note		★	★			
Paragraph			★	★		★
Persuasive paragraph					★	★
Picture map	★					
Poem		★	★		★	
Poster			★			
Realistic story						★
Riddles	★		★			
Sentences	★	★				
Sentences that compare	★					
Story		★	★			★
Summary			★	★		★
Tongue twister		★				

Skills Index

The following chart shows the lessons where the Focus Skills and the Maintenance Skills are presented in the Student's Edition and Teacher's Guide of Level E.

The first column lists the skills. The second column lists in boldface type the lesson numbers where the Focus Skills are presented. The third column lists the lesson numbers where the Maintenance Skills are presented.

Each Focus Skill is presented in the Strategy section of the lesson in the Student's Edition. The "On Your Own" section, which begins with a reading selection, provides further opportunities to apply the Focus Skill to a new context. The Maintenance Skills included in each lesson are those skills that were presented as Focus Skills in earlier lessons in Level E, as well as Levels A, B, C, and D.

Strategies and Skills	Focus Skills	Maintenance Skills
Comprehension		
Author's purpose	11	4
Author's viewpoint	16	
Cause and effect	6	2, 3, 10, 13, 18, 25, 29, 33
Comparing and contrasting	8	4, 7, 10, 16, 18, 27
Context clues	7	
Drawing conclusions	2	5, 6, 8, 12, 14, 23, 25, 26, 29, 30, 31, 32, 33, 34
Fact and opinion	12	
Main idea		9, 15, 17, 19, 20, 21, 26
Main idea and details	1	13
Making generalizations	17	
Making judgments	13	7, 9, 11, 15, 16, 19, 24, 27, 28
Outlining	18	
Paraphrasing	10	
Persuasive devices and propaganda	19	
Point of view	14	
Predicting outcomes	5	1, 2, 22, 34
Sequence: order of events	3	
Sequence: steps in a process	4	
Summarizing	9	1, 3, 6, 11, 12, 17, 28, 32
Text structure	15	
Story Structure		
Character	20	8, 14, 22, 23, 30
Plot	21	5, 24, 31
Setting	22	20
Theme	23	21
Word Study		
Antonyms	25	
Connotation and denotation	28	
Homonyms	26	
Synonyms	24	
Using Figurative language	27	
Research and Study Skills		
Library card catalog/the Internet	34	
Understanding charts and tables	30	
Using a dictionary	32	
Using an encyclopedia	33	
Using graphs	31	
Using maps	29	

Using the Comprehension Plus Tests

Assessment Tests are provided in the Teacher's Guide for each level of the program. There are six tests in Level A, five tests in Levels B–D, and six tests in Levels E and F. Each test is designed to measure students' proficiency on four to six skills taught at each level. The tests may be used as pretests or posttests depending on the students' needs and the teacher's instructional style. If students answer two out of the three tested items correctly, they are considered to have mastered that skill.

In addition to the tests, *Comprehension Plus* provides the following management tools:
• Class Record-Keeping Chart (pages T14–T15)
• Progress Record Chart (pages T16–T17)

There are a total of six tests offered for this level of *Comprehension Plus*. You may want to use them to evaluate how well students have mastered the 34 focus skills taught in the lessons. As the following chart summarizes, each test includes three passages. Students will answer six comprehension questions for each passage. Each set of six questions will test students' understanding of two focus skills.

To administer the test:

• Make as many copies of a test as you need.

• Have students write their names on each page.

• Explain that students will read three test passages and answer six questions for each passage.

• After students read the first passage, you may want to review their answers to the first test item to make certain they understand what is expected of them.

• Use the Answer Key on pages T12–T13 to score each test.

• You may want to record the test results on the Class Record-Keeping Chart on pages T14–T15.

Test	Passage Number	Lessons	Skills
1	1	1 & 2	• Main idea and details • Drawing conclusions
	2	3 & 6	• Order of events • Cause and effect
	3	4 & 5	• Steps in a process • Predicting outcomes

Using the Comprehension Plus Tests, continued

Test	Passage Number	Lessons	Skills
2	1	7 & 8	• Context clues • Comparing and contrasting
	2	9 & 11	• Summarizing • Author's purpose
	3	10 & 12	• Paraphrasing • Fact and opinion
3	1	13 & 14	• Making judgments • Point of view
	2	15 & 16	• Text structure • Author's viewpoint
	3	17 & 18	• Making generalizations • Outlining
4	1	20 & 24	• Character • Synonyms
	2	21 & 22	• Plot • Setting
	3	23 & 26	• Theme • Homonyms
5	1	19 & 25	• Persuasive devices and propaganda • Antonyms
	2	27 & 28	• Using figurative language • Connotation and denotation
	3	31 & 33	• Using graphs • Using an encyclopedia
6	1	30 & 32	• Using charts and tables • Using a dictionary
	2	29 & 34	• Using maps • Using a library card catalog/ the Internet

Answer Key

Test 1 (Passages 1, 2, and 3 numbered sequentially)

1. **Zoo animals are living longer, so they need special medical care.** Main idea and details
2. **The gorilla needs vitamins to boost her energy.** Main idea and details
3. **Zookeepers appreciate their older animals** Main idea and details
4. **Elephants can hurt their handlers.** Drawing conclusions
5. **the doctor is helping her.** Drawing conclusions
6. **old zoo animals have different lives than wild animals** Drawing conclusions
7. **John had some difficulty getting the car to start.** Sequence: Order of events
8. **someone said, "What took you so long?"** Sequence: Order of events
9. **did fast turns in the air.** Sequence: Order of events
10. **They had trouble with their car and model plane.** Cause and effect
11. **John fooled around with the controls.** Cause and effect
12. **he doesn't want the plane to crash again** Cause and effect
13. **being an egg** Sequence: Steps in a process
14. **after hatching from the egg** Sequence: Steps in a process
15. **fill out your folded wings** Sequence: Steps in a process
16. **The story is going to be about the stages of a butterfly's growth.** Predicting outcomes
17. **The butterfly will eventually lay eggs of her own.** Predicting outcomes

Test 2 (Passages 1, 2, and 3 numbered sequentially)

1. **run** Context clues
2. **We sang a rhyme to the beat of our feet.** Context clues
3. **by saying, "I'm right behind you."** Context clues
4. **The students exercise every day.** Comparing and contrasting
5. **Raising and climbing ladders is harder.** Comparing and contrasting
6. **Fighting real fires will be more dangerous than firefighting school.** Comparing and contrasting
7. **Tilden's robots have simple wiring rather than computer chips.** Summarizing
8. **Tilden's robot bug turns, steps high, and finally finds the leg movement to get free.** Summarizing

9. **Scientist Mark Tilden builds robots that don't run by computer programs.** Summarizing
10. **The article gives information about something.** Recognizing author's purpose
11. **to inform** Recognizing author's purpose
12. **The author would have listed reasons people should learn about these robots.** Recognizing author's purpose
13. **The *Columbia* shuttle was hit by more than a hundred flying objects during one flight.** Paraphrasing
14. **Space trash can burn up as it falls to Earth.** Paraphrasing
15. **It restates the meaning of the original sentences in different words.** Paraphrasing
16. **Satellites should be built so that they don't explode.** Fact and opinion
17. **An exploding rocket can send out hundreds of bits of metal.** Fact and opinion
18. **You cannot prove that it's scary or not.** Fact and opinion

Test 3 (Passages 1, 2, and 3 numbered sequentially)

1. **Bill, a farm boy** Point of view
2. **The narrator refers to himself as I.** Point of view
3. **The boy told Bill that his master planned to sell him.** Point of view
4. **All slaves should try to escape.** Making judgments
5. **Their master was going to sell Sam.** Making judgments
6. **He thinks Sam would be a good friend.** Making judgments
7. **chronological order** Text structure
8. **the past couple of nights, this morning** Text structure
9. **It might have discussed how different members of the family felt about the trip.** Text structure
10. **She's excited and happy.** Author's viewpoint
11. **She's worried about whether the family will be safe.** Author's viewpoint
12. **A bear leaves scratches on a nearby tree.** Author's viewpoint
13. **Curlers are fine athletes.** Making generalizations
14. **Men, women, and children often play on the same team.** Making generalizations
15. **The passage tells about a sport that is probably unfamiliar to most Americans.** Making generalizations

T12 **Comprehension Plus • Level E**

Answer Key, *continued*

16. **The History of Curling** Outlining
17. **Rules of Curling** Outlining
18. **Use of the Broom** Outlining

Test 4 (Passages 1, 2, and 3 numbered sequentially)

1. **smacked** Synonyms
2. **fascinated** Synonyms
3. **cold, damp, cement floor** Synonyms
4. **He jokes about the missing guitar.** Character
5. **She disagrees with the other group members.** Character
6. **somewhat lazy about playing music** Character
7. **Every nine years, Athens must send fourteen youths to Crete to the Minotaur.** Plot
8. **Theseus takes Ariadne away.** Plot
9. **Minos hated Athens because his only son had died while a guest of the Athenians.** Plot
10. **He lived on the Greek island of Crete.** Setting
11. **Daedalus** Setting
12. **The story happens in a time and place where half-human monsters and heroes could be found together.** Setting
13. **bit** Homonyms
14. **different spellings and meanings, but the same pronunciation** Homonyms
15. **the same spelling but different meanings and pronunciations** Homonyms
16. **She learns that she can ride a horse.** Theme
17. **You can learn to do new things if you are willing to try.** Theme
18. **As Michelle gets over her nervousness, she rides successfully.** Theme

Test 5 (Passages 1, 2, and 3 numbered sequentially)

1. **testimonial** Persuasive devices and propaganda
2. **bandwagon** Persuasive devices and propaganda
3. **loaded words** Persuasive devices and propaganda
4. **unruly** Antonyms
5. **benefit** Antonyms
6. **old** Antonyms
7. **a simile** Using figurative language
8. **Mrs. Weld was extremely nervous.** Using figurative language
9. **excited** Using figurative language
10. **walked** Connotation and denotation
11. **ate greedily** Connotation and denotation
12. **busy** Connotation and denotation
13. **lawyers** Using graphs
14. **21** Using graphs
15. **farmers** Using graphs
16. **Lyndon Johnson** Using an encyclopedia
17. **U.S. History** Using an encyclopedia
18. *President* and *Pretoria* Using an encyclopedia

Test 6 (Passages 1 and 2 numbered sequentially)

1. **Amphibian** Using charts and tables
2. **Bird** Using charts and tables
3. **Reptile** Using charts and tables
4. **weasel** Using a dictionary
5. **hunt** Using a dictionary
6. **Mammal** Using a dictionary
7. **I-5** Using maps
8. **Puget Sound** Using maps
9. **British Columbia** Using maps
10. **Mt. St. Helens** Using a library card catalog/the Internet
11. **Mount Rainier National Park** Using a library card catalog/the Internet
12. **Olympia** Using a library card catalog/the Internet

Class Record-Keeping Chart

The following chart can be used to record the number of items each student has answered correctly for each skill tested. Students need to answer correctly two out of the three tested items per skill to be considered to have mastered that skill. Write in each cell the number of items answered correctly by the student. Add the total of correct answers in the bottom cells.

Name

Test	Items	Strategies and Skills									
1	1–3	Main idea and details									
	4–6	Drawing conclusions									
	7–9	Sequence: order of events									
	10–12	Cause and effect									
	13–15	Sequence: steps in a process									
	16–17	Predicting outcomes									
2	1–3	Context clues									
	4–6	Comparing and contrasting									
	7–9	Summarizing									
	10–12	Author's purpose									
	13–15	Paraphrasing									
	16–18	Fact and opinion									
3	1–3	Point of view									
	4–6	Making judgments									
	7–9	Text structure									
	10–12	Author's viewpoint									
	13–15	Making generalizations									
	16–18	Outlining									
4	1–3	Synonyms									
	4–6	Character									
	7–9	Plot									
	10–12	Setting									
	13–15	Homonyms									
	16–18	Theme									
		Total Correct									

Class Record-Keeping Chart, *continued*

Test	Items	Strategies and Skills	Name									
5	1–3	Persuasive devices and propaganda										
	4–6	Antonyms										
	7–9	Figurative language										
	10–12	Connotation and denotation										
	13–15	Using graphs										
	16–18	Using an encyclopedia										
6	1–3	Using charts and tables										
	4–6	Using a dictionary										
	7–9	Using maps										
	10–12	Using a library card catalog/the Internet										

Total Correct

Progress Record Chart

Name_____

The following chart can be used to record students' progress upon completion of the Comprehension/Study Skills, the Vocabulary Skill, and the Writing Skill activities for each lesson. The symbol ✔, +, or – can be used or any numerical system devised by the teacher to indicate students' work as satisfactory (✔), very good (+), or needs improvement (–). Page references for each Strategy and Skill are provided for convenient reference.

Lesson	Focus Skill	Comprehension Study Skills		Vocabulary Skills		Writing Skills	
		PAGE	✔, +, –	PAGE	✔, +, –	PAGE	✔, +, –
1	Main idea and details	5–6, 8–9		10		10	
2	Drawing conclusions	11, 13		14		14	
3	Sequence: order of events	15–16, 18–19		20		20	
4	Sequence: steps in a process	21, 23		24		24	
5	Predicting outcomes	25, 27		28		28	
6	Recognizing cause and effect	29, 31		32		32	
7	Using context clues	33, 35		36		36	
8	Comparing and contrasting	37, 39		40		40	
9	Summarizing	41–42, 44–45		46		46	
10	Paraphrasing	47, 49		50		50	
11	Author's purpose	51–52, 54–55		56		56	
12	Statements of fact and opinion	57, 59		60		60	
13	Making judgments	61, 63		64		64	
14	Point of view	65–66, 68–69		70		70	
15	Text structure	71–72, 74–75		76		76	
16	Understanding author's viewpoint	77, 79		80		80	
17	Making generalizations	81, 83		84		84	
18	Outlining	85, 87		88		88	
19	Persuasive devices and propaganda	89–90, 92–93		94		94	
20	Literary elements: character	95, 97		98		98	
21	Literary elements: plot	99, 101		102		102	
22	Setting	103, 105		106		106	
23	Literary elements: theme	107, 109		110		110	
24	Synonyms	111, 113		114		114	
25	Antonyms	115, 117		118		118	
26	Understanding homonyms	119, 121		122		122	
27	Using figurative language	123, 125		126		126	
28	Connotation and denotation	127, 129		130		130	
29	Using maps	131, 133		134		134	
30	Understanding charts and tables	135, 137		138		138	

Progress Record Chart, *continued*

Name_____

The following chart can be used to record students' progress upon completion of the Comprehension/Study Skills, the Vocabulary Skill, and the Writing Skill activities for each lesson. The symbol ✔, +, or – can be used or any numerical system devised by the teacher to indicate students' work as satisfactory (✔), very good (+), or needs improvement (–). Page references for each Strategy and Skill are provided for convenient reference.

Lesson	Focus Skill	Comprehension Study Skills PAGE	✔, +, –	Vocabulary Skills PAGE	✔, +, –	Writing Skills PAGE	✔, +, –
31	Using graphs	139, 141		142		142	
32	Using a dictionary	143, 145		146		146	
33	Using an encyclopedia	147, 149		150		150	
34	Using a library card catalog/the Internet	152–153, 155		156		156	

Read the story below. Then answer the questions on the next page.

Say, "Aah," Panda

The panda is old. He can't move as fast as he used to. There's pain in his bones. He takes a pill for it. The doctor hides the pill in a muffin. Blueberry is the panda's favorite flavor. If the muffin isn't blueberry, the panda won't eat it. In fact, if it's the wrong brand, the panda won't eat it.

The gorilla's fur has turned gray. She's very old, too. She walks slowly. Her gums hurt. She gets vitamins to boost her energy.

The old seals can't swim as fast as they once did. Their sleek fur is sprinkled with silver. Their muscles hurt, and they're getting thin. They don't feel like eating very much. One seal has no teeth. The doctor gives them vitamins and medicine for the muscle pain. Not having teeth isn't a big problem, though. Zoo seals don't have to catch their own food. A keeper gives it to them by hand. They swallow the fish whole so they don't really need teeth.

Then there's the elephant. She's 45 years old. She's the chief elephant at this zoo, but she has an infected toe. How do you treat an elephant with a bad toe? Well, you'd better treat her very carefully.

The doctor gives the elephant a shot in the toe. She also gives the elephant a lot of peanuts. The elephant gets these shots three times a week. She's used to them. She knows they ease the pain.

"What a good elephant," the doctor thinks. "She's not stepping on me. She's not slapping me away with her trunk. I hope she teaches the other elephants how to act. I wish the tiger was this easy."

A good zoo doctor can tell what an animal is feeling. She can sense when the animal is going to get angry, and she knows how to calm it down. Animals can't say, "My throat hurts," so a good zoo doctor needs to be able to figure out what's wrong.

These days, zoo doctors are very busy. That's because zoos are better at keeping animals alive. Zoo animals live longer than wild animals do. Old zoo animals have illnesses that wild animals rarely have. A wild animal with a bone disease would soon die. A zoo animal gets treated for it. She can stay alive, just as a human would. But the zoo must find money to pay for her treatment.

Zookeepers appreciate their older animals, but older animals present some new challenges.

Name _____

Fill in the circle next to the words that answer the question or complete the sentence.

1. Which of the following statements best states the main idea of this story?

○ Treating older animals costs a lot of money.

○ When a wild animal gets sick, it usually dies in a matter of days.

○ To become a zoo doctor, you must study hard for many years.

○ Zoo animals are living longer, so they need special medical care.

2. Which of the following statements supports the main idea of this story?

○ The elephant doesn't slap with her trunk.   ○ Zoo seals don't have to catch their food.

○ Blueberry is the panda's favorite flavor.   ○ The gorilla needs vitamins to boost her energy.

3. Which of the following statements does NOT support the main idea of this story?

○ The elephant gets three shots a week.   ○ Old seals lose interest in food.

○ The panda has pain in his bones.   ○ Zookeepers appreciate their older animals.

4. Why would you need to treat an elephant with an infected toe very carefully?

○ Elephants use all of their toes for walking.   ○ Elephants can hurt their handlers.

○ Elephants are important animals.   ○ Elephants have big feet.

5. The old elephant seems to know that _____.

○ the doctor is helping her   ○ the doctor trained for many years

○ the doctor is bothered by the tiger   ○ the doctor is afraid of her

6. A conclusion you can draw from this passage is that _____.

○ old animals can't be saved   ○ old animals are very popular animals

○ old zoo animals have different lives than wild animals

○ old zoo animals don't always get the best of care

Read the story below. Then answer the questions on the next page.

Tiny Planes

At first, everything seemed to go wrong. The tail fell off Chris's model plane. It took ten minutes to glue it back on. Then John's car wouldn't start.

"Come on," Chris urged his older brother. "Get this thing to start. We'll miss the whole day of flying if you don't."

"Stop worrying," John said. "I know cars like you know model planes."

"Yeah? Well, what do you know about starting *this* car?"

John thought for a second. Quietly he said, "I think we need a jump start. Last week, Dad showed me how to use the cables. I think I remember."

John did remember. He jump-started the car in just a few minutes. The two brothers drove off, heading for the large, grassy field at the edge of town. That was where the Model Airplane Club met every weekend.

The other club members were already there. Above one end of the field, a tiny yellow plane did loops. At the other end, a tiny blue plane climbed and dove.

"What took you so long?" someone asked Chris.

Chris grumbled to himself. He walked over to a group of people with model planes. A mother and her son had a World War II fighter plane. They had built it together from a kit. A girl in a wheelchair held a tiny helicopter in her lap. A man with a brown beard was fixing his plane on the grass. Each owner had a remote control to work the plane. Each remote control had two control sticks.

"All right, it's my turn," Chris finally said. He turned the propeller to start his plane. The plane rolled forward on the grass. As it picked up speed, Chris pulled a control stick back. The plane climbed into the air.

"Watch this loop," Chris said. He moved the control sticks back and forth. His plane began to turn in a tight circle.

"You're turning too fast," John told him. "You have to slow down."

"Don't talk to me while I'm flying!" Chris yelled.

Chris's little red plane spun to the ground and crashed.

"It's because you were talking to me," Chris said. "I forgot which stick to use."

John said, "No, it's because you were turning too fast."

They spent half an hour fixing the little plane. Finally, it was ready to fly again.

"This time, make your turns slower," John said.

"Keep quiet," Chris said. But he did make his turns slower. His loops worked. He spent the next half-hour flying his plane perfectly. Then he let John try.

The two brothers smiled. The red plane danced in the wind. It was a good day after all.

Name _____ **TEST 1,** *continued*

Fill in the circle next to the words that answer the question or complete the sentence.

7. Which of the following events happened first?

○ Trying to do a loop, Chris crashed his plane.

○ Chris and John put the tail back on the plane.

○ John had some difficulty getting the car to start.

○ The brothers were late for the Model Airplane Club meeting.

8. Soon after John and Chris reached the field, _____.

○ Dad showed them something important   ○ the other members arrived

○ someone said, "What took you so long?"   ○ they went home again

9. Before the tiny plane crashed, it _____.

○ lost its tail   ○ ran out of fuel

○ hit another plane   ○ did fast turns in the air

10. Why were the boys late for the club meeting?

○ They didn't know the directions to the field.

○ They had trouble with their car and model plane.

○ The others arrived before they did.

○ Their father taught them how to use jumper cables.

11. Which of the following is NOT a possible cause of the model plane crash?

○ John talked to Chris.   ○ Chris tried to turn too fast.

○ John fooled around with the controls.   ○ Chris forgot which control stick to use.

12. Chris turns the plane more slowly on his second flight because _____.

○ John says that he should   ○ he is talking to John

○ he wants to let John try   ○ he doesn't want the plane to crash again

Comprehension Plus • Level E   **T21**

Read the story below. Then answer the questions on the next page.

How to Become a Butterfly

First, you start out as an egg glued to a leaf. Inside the egg, you grow. A week later, you're big enough to break the egg. You move, and the shell cracks. Your six legs crawl over the edge of the shell. You're out! You plop onto a soft, bouncy floor. It's a leaf. You can't see that it's green because you can't see colors. But you look around.

You think, "I must be a caterpillar."

Then you think, "I'm hungry."

Caterpillars are always hungry! Tiny as you are, you have mighty jaws. You munch your way across your first leaf. To move, you scrunch up your body into a hump. Then you push forward. Scrunch, push, eat, scrunch, push, eat, day after day after day. And everywhere you go, you drag a silky thread behind you. You spin it from a gland in your mouth.

Why spin a silky thread? Well, look, here's the end of the leaf. What are you going to do? Jump? Yes! You drop down to another leaf, hanging by your silky thread. You can escape from danger in the same way.

Your soft, wormlike body grows bigger and bigger. Finally, you get too big for your own skin! No problem, you'll get rid of that old skin. Just shrug it off and grow a looser one.

You do this five or six times while you're a caterpillar. It's like buying a new wardrobe because you've gained weight. The only dif-

ference is that you don't have to pay for it.

One day, you're three weeks old. At last, you can stop eating. You find a safe branch and settle down. You hang upside down, sticking to the branch with your silk. Then you shed your skin one more time. This time, your new covering is hard.

You're not a caterpillar anymore. You're a pupa. You spend two weeks in your upside down hiding place. You don't move. You don't eat. But strange things are happening to you. Some of your organs are shrinking away. New organs are growing. What do you feel? Are you afraid, excited, content? If only you could tell humans how you feel!

Finally you break your hard skin and struggle out. You're an adult, but you're wet all over. You have two pairs of wings, but you can't fly yet. Your wings are folded behind you. You have to fill them out with fluid from your body.

Ah, that's better. The fluid has hardened; your wings are dry and are covered with tiny, powdery scales. You fly toward a flower. You need to suck out the flower's nectar with your long, curled tongue. Your wings flap lightly up and down. They are bright blue, green, red, and yellow. You can see colors now.

Do you know that you are a beautiful butterfly?

Fill in the circle next to the words that answer the question.

13. What is the first step in the process of becoming a butterfly?

   ○ being a moth   ○ being an egg

   ○ being a caterpillar   ○ being a pupa

14. When do you go through the caterpillar stage?

   ○ while changing inside your hard case

   ○ after hatching from the egg

   ○ after learning to fly

   ○ before leaving the eggshell

15. After emerging as an adult butterfly, what do you do first?

   ○ hatch your own eggs   ○ start eating again

   ○ learn to fly   ○ fill out your folded wings

16. What might a reader logically predict after reading the title and first paragraph of this story?

   ○ The butterfly is going to hatch more eggs at the end.

   ○ Something terrible is going to happen to the caterpillar.

   ○ The butterfly in this passage will talk.

   ○ The story is going to be about the stages of a butterfly's growth.

17. Based on your own experiences and information learned in this story, what can you logically predict will happen in the future?

   ○ The butterfly will eventually lay eggs of her own.

   ○ The butterfly will be caught in a net.

   ○ The butterfly's habitat will be destroyed.

   ○ The butterfly will become a caterpillar again.

Read the story below. Then answer the questions on the next page.

Firefighting School

June 22

Dear Diary,

I've just finished my first week at firefighting school. It's been the hardest and hottest week of my life, but it's also been the best. I'm learning so much and having a great time.

Today began like every other day—with exercise. We stretched, we did push-ups, and we did sit-ups. Then we ran three miles. While we ran, we sang a rhyme to the beat of our feet. We chanted, "We'll be here tomorrow. We were here yesterday. We'll never quit, there's just no way."

After exercising, we went to class. We learned about what happens when water hits fire. Sometimes, blasting water at fire is the wrong thing to do. The force of the water can make the fire spread or turn the water into boiling steam.

There's so much to learn and remember! When we make a mistake in class, we have to sprint up and down the stairs of Slim Jim. Slim Jim is a six-floor building. It's a practice building for fighting fires. Just try running up and down the stairs of that building a few times! You'll be sure to study harder next time.

Today's lunch was great, as usual. We are allowed to eat as much as we want, and we have half an hour to chat. I'm making some really good friends here. We're all going through the same thing. When it gets hard, we encourage each other by giving hints or by saying, "I'm right behind you. You can do it."

We needed the food and the rest. Right after lunch, it was time to hit Mud Street. This is a road that is covered in ankle-deep mud. The instructors give us a hose to pull and then turn it on. We have to pull the hose a hundred feet through the mud while we aim the water at a target. We have to work hard so we won't get knocked off our feet. It's like dragging a huge snake that's trying to escape.

Mud Street is the hardest thing I've done so far. But I've heard that harder things are coming up. Raising and climbing ladders is harder. Finding your way out of a strange building, blindfolded, before your air runs out, is harder. Working with real fire is harder. Even though it's only school, we're going to work with real flames before it's all over.

In twenty weeks, my school days will end. I know that fighting real fires will be more dangerous than the experiences I'm having in school, but I'm not afraid. I've wanted to be a firefighter all my life, and I think I'll be prepared. Will my dream really come true?

Name _____ **TEST 2,** *continued*

Fill in the circle next to the word or words that answer the question or complete the sentence.

1. Which word is a synonym for *sprint?*

   ○ *run*   ○ *study*

   ○ *fight*   ○ *practice*

2. Which sentence from the story helps you define *chant?*

   ○ Today began with exercise.   ○ We sang a rhyme to the beat of our feet.

   ○ We stretched and we did sit-ups.   ○ After exercising, we went to class.

3. Which of the following are examples of ways firefighting students *encourage* each other?

   ○ running three miles, then going to class   ○ by saying, "I'm right behind you."

   ○ racing up and down Slim Jim   ○ finding their way through a building

4. How are all the days at firefighting school the same?

   ○ The students exercise every day.   ○ The students climb ladders every day.

   ○ The students work with fire every day. ○ The students go up and down stairs every day.

5. How does the author say pulling a hose down Mud Street is different from raising and climbing ladders?

   ○ Pulling a hose is harder.   ○ Raising and climbing ladders is harder.

   ○ Pulling a hose is more fun.   ○ Raising and climbing ladders takes longer.

6. How does the author think that fighting real fires will be different than firefighting school?

   ○ Fighting real fires will not be as hard as firefighting school.

   ○ At firefighting school, students work with real flames.

   ○ When fighting real fires, water will have to be used.

   ○ Fighting real fires will be more dangerous than firefighting school.

Read the article below. Then answer the questions on the next page.

Robots on Their Own

A bug is walking across the desert sand. Its eyes sense the land ahead of it. Its legs sense the land beneath. When it comes to a rock, the bug stops. Soon it finds the right way to walk around the rock.

Then the bug comes to a roll of tape in the sand. One of the bug's legs steps into the center hole of the tape. It's trapped! It tries turning. It tries stepping high. Finally, it gets free. It has found the right leg movements to help it escape.

That's what a real bug would do. But the bug in this case is made with electric wire and a battery. It's a robot.

When you think of the word *robot,* you probably think of something with a powerful computer brain, but this robot bug has no computer. It's wired the old-fashioned way. This robot is so simple that people can't understand how it works. Its inventor, scientist Mark Tilden, is trying to explain the concept.

Many scientists have tried to invent robots based on computers. The problem is, a computer can only do things it's programmed to do. If it comes across a problem it hasn't been programmed for, it can't solve the problem.

That's the opposite of the way real creatures work. Insects have very simple brains.

Their bodies are just very good at finding a way around things. They can find food and water and shelter. They can avoid enemies. They can survive.

Real creatures survive without a lot of programming. They test out the world around them. They face problems and find solutions. But they don't always use the same solution. The next time, they might try something new. Being able to try new things helps them survive.

Mark Tilden thinks that robots should be built the same way. He doesn't want a robot that can do high-level math. He wants a robot that can find its own way and keep going. He wants to make a robot that can do its work without being told exactly how.

Tilden has built a robot snake. The snake crawls up a person's body and crawls down again. It isn't programmed for these actions. It just starts moving and finds the best way to its goal. It seems almost alive. It doesn't move exactly the same way each time. Like a real snake, it can choose different paths.

Some scientists don't know what to make of Tilden's robots. They think, "Where are the computer chips?" But Tilden keeps building better and better robots. He wants his robots to think the way living things do, not the way computers do.

Name _____

Fill in the circle next to the correct answer.

7. Which detail is important and should be included in a summary of the article?

   ○ Tilden's robots have simple wiring rather than computer chips.

   ○ The robot bug has an antenna that helps it find things.

   ○ The robot bug gets stuck on tape.

   ○ The robot snake seems almost alive.

8. Which detail is NOT important enough to put in a summary?

   ○ A Tilden robot can solve the same problem in more than one way.

   ○ Tilden's robots find their way around in complex environments.

   ○ A Tilden robot doesn't need to be programmed for every problem it might meet.

   ○ Tilden's robot bug turns, steps high, and finally finds the leg movement to get free.

9. Which is the best summary of this article?

   ○ Mark Tilden designs robots.

   ○ Mark Tilden is a very smart scientist.

   ○ Today, scientists are building things that can act like real bugs.

   ○ Scientist Mark Tilden builds robots that don't run by computer programs.

10. Which of the following statements describes this article best?

   ○ The article tells a story.

   ○ The article creates a mood or feeling.

   ○ The article is humorous.

   ○ The article gives information about something.

11. Based on your answer to question 10, what is the *most* important purpose of the article?

   ○ to entertain   ○ to express   ○ to inform   ○ to persuade

12. How might this passage have been different if the author's purpose had been to persuade?

   ○ The author would have told funnier stories about the robots.

   ○ The author would have compared and contrasted Tilden's robots.

   ○ The author would have listed reasons people should learn about these robots.

   ○ The author would have described his own personal experiences with Tilden robots.

Comprehension Plus • Level E

Read the article below. Then answer the questions that follow.

Space Garbage

Outer space is beautiful. Looking out the window of a space shuttle, you can see the stars more clearly than you can from Earth. It's a thrilling view. However, what's out there can be dangerous, too. And the dangerous things are often too small to see.

Above Earth, where space shuttles orbit, there are thousands of chunks of space garbage. They are flying as fast as spaceships, at about 17,000 miles per hour. Sometimes they hit spaceships. On one flight of the shuttle *Columbia,* the ship was hit 106 times. Most of those hits were not caused by rocks. They were caused by pieces of space garbage.

What kinds of objects are floating in space today? Some are satellites that are no longer working. Others are pieces of rockets that exploded. The first explosion of a rocket in space took place in 1961. Since then, many others have occurred. An exploding rocket can send out hundreds of bits of metal.

Space garbage also results from everyday events. Let's say an astronaut walks outside a shuttle, taking pictures. What if he drops the camera lens cap? It becomes a piece of orbiting junk.

A flying bolt may not sound like much. If it's flying ten times as fast as a bullet, though, it can be pretty scary.

Some space trash burns up by falling toward Earth. If it's high up in space, though, it won't fall to Earth. It will stay in orbit.

What can be done about space trash? This may be one of the most important questions now facing NASA. One answer is to keep track of it. Radar can track a piece of space junk as small as a softball. Before launching a flight, NASA makes sure no other ships or satellites will be in the way. They could also make sure no large pieces of space junk were in the flight's path.

But what about smaller things? What about a piece of metal as small as a pebble? One solution is to invent armor for spaceships. Another is to leave less garbage up there.

So far, no spaceship has been destroyed by flying junk, but it could happen someday. That's why we should all work together to come up with a plan for space junk. We don't want to wait until it is too late.

Fill in the circle next to the words that answer the question.

13. Which of the following choices is the best paraphrase of this sentence from the article?

On one flight of the shuttle *Columbia,* the ship was hit 106 times.

○ The space shuttle was hit by flying rocks as it went through space.

○ There's a chance that the space shuttle is going to be hit by a piece of space garbage.

○ The *Columbia* shuttle was hit by more than a hundred flying objects during one flight.

○ The space shuttle has had some problems that have been in the news.

14. Which choice is the best paraphrase of this sentence?

Some space trash burns up by falling toward Earth.

○ Many objects in space burn up in orbit.   ○ An object in orbit can fall toward Earth.

○ Some space trash burns up by falling toward Earth.   ○ Space trash can burn up as it falls to Earth.

15. Explain your answer to question 14.

○ It uses the writer's original sentence.   ○ It includes the author's opinion.

○ It restates the meaning of the original sentence in different words.   ○ It gives a summary of the most important idea.

16. Which of the following is a statement of *opinion?*

○ Satellites should be built so that they don't explode.

○ Radar can track pieces of space junk as small as a softball.

○ On one flight of the shuttle *Columbia,* the ship was hit 106 times.

○ They are flying as fast as spaceships, at about 17,000 miles per hour.

17. Which of the following is a statement of *fact?*

○ Outer space is beautiful.   ○ It's a thrilling view.

○ That's why we should all work together to come up with a plan for space junk.   ○ An exploding rocket can send out hundreds of bits of metal.

18. Why is the following a statement of *opinion?*

When a flying bolt is flying ten times as fast as a bullet, it can be pretty scary.

○ Space junk doesn't fly that fast.   ○ You cannot prove that it's scary or not.

○ A flying bolt is not scary.   ○ What the author is saying is true.

Read the story below. Then answer the questions on the next page.

Moving Through the Night

Late last night, just after midnight, there was a loud knock on our door. I could tell how late it was by how low the moon was in the sky.

Nobody ever knocks on our door that late. In fact, hardly anyone ever knocks on our door at all. Our little farm is in the hills of Tennessee, and the nearest neighbors are more than two miles down the road.

I didn't get out of bed because I was supposed to be asleep. I looked and listened, though. I saw Dad open the wooden door, and I immediately noticed three black people standing outside: a man, a woman, and a boy about my size. They were damp from the rain, and they looked very tired. Dad motioned for them to come inside. Without a word, he sat them down on the rug near the fireplace, and Mom brought them some bread and a jug of milk. They ate ravenously.

Soon Mom checked to see if I was still sleeping, and of course I couldn't trick her. I opened my eyes and asked, "Who are they?"

"They were slaves on a plantation near here," she said. "They're escaping."

Next morning's breakfast was especially enjoyable because the table was so crowded—Mom, Dad, the three runaway slaves, and me!

"Bill," Dad told me, "this must remain an absolute secret, for if you accidentally tell anyone about this, we could go to jail. Our guests will stay with us for the day, and then they'll sneak out again tonight. Leaving now would be too risky, with the sheriff's men and dogs out scouring the woods."

"Why did they come here?" I asked.

My father explained that we were now part of the Underground Railroad. Our house was a "station" in a heroic "train" that assists runaway slaves.

I did my chores thoughtfully, and when I returned, the boy was sitting looking at the fire. "My name's Bill," I said. "Want to play jacks?"

He was so suspicious that he didn't say anything until his mother nodded for him to answer. "I'm Sam," he said.

"Why are you running away?" I asked Sam. "Did your master whip you?"

"Not as much as some," Sam said. "There are lots of worse masters. But we found out he was planning to sell me, and Mom and Dad didn't want our family split up. We had to leave. Anyway, it's not right to have slaves. All slaves should try to escape."

I thought about that. Then I said, "I guess you're right."

I taught Sam to play jacks, and then I showed him my rock collection. The next morning, he was gone with his family.

"I wish he could live around here and be my friend," I said.

Dad looked at me. "Maybe that will happen someday."

Comprehension Plus • Level E

Name _____ **TEST 3,** *continued*

Fill in the circle next to the words that answer the question.

1. Who is the narrator of the story?

   ○ the author   ○ Bill's dad

   ○ Sam, the young slave   ○ Bill, a farm boy

2. How can you tell that the story is told from the first-person point of view?

   ○ The narrator speaks first.   ○ The narrator refers to himself as *I*.

   ○ The narrator knows the thoughts of all the characters.   ○ The narrator is the most important character in the story.

3. Which sentence might have been included in the story if it had been written in the third-person point of view?

   ○ The boy was just about my size.   ○ My mom and dad helped the family.

   ○ The boy told Bill that his master planned to sell him.   ○ I really enjoyed having breakfast with all our new friends.

4. What judgment does Sam make about slavery?

   ○ Slaves should only try to escape if their masters are very mean.   ○ It makes no difference whether a master is nice or mean.

   ○ All slaves should try to escape.   ○ It is fine if a slave's master is nice.

5. What detail supports the judgment that the family ought to escape from slavery?

   ○ The sheriff sent men and dogs to search for them.   ○ Their master was not as bad as some other masters.

   ○ Bill and his family were helping them.   ○ Their master was going to sell Sam.

6. What is Bill's judgment of Sam?

   ○ He thinks Sam would be a good friend.   ○ He thinks Sam talks too much.

   ○ He thinks slavery is wrong.   ○ He thinks Sam is too young.

Read the journal entries below. Then answer the questions on the next page.

Wilderness Journey

June 10

Today was the greatest day of my life so far. We began our hiking trip. We're going north from Yellowstone National Park through Montana. Our whole family—Mom, Dad, Nick, and our dog, Mr. Novak—is traveling as a team. We are each carrying a heavy backpack. Even Mr. Novak has a backpack. He's carrying his own dog food. Dad said he wouldn't take the dog along any other way.

We're hiking on trails through back country, in high valleys, between snowy mountain peaks, and across meadows. There are wildflowers everywhere, beautiful yellow, white and purple ones. Mom told us not to pick any, although when we came to a massive field of flowers even she picked a few. (So now we're all stomping around with flowers in our caps.) At this time of year, snow and ice are melting from the summits, which means the streams and rivers are running full. We keep coming across signs of animal life. This afternoon I saw tracks that Dad thought belonged to a wolf! I just hope we don't meet any grizzly bears.

June 12

I haven't slept too well the past couple of nights because I'm not used to sleeping on hard ground. But the stars here are so bright and clear that it's fun just to stay awake and gaze up at them. Each night, when we set up camp, we have to make sure we don't leave any items that might attract bears. For example, we put our food in metal containers and hang it on a line in the trees.

June 18

We've been traveling about ten miles a day. That's a lot when you consider that we're hiking with full packs on rough trails at high altitude. Today we saw a beautiful waterfall with two eagles flying above it.

I haven't written as much in this journal as I'd hoped because at the end of a day's hike, all I want to do is eat and rest. I do want to mention that something disturbing happened last night. Mr. Novak started running around, barking and whining. Mom and Dad exchanged meaningful looks. I asked if they thought a bear might be around. Mom said, "Of course not," to which Dad replied, "It's not likely, anyway." Then Mom suggested that we all start making noise so we banged pots and blew the whistles that we had brought along to scare bears.

Then this morning, there were big scratches on the tree where our food was hung. Dad looked at them and said, "Bear claws."

We're going to move far away from here before nightfall. I'm anxious to get moving. I've been pestering my parents all morning. I don't want to be around if those bears come back.

Name _____

Fill in the circle next to the words that answer the question.

7. What is the text structure of this selection?

- ○ main idea and details
- ○ cause and effect
- ○ chronological order
- ○ problem and solution

8. Which clue words help you identify the text structure of this selection?

- ○ greatest, fun, beautiful
- ○ disturbing, scare, barking, and whining
- ○ the past couple of nights, this morning
- ○ of course not, it's not likely

9. How might this selection have been different if it had used compare and contrast text structure?

- ○ It might have shown how the author and her family dealt with the problem of bears.
- ○ It might have shown events in the order in which they happened.
- ○ It might have described something the family did, and the results of that action.
- ○ It might have discussed how different members of the family felt about the trip.

10. How does the author feel when she starts out on the journey?

- ○ She's excited and happy.
- ○ She wishes she were back home.
- ○ She's bored by nature.
- ○ She's angry that she has so much to carry.

11. How does the author feel at the end of the story?

- ○ She realizes that she loves nature after all.
- ○ She's worried about whether the family will be safe.
- ○ She feels closer to her family than ever.
- ○ She's still angry.

12. What story event changes the author's viewpoint?

- ○ The dog goes wild.
- ○ The family has fun making noise.
- ○ The bear eats their food.
- ○ A bear leaves scratches on a nearby tree.

Comprehension Plus • Level E

Read the article below. Then answer the questions on the next page.

Curling

Curling is a sport you may never have heard of, yet it's played by more than a million people around the world. It's a winter sport, played on ice, so it's most popular in northern countries like Canada. Curling is played in the United States by about 15,000 people, mostly in northern states with long, cold winters, such as Wisconsin, Minnesota, and North Dakota.

Curling probably began in Scotland in the 1500s or earlier. Scottish winters were long, and there were few forms of entertainment, so people began making a sport out of sliding heavy stones on the frozen lakes. Someone must have gotten the idea of giving points to the players whose stones slid closest to a goal. The game spread, and in the 1700s, curling clubs formed. Then Scottish soldiers brought the sport to North America.

Curling is played by teams of four people. Men, women, and children often compete on the same team—assuming that they can slide a forty-pound stone down the ice! The frozen court is approximately twice as long as a bowling alley. There's a goal at each end, called a "tee." Each player is equipped with two polished, flat-bottomed, granite stones. Both teams slide their stones toward the same goal, just like in horseshoes. After all

sixteen stones have been cast, the team whose stone has slid closest to the goal gets one point. Then play begins in the other direction.

The rules are easy to learn, but playing the game is hard. The ice is so slick and the stone is so heavy that even the smallest misjudgment in a throw can make the stone slide much too far or stop much too suddenly. Any rough or uneven patch in the ice can change the direction in which the stone is moving. Also, the melting of the ice makes things tricky for the curlers. Water helps the stone slide, but it can also alter the stone's path. In curling, a broom is part of each player's equipment. Players can sweep the ice in front of a stone as it moves, to help it go down the court.

A good curler must know how much force to use. He or she must also know how to send the stone curling around the other teams' stones if they are blocking the way. The player must know the exact conditions of the ice on the court—conditions that change throughout the game. In other words, a good curler must be a fine athlete. That may explain why the International Olympic Committee decided to make curling an Olympic sport in 1998.

Fill in the circle next to the words that answer the question.

13. Which statement is a generalization you might make after reading this article?

○ Curlers are fine athletes.   ○ Curling is a funny-looking sport.

○ Curling is played in places where it is cold.

○ Curling probably began in Scotland in the 1500s.

14. Which statement is a generalization about curling teams?

○ Each member of a team gets two stones.

○ Men, women, and children often play on the same team.

○ Teams began to form in the 1700s.   ○ A curling team has four players.

15. Which statement is a generalization about the passage?

○ The passage is about a new Olympic sport, curling.

○ The passage is informational, and it's easy to read.

○ The passage is written in the third-person point of view.

○ The passage tells about a sport that is probably unfamiliar to most Americans.

16. If you were making an outline of this passage, what would be the main topic of paragraph 2?

○ How to Curl   ○ Curling Equipment

○ The History of Curling   ○ Why Curling Is Popular

17. What would be the main topic of paragraph 3?

○ Curlers—A Special Kind of Athlete   ○ Rules of Curling

○ Curling Across the U.S. and Canada   ○ Secrets of Sliding the Stone

18. Suppose one of your main topics is *How to Play the Game.* Which of the following might be a subtopic under that heading?

○ Curling and the Olympics   ○ Curling in Canada

○ Use of the Broom   ○ Where to Find Curling Teams in the U.S.

Comprehension Plus • Level E   **T35**

Read the story below. Then answer the questions on the next page.

The Case of the Missing Guitar

The band was setting up for rehearsal in Jodi's basement. All four members were present: Carl the bassist, Shannon and Kyoko the guitarists, and Jodi herself, the drummer. Jodi, always eager to get started, began hitting the drums with her sticks. She smacked the snare drum a few times, then rattled off a brisk roll.

"Yo, let's get going!" she urged the others as she pounded the snare with her foot.

"Don't rush us, girl," Kyoko said, flicking open the latches of her guitar case. "All you have to do is sit in front of your drums; but we have to plug in our amps, tune up our instruments, and—hey, what's going on?"

"What?" asked Carl, suddenly enthralled now that there seemed to be a mishap.

Kyoko displayed the interior of her guitar case, which was empty. "Okay, who's hiding my guitar?"

"I am—it's right here in my back pocket," Carl laughed.

"Stop being silly, Carl," Kyoko said. "The guitar was in the case when I came here. I'm sure of it. If the case had been empty, it would have been much lighter." She glared suspiciously at her bandmates. "Answer me, where is it?" In frustration, she flung the guitar case shut and threw herself on the cold, damp, cement floor of the cellar. "Okay, that does it, I'm quitting—I resign. None of you care about anyone but your-

selves. You don't care if I lose an expensive guitar; you just want to make jokes."

"*I'm* being serious," Jodi said, descending from her stool. "Come on, everyone. Let's all try to find Kyoko's guitar."

"Will someone please have a moment's patience?" Shannon complained. "I just *got* here and I haven't had time to get my own guitar out, and—hey!" she exclaimed, as she pulled a jade-green, slender-bodied guitar from her case. "This isn't mine, it's Kyoko's!"

Carl cackled. "So if Kyoko's guitar's in Shannon's case, where's Shannon's guitar?"

All four partners stared at one another silently. Then, in the stillness, they heard a strumming of strings, coming from the video room.

Jodi ran toward the strumming. A moment later, she returned, dragging her five-year-old sister Stevie behind her. On Stevie's face was a confused, excited expression, and in her arm was Shannon's red guitar.

"I was just learning how to play," Stevie whined.

"Okay, that solves one mystery," Jodi said. "But how did the guitars get in the wrong cases? If the switch was made after our last session and you didn't notice until now, it means neither of you practiced all week."

Shannon and Kyoko suddenly looked embarrassed.

Name _____

Fill in the circle next to the word or words that answer the question or complete the sentence.

1. Which word in the story is a synonym for *hit?*

   ○ strumming   ○ extracted   ○ smacked   ○ cackled

2. Which of the following words is a synonym for *enthralled?*

   ○ embarrassed   ○ fascinated   ○ joking   ○ angry

3. Which word or words near the word *cellar* would help you understand that it is a synonym for *basement?*

   ○ suspiciously   ○ cold, damp, cement floor

   ○ threw herself   ○ I'm quitting—I resign

4. How can you tell that Carl is the clown of the group?

   ○ He is the only boy in the band.   ○ He jokes about the missing guitar.

   ○ The author states that Carl is the clown of the group.

   ○ Since the other characters are serious, Carl must be the clown.

5. Which detail does NOT show that Jodi likes to be a leader?

   ○ She pushes everyone to get started.

   ○ She suggests that everyone help find the guitar.

   ○ She goes to investigate when she hears the sound of a guitar.

   ○ She disagrees with the other group members.

6. Shannon is slow to get started, she complains, and she has not practiced all week. These facts show that she is _____.

   ○ a terrible person   ○ more serious than the others

   ○ somewhat lazy about playing music   ○ not very talented

Read the story below. Then answer the questions on the next page.

The Myth of Theseus and the Minotaur

Theseus, the young prince of Athens, loved danger. This bold young man wanted so much to be a hero that he always refused to travel by the safe route. He insisted on taking roads where there were lots of bandits he could kill. When he heard about the Minotaur, he longed to fight that monster to the death—which was just the opposite of what almost any other human being would have felt, except perhaps for Theseus's cousin Hercules.

The Minotaur was half man, half bull, and all fierce. He lived on the Greek island of Crete, where he was sort of the pet, and sort of the prisoner, of King Minos. His home, or prison, was an incredibly complicated maze called the Labyrinth. None of those who entered the Labyrinth could find their way out again.

Now, Minos hated Athens because his only son had died while a guest of the Athenians. Minos had taken revenge by capturing the city of Athens. He had declared that he would destroy the city unless it sent seven young men and seven young women to Crete, to be shoved into the Labyrinth. There, they would be killed and eaten by the Minotaur. Athens had to send this human tribute to Crete once every nine years.

When Theseus first heard about the Minotaur, he immediately volunteered to be sent into the Labyrinth so he could try to kill the monster. His father, the king, agreed, and so Theseus boarded the sailing ship with thirteen other young people, all headed for Crete.

Theseus was handsome as well as courageous and strong. When he landed in Crete, the princess there, Ariadne, spotted him among the Athenian prisoners. She fell in love with him at first sight. Ariadne ran to talk to the architect who had built the Labyrinth, a great inventor named Daedalus. "Tell me the secret of how to get out of the Labyrinth," she pleaded. Daedalus gave her a ball of thread to give to Theseus. When Theseus entered the Labyrinth, he could unroll the ball as he walked and then find his way out by following the thread back.

Ariadne took the ball of thread to Theseus and gave it to him on condition that if he got out alive, he would marry her. Of course, he agreed. Then he entered the Labyrinth, unrolling the thread as he went. He found the Minotaur somewhere near the center and attacked and killed the monster with his bare hands. Theseus led the other thirteen youths out of the Labyrinth and set sail toward Athens with them and Ariadne.

Fill in the circle next to the words that answer the question.

7. What is the main problem that faces the characters in the story?

○ They have to reach Crete from Athens.   ○ Theseus asks to be sent to Crete.

○ Ariadne falls in love with Theseus at first sight.

○ Every nine years, Athens must send fourteen youths to Crete to the Minotaur.

8. Which of the following is NOT part of the background of the story?

○ Theseus loves danger.   ○ The Minotaur is half man and half bull.

○ Theseus takes Ariadne away.   ○ King Minos seeks revenge upon the city.

9. Which sentence shows a flashback to an event that happened before the story begins?

○ Minos hated Athens because his only son had died while a guest of the Athenians.

○ When Theseus first heard about the Minotaur, he wanted to kill the monster.

○ Ariadne spotted Theseus among the Athenian prisoners and fell in love with him.

○ Theseus entered the Labyrinth, found the Minotaur, attacked and killed the monster.

10. Which words from the story help you learn the story's setting?

○ He lived on the Greek island of Crete.   ○ handsome and strong

○ half man, half bull, and all fierce   ○ killed the monster with his bare hands

11. Which of the following does NOT describe the story's setting?

○ King Minos's island   ○ Daedalus   ○ the Labyrinth   ○ ancient times

12. What is the most important effect the setting has on the story?

○ The story happens in a time and place where half-human monsters and heroes could be found together.

○ Because it is set in ancient Greece, the characters must all wear Greek clothing.

○ The characters are more intelligent because they live in ancient Greece.

○ When a story is about gods and goddesses, unusual events take place.

Read the story below. Then answer the questions on the next page.

First Ride

"I don't know if I've ever seen a live horse before," Michelle said tensely, as she looked at the big, heavy animals gathered in the corral. The way they were tossing their heads, snorting, and switching their tails, she didn't know how she could ever get up on one of them and go for a ride.

"Don't worry," her best friend Joni said. "Just do what I do and you'll be okay."

"But you've never ridden one either!" Michelle protested.

"What difference does that make?" Joni said defiantly. Michelle wondered how her friend got to be that way—always sure of herself in every situation.

"Okay," called the camp counselor in a loud, hoarse voice. "Everybody get your helmets on. One of the handlers will lead you to a horse and help you get into the saddle."

"Remember, just let it happen," Joni whispered, as the two of them were led separately to their mounts.

Michelle was still strapping her helmet onto her chin, when her left foot was suddenly being hoisted into a stirrup by somebody's big hand. Her right leg was swung over the horse's back. She thumped down onto the saddle, sitting straight, though she felt a little shaky. Her horse was a pale, tan color, almost yellow, with a gray-white mane,

and it kept dipping its neck to shake the flies away.

"How ya doing?" the man who had helped her asked.

At first Michelle mumbled nervously, "Oh, I don't know," but then she remembered to straighten her posture. "Actually, I'm doing fine," she said in a firmer, more confident voice. "What's that metal rod in his mouth?"

"That's called the bit, and it's what you'll be pulling on when you pull the reins," the man answered. "Don't worry, you won't hurt him; a tame horse likes the feel of the bit in its mouth. Besides, these horses all live here at the camp. They get ridden every day. They're used to kids like you."

Michelle wanted to ask him more questions, but the lead rider had called out, "Yee-hah!" as a signal to move. The pack of horses, twenty-four altogether, stretched out as it moved down the bridle path, the faster riders inching ahead and the slower ones, like Michelle, lingering toward the rear.

"Hey, this is fun!" Michelle said aloud.

She tapped her horse's side with her heels and clicked her tongue. "Come on!" she urged, and trotted up the road to arrive beside Joni.

Name _____ **TEST 4,** *continued*

Fill in the circle next to the word or words that answer the question or complete the sentence.

13. Which of the following words from the story has a homonym—a word with the same spelling and pronunciation but a different meaning?

○ *rein*   ○ *mane*   ○ *bit*   ○ *stretched*

14. *Horse* and *hoarse* are homophones because they have

○ the same pronunciation and spelling.   ○ the same meaning and pronunciation.

○ different spellings and meanings, but the same pronunciation.

○ different meanings, different spellings, and different pronunciations.

15. Find the word *live* two times in the story. These words are homographs because they have

○ different meanings, spellings, and pronunciations.

○ the same spelling and meaning.   ○ the same spelling and pronunciation.

○ the same spelling but different meanings and pronunciations.

16. What does Michelle learn in this story?

○ She learns that horses are scary.   ○ She learns to talk to a horse.

○ She learns that Joni is a good guide.   ○ She learns that she can ride a horse.

17. Which is a theme, or central idea, of this story?

○ You can learn to do new things if you are willing to try.

○ Listen to your friends' ideas because they're probably better than your own.

○ Horses are intelligent animals.   ○ Listen to people's ideas.

18. Which detail gives you the best evidence for the theme?

○ Michelle rides next to Joni.   ○ The horses were tossing their heads.

○ The man who helps Michelle into the saddle is courteous.

○ As Michelle gets over her nervousness, she rides successfully.

Read this editorial from a school newspaper. Then answer the questions on the next page.

Support School Sports

You cannot underestimate the benefits of school sports. School sports can help build a loyal student body. They can help set up strong ties with the people in town. They can guarantee that kids will become disciplined adults. Students can develop special talents and skills. Students who might be at risk for bad behavior can find a place. Sports turn effort into excellence.

Dan Jones is a track star at East Valley High. He has this to say: "I love being part of the track team. It has changed my life. Before I tried out for track, I was on a slick slope. I was heading for trouble. I let my grades slide. I had lots of time to waste. I got into things that were just plain bad. Coach Wilkes helped me turn my life around. I hate to think where I might be if it were not for track. Now I hope to win a college scholarship. I can participate in track while I study to become a vet. It will be a dream come true. All kids should get into sports. If they don't, they will be missing out on the opportunity of a lifetime."

When money for school sports is cut, students and local citizens suffer drastically. Yes, students need up-to-date technology,

and students need new textbooks. Schools need to hire more teachers. Schools need to be repaired so that they will be safe. But none of these things should take away from the money spent on sports. Students need fields, tracks, pools, and gyms. They need the best equipment. Being involved in sports builds character. It encourages good health habits. It helps start lasting relationships. Can you say that of a math class? No, you cannot.

"I like school, but I love swimming!" So says Mandy Ng. She is a member of the swim team at Piney Glen High School. Mandy swims the 100-meter backstroke. Her speed may give her a spot on the state team. Mandy has a bright future in the water.

When the debate to cut money for sports in your hometown begins, pay attention. Think about what kids need to make their lives interesting, rewarding, and fun. Think about what makes kids well-rounded and fit. Think about how sports can bring people together. Become a positive voice for more sports funding. Kids all over the state need your help.

Fill in the circle next to the word or words that answer the question or complete the sentence.

1. Dan Jones's quote is an example of _____.

    ○ testimonial   ○ bandwagon

    ○ loaded words   ○ facts and statistics

2. "All kids should get into sports. If they don't, they will be missing out on the opportunity of a lifetime" is an example of _____.

    ○ testimonial   ○ bandwagon

    ○ loaded words   ○ facts and statistics

3. "When money for school sports is cut, students and local citizens suffer drastically" is an example of _____.

    ○ testimonial   ○ bandwagon

    ○ loaded words   ○ facts and statistics

4. An antonym for *disciplined* is _____.

    ○ *successful*   ○ *unhappy*

    ○ *unruly*   ○ *careful*

5. An antonym for *suffer* as it is used in this selection is _____.

    ○ *give*   ○ *torture*

    ○ *benefit*   ○ *happy*

6. Which word is an antonym for *up-to-date?*

    ○ *old*   ○ *used*

    ○ *recycled*   ○ *long-lost*

Read the letter below. Then answer the questions on the next page.

Choir in Washington, DC

Dear Uncle Rich and Aunt Chris,

Our choir trip to Washington, DC, has been very hectic but fun. We are as busy as bees all day long. Then we have a concert each night. Miss Weld tries to get us to rest in the afternoon, but it's very hard to settle down. There is so much to see and do.

We have trudged up and down the National Mall. It feels like our legs are going to fall off! Yesterday we toured the Capitol and met our state senator, Senator Smith. It was very exciting. He is taller in person than he is on TV. Mary says that on TV everyone is a shrimp. On TV, people are only 9 inches tall! (That's a joke.) Anyway, he was nice. He gave us some good tips on where to eat lunch.

Today we went to see the Lincoln Memorial. We got our picture taken on the steps. Miss Weld had us sing "America the Beautiful." We did it to honor Marian Anderson, an African-American opera singer. She was barred from singing in Constitution Hall so she sang on the steps. It gave us chills to be there. Of course, she sang for 75,000 people, and we sang for only about 20. Most of them didn't even wait for verse two!

After that we had a picnic. We stuffed ourselves. Miss Weld read from the guide book. She told us about Maya Lin. Ms. Lin designed the Vietnam Veterans Memorial. After lunch we went to get a close look at it. I was honored to sing there. We sang "America" and "Danny Boy." I found Uncle Nick's name on the wall. We took some pictures there, too. I will send you one.

Now we're going to have dinner and get ready to sing at tonight's outdoor concert. Tomorrow morning we will tour the White House. This will be the high point of the trip. We will sing for the First Lady. I am on pins and needles just thinking about it. Miss Weld is as nervous as a cat, but she says we'll pull it off without a hitch.

You should plan a trip here. You would like it. There is history in every step. And I know where our senator buys his sandwiches!

I'll call you when I get home.

Love,

Katy

Fill in the circle next to the word or words that answer the question or complete the sentence.

7. "Katy and her friends were as busy as bees" is an example of _____.

○ a simile   ○ a metaphor

○ personification   ○ a synonym

8. "Miss Weld was as nervous as a cat" means that _____.

○ Mrs. Weld was not very nervous   ○ Mrs. Weld was extremely nervous

○ Mrs. Weld wasn't usually nervous ○ Mrs. Weld looked like a cat

9. The expression "Katy is on pins and needles" means that Katy is very _____.

○ hungry   ○ uncomfortable

○ tired   ○ excited

10. In the second paragraph, the connotation of the word *trudged* is _____.

○ walked   ○ worked

○ tired   ○ energetic

11. In the fourth paragraph, the connotation of *stuffed* is _____.

○ ate slowly   ○ ate quickly

○ ate very little   ○ ate greedily

12. Which word is the denotation of *hectic?*

○ boring   ○ restful

○ busy   ○ tiring

Read this section from an encyclopedia entry and study the accompanying graph. Then answer the questions on the next page.

President   **Pretoria**

President

Anyone born in the United States can grow up to be the president. A president can come from any walk of life.

Presidents' Occupations

Half the men who have taken office have studied law, which is the U.S. Constitution at work. However, that is not the only job that the presidents have held. Jimmy Carter was a peanut farmer, and Lyndon Johnson had a cattle ranch. In fact, seven of our presidents have spent part of their lives working on the land. Seven of our presidents held other elected offices first. Bill Clinton and Ronald Reagan were governors. John Kennedy served as a congressman and a senator. Some of our presidents were soldiers, including Ulysses S. Grant and Dwight D. Eisenhower. They were generals in the army. William Taft and Warren G. Harding both worked as newspaper editors. Herbert Hoover was an engineer. Some of our presidents taught school. Andrew Johnson was a tailor.

All of the men who have been president have one thing in common. They were chosen by the American people to serve our nation.

See also **U.S. History.**

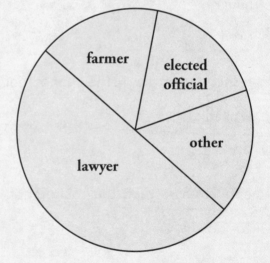

Occupations of 42 U.S. Presidents, 1789–2000

Fill in the circle next to the word or words that answer the question or complete the sentence.

13. According to the graph, what occupation did the largest number of presidents have?

    ○ farmers   ○ elected officials

    ○ lawyers   ○ other

14. According to the graph, how many presidents have been lawyers?

    ○ 10   ○ 12

    ○ 17   ○ 21

15. According to the graph, one-sixth of the 42 presidents were _____.

    ○ lawyers   ○ teachers

    ○ soldiers or newspaper editors   ○ farmers

16. Which president had a cattle ranch?

    ○ Andew Johnson   ○ Andrew Jackson

    ○ Lyndon Johnson   ○ Jimmy Carter

17. If you wanted to find out more about this topic, where might you look?

    ○ Pie Graphs   ○ President's Occupations

    ○ Pretoria   ○ U.S. History

18. The guide words on this encyclopedia page are _____.

    ○ President and Occupation   ○ President and Pretoria

    ○ Johnson and Kennedy   ○ *See also* U.S. History

Look at the chart and read the dictionary definition below. Then answer the questions on the next page.

Our Animals

The students in Ms. Fong's class love animals. They made a chart to show the kinds of pets they have. The chart also helped them group different categories of animals.

One day Rick came to school. He announced that he had just gotten a pet ferret named Telly. The students wanted to add it to the chart. But they had to find out exactly what a ferret was first! They looked it up in the dictionary and then knew right where it belonged.

fern ► fertilize

fer-ret (fer ′ it) *n.* An animal of the weasel family. It is about 14 inches in length. It has pale yellow or white fur and red eyes. It is a native of Africa but has been domesticated in Europe. Ferrets are used to drive rats or rabbits out of their holes. *The black-footed ferret chased the rabbit from its den.*
v. 1. To hunt or drive out of a hiding place.
2. To search, often used with *out. I had to ferret out the answer to the math problem.*

Animal Families

Mammal	Reptile	Amphibian	Bird	Fish
cat	turtle	salamander	canary	goldfish
dog	iguana	frog	finch	guppy
hamster	snake		cockatiel	
gerbil			parrot	
hedgehog				

Name _____ **TEST 6,** *continued*

Fill in the circle next to the word or words that answer the question or complete the sentence.

1. A toad is related to frogs and salamanders. In what column of the chart would it belong?

   ○ Mammal   ○ Reptile

   ○ Fish   ○ Amphibian

2. A budgie is a small parrot. In what column of the chart would it belong?

   ○ Mammal   ○ Reptile

   ○ Bird   ○ Amphibian

3. A striped racer is a kind of snake. In what column of the chart would it belong?

   ○ Mammal   ○ Reptile

   ○ Bird   ○ Amphibian

4. What family is the ferret a member of?

   ○ rabbit   ○ African

   ○ weasel   ○ European

5. Ferrets are trained to _____.

   ○ hunt   ○ solve problems

   ○ attack   ○ protect

6. Based on what you learned about the ferret, in what column would it belong?

   ○ Mammal   ○ Reptile

   ○ Bird   ○ Amphibian

Read the passage. Then look at the map below. Use the map and the passage to answer the questions on the next page.

Washington, the Evergreen State

The state of Washington was the 42nd state to join the United States of America. It is located in the Pacific Northwest. Its northern side borders Canada. To the west are Puget Sound and the Pacific Ocean. Chains of islands dot the bays and coves down the coast. The state of Oregon is to the south. The Columbia River flows along this state line. Idaho is to the east of Washington. The Cascades run down the middle of the state. This mountain range splits the state into two parts. On the west side of the mountains, there are pine forests. They cover the steep slopes. The land east of the mountains is very fertile. Farmers produce many crops there, including apples, wheat, and grapes. Washington is known as the Evergreen State.

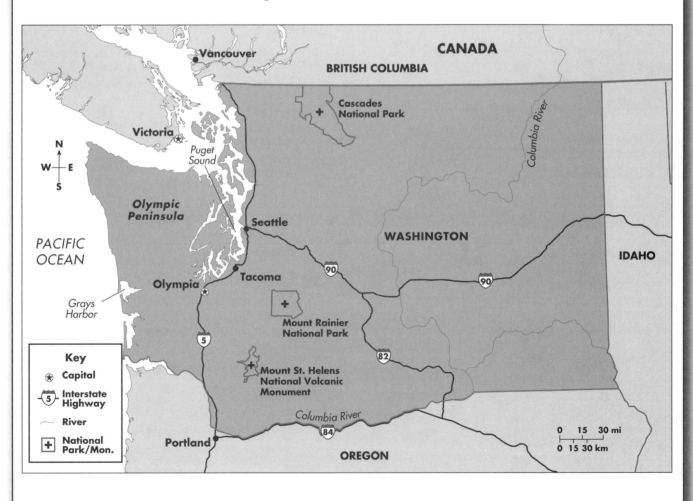

Name _____ **TEST 6,** *continued*

Fill in the circle next to the word or words that answer the question.

7. Which interstate highway would you take to get from Seattle to Portland?

  ○ I-5   ○ I-82

  ○ I-84   ○ I-90

8. What is the body of water between Seattle and the Olympic Peninsula?

  ○ Pacific Ocean   ○ Puget Sound

  ○ Grays Harbor   ○ Columbia River

9. What Canadian province is on the northern boundary of Washington?

  ○ Oregon   ○ Victoria

  ○ Vancouver   ○ British Columbia

10. If you wanted to find out more about volcanoes in Washington, what keyword or subject would you look under?

  ○ mountain   ○ eruptions

  ○ Mount St. Helens   ○ national monuments

11. What keyword or subject would help you find information about backpacking?

  ○ Grays Harbor   ○ Columbia River

  ○ Olympic Peninsula   ○ Mount Rainier National Park

12. What keyword or subject would you look up to find information about the capital?

  ○ Seattle   ○ Tacoma

  ○ Olympia   ○ Vancouver

Main Idea and Details (pages 5–10)

Objective: Students can identify the main idea and supporting details in a text.

Teaching TIPS

- Students better understand a text when they identify its main idea.

- Students learn to organize and prioritize information when they identify the main idea and supporting details.

Skills Reviewed and Maintained

Comprehension

Summarizing	See Checking Comprehension
Making Predictions	See Checking Comprehension

Phonics

Digraph *ch*	See Practicing Vocabulary, Phonics Mini-Lesson

Writing

Character Sketch	See Making the Reading and Writing Connection

Teach

Tell students that the main idea of a paragraph is the paragraph's most important idea. Details, such as facts or examples, support the main idea.

- Write the following paragraph on the board.

    Summertime is swimming time! Here are some rules to follow when you swim: Only swim if there is a lifeguard; always swim with a buddy; don't splash other swimmers; never push someone under the water. If you follow the rules, swimming can be safe and fun.

- Copy and distribute the Graphic Organizer on page T106 of this Guide. Help students identify the main idea and details of the paragraph. Fill in the organizer together.

Main Idea	Swimming can be safe and fun if you follow certain rules.
Detail	Swim where there is a lifeguard.
Detail	Swim with a buddy.
Detail	Don't splash.

- Ask students to explain how the main idea differs from the supporting details. *(the main idea is more general)*

- Direct students to read the passages on pages 5 and 6. Remind them that the main idea is not always stated directly. It must be inferred from details in the text.

- Have students complete the exercises. Check for understanding by asking them to restate the main idea of each passage in their own words.

On Your Own Practice

Introducing Vocabulary

Before students read the article, introduce the vocabulary words *(achievement, anchors, deteriorate, devised, motivational, nuisance, valid)* and discuss their meanings. Have students look up each word in the Glossary.

Reading the Passage

Have students read the title and look at the photograph. Ask them to suggest what "challenges" Erik Weihenmayer might face.

Checking Comprehension

- Explain that a summary retells only the most important ideas and events. Guide students in choosing two or three main points that tell how Erik meets the challenges of blindness.

- Remind students that they should use evidence from the article as well as their own knowledge and experience to make predictions about Erik's future activities.

Practicing Comprehension Skills

Remind students to look carefully at the supporting details as they formulate a main idea sentence. They should ask themselves, *"Does my main idea make sense? Does it cover all the important details?"*

Practicing Vocabulary

Review the vocabulary words. Ask students to identify the two words with the digraph *ch*. *(achievement, anchors)* Have students complete the vocabulary exercise independently. Then review the answers as a group.

Apply

Making the Reading and Writing Connection

Ask volunteers to read their character sketches aloud. Listeners can then identify the stated or implied main idea.

You may want to use pages 116–118 in *The Write Direction*, Grade 5 for additional opportunities in writing character sketches.

MEETING INDIVIDUAL NEEDS

Phonics: Digraph *ch*

On the board, write the vocabulary words that contain the digraph *ch: achievement, anchors.*

- Say both words, stressing the sound of *ch.* Have students repeat the words.

- Ask students what sound the letters *ch* represent in each word. Explain that the letters *ch* can stand for the /k/ or /sh/ sounds.

- Brainstorm other words that contain the digraph *ch.* List the words on the board, sorted according to the place of the *ch* in the word.

You may want to use to pages 7–8 in *MCP Phonics,* Level E for additional practice with the digraph *ch.*

ESL Strategy

Have students write a caption for a magazine picture. In their captions, students should tell what point or idea the picture shows. Ask them to point out details in the picture that support their captions.

Multiple Intelligences: Verbal-Linguistic

Have small groups of students research scientific and technological inventions that make life easier for people with visual impairments. Have groups present their findings to the class.

Home-School Connection

Have students read a newspaper article or watch a news story with a family member. They can then write a sentence that presents the story's main idea.

LESSON 2 Drawing Conclusions (pages 11–14)

Objective: Students can draw conclusions about a story or an article.

Teaching TIPS

- Students synthesize and evaluate information when they draw conclusions.

- Students who draw conclusions get more ideas from what they read and better understand the author's point.

Skills Reviewed and Maintained

Comprehension

Making Predictions	See Checking Comprehension
Cause and Effect	See Checking Comprehension

Phonics

Words with *gn*	See Practicing Vocabulary, Phonics Mini-Lesson

Writing

Informative Paragraphs   See Making the Reading and Writing Connection

Teach

Ask students to watch carefully as you act out a situation. Then pantomime an activity, such as searching for your reading glasses. *(Hold the book at arm's length, squint, pat pockets, check under papers, and so on.)*

- Ask students what you were doing and how they figured it out. Then point out that they drew a conclusion by combining visual details with their previous experiences and knowledge.

- When a person infers something that isn't directly stated, he or she is drawing a conclusion. A conclusion is a sensible decision, which is made after thinking about details and facts. Help students realize that they draw conclusions constantly in their daily activities.

- Tell students that readers, too, make logical decisions based on information in the text as well as their own experiences.

- Have students read the passage about a famous artist. Encourage them to draw conclusions about the technique that he developed.

- Invite students to complete the exercise. Then discuss how they drew their conclusions.

On Your Own Practice

Introducing Vocabulary

Before students read the article, introduce the vocabulary words (*aligned, cartoonist, gnarled, illusion, optical, shoulder, stimulation*) and discuss their meanings. Have students use the words in oral sentences.

Reading the Passage

Have students read the title and look at the pictures. Ask them how the term *optical illusion* relates to the article's title, "Fooling the Eye."

Checking Comprehension

- A valid prediction must be supported by information in the article. Have students point out details that helped them speculate about computer screens.

- Review cause-and-effect relationships. Encourage students to use the word *because* in their answers to link cause and effect.

Practicing Comprehension Skills

Although a conclusion is a decision or opinion made by the reader, it must be based on information in the passage. To check, students can ask, *"What assumptions did I make in reaching my conclusion?"*

Practicing Vocabulary

- Review the vocabulary words. Have students identify the two words with the letters *gn*. (*aligned, gnarled*)

- Invite students to complete the vocabulary exercise independently. Review the answers with the group.

Apply

Making the Reading and Writing Connection

Let volunteers read their paragraphs aloud. Have listeners identify the incorrect and the correct conclusion, and tell why the incorrect one may have been drawn first.

You may want to use pages 134–135 in *The Write Direction*, Grade 5 for additional opportunities in writing an informative paragraph.

MEETING INDIVIDUAL NEEDS

Phonics: Words with *gn*

On the board, write the vocabulary words with *gn*: *aligned, gnarled.*

- Say both words and have students repeat them. Ask what letter is silent. *(g)*

- Write other *gn* words on the board: *sign, reign, gnaw, gnome, gnu, gnash, gnat.* Have volunteers say the words.

- Ask students to copy the words from the board, and underline the letters that represent the sound /n/ in each word. Challenge them to add other *gn* words to their lists. Encourage them to use a dictionary.

You may want to use pages 19–20 in *MCP Phonics*, Level E for additional practice with *gn*.

ESL Strategy

Write some words that describe feelings on the board. (Possible words: *happy, sad, angry, excited, scared, proud*) Make sure students know the meaning of each word. Then pantomime faces and gestures that suggest one of the feelings. Have students draw a conclusion about which feeling you are portraying.

Multiple Intelligences: Logical-Mathematical, Interpersonal

Have students analyze the multiple-choice test questions on pages 11 and 13 of this lesson. They can discuss why each answer choice is or is not a logical conclusion.

Home-School Connection

Suggest that students watch a television show with a family member. Midway through the show, they can draw conclusions about why the characters are acting in a certain manner or doing certain things.

Sequence: Order of Events (pages 15–20)

Objective: Students can track the order of events in a text.

Teaching TIPS

- Students realize that keeping track of a sequence of events is essential to the understanding of some kinds of texts.

- Students use clue words to follow the order of events when reading and organize the order of events when writing.

Skills Reviewed and Maintained

Comprehension
Summarizing   See Checking Comprehension
Cause and Effect   See Checking Comprehension

Word Study
Prefix *re-*   See Practicing Vocabulary, Word Study Mini-Lesson

Writing
Play   See Making the Reading and Writing Connection

Teach

Ask two volunteers to demonstrate each of the following situations: *(1) Bo snatches a cookie <u>while</u> Jo's back is turned. (2) Jo turns around <u>before</u> Bo has a chance to snatch a cookie. (3) Bo snatches a cookie <u>right after</u> Jo turns around.*

- Discuss how the clue words *while, before,* and *right after* helped the two actors know when to do something.

- Explain that in some stories and articles, the sequence of events, or order in which things happen, is crucial. A story might end differently if the events had happened in a different order.

- List other words and phrases that are clues to sequential order: *first, next, later that day, at two o'clock, finally, as soon as.* Point out that dates and times of day can also be clues to the order in which things happen.

- Have students read the passages on pages 15 and 16 and complete the exercises. Make sure they understand the concept of *flashback.*

On Your Own Practice

Introducing Vocabulary
Before students read the play, introduce the vocabulary words *(contemplate, exaggerate, frantically, incline, precious, reappear, reassuringly)* and discuss their meanings. For each word, have students demonstrate an action or give an example.

Reading the Passage
Have students use the title and illustration to predict what "A Long Walk Home" might be about. Explain play conventions: Setting and stage directions are written in parentheses and italics; a character's name is followed by a colon. Encourage students to visualize the action.

Checking Comprehension

- Clarify that a story summary usually includes the characters' main problem and the reasons for it. It does not include the reader's opinions or suggestions.

- Review cause-and-effect relationships. Then invite students to reread the part of the play just before Brianna offers her arm to her sister. Discuss possible causes of that action. Ask students to think about their own family experiences.

Practicing Comprehension Skills
To help students keep track of the sequence of events, suggest that they picture the story action in their minds. Visualizing is often an effective way to track sequence. Explain that another method is to draw a time line.

Practicing Vocabulary

- Review the vocabulary words. Have students identify the two words with the prefix *re-. (reappear, reassuringly)*

- Invite students to complete the vocabulary exercise independently. Go over the answers together.

Apply

Making the Reading and Writing Connection

Partners should read each other's plays, summarize the characters' problem and their solution for it, and find examples of sequence clue words.

You may want to use pages 92–96 in *The Write Direction*, Grade 5 for additional opportunities in writing a play.

MEETING INDIVIDUAL NEEDS

Word Study: Prefix *re-*

On the board, write the vocabulary words *reappear* and *reassuringly*. Circle the prefix *re-*. Say each word and have students repeat it.

- Remind students that *re-* means "again." Ask how that meaning applies to the two vocabulary words. (When something *reappears*, it appears again; when you talk or act *reassuringly*, you assure someone again.)

- Write these base words on the board: *do, test, apply,* *build, cycle, heat*. Have students copy them, adding the prefix *re-*. Volunteers can explain the meaning of each new word.

You may want to use pages 77–78 in *MCP Phonics*, Level E for additional practice with the prefix *re-*.

ESL Strategy

Have students acquiring English work with a peer tutor to review sequential order. Partners can read a short story and draw a time line illustrating what happens *first, next, after that,* and *finally*.

Multiple Intelligences: Bodily-Kinesthetic, Verbal-Linguistic, Interpersonal

Students can perform "A Long Walk Home" or one of the student plays from the Reading and Writing Connection.

Home-School Connection

As students and a family member do a chore together, they can discuss the sequence of steps involved. For example: *First, we separate the whites and the colors. Then we put the whites in the washing machine. Next we add detergent and bleach . . .*

LESSON 4 Sequence: Steps in a Process (pages 21–24)

Objective: Students can identify and order the steps in a process.

Teaching TIPS

- Students are able to make and do things independently when they learn how to follow a set of ordered instructions.

- Students use steps in a process across content areas.

Skills Reviewed and Maintained

Comprehension

Author's Purpose	See Reading the Passage, Checking Comprehension
Comparing and Contrasting	See Checking Comprehension

Phonics

Letter Combination *old*	See Practicing Vocabulary, Phonics Mini-Lesson

Writing

Directions	See Making the Reading and Writing Connection

Teach

Remind students that making or doing many things requires following certain steps, which usually must be done in a particular order. Point out to students that they follow a sequence when they get ready for school, brush their teeth, or wash the dishes. Have volunteers suggest other examples.

- Ask a volunteer to demonstrate a simple task, such as folding a paper airplane. Have the student explain the steps as he or she demonstrates the process.

- As the volunteer describes the steps, write clue words on the board: *first, then, next, after that, finally.*

- Tell students that when instructions are written, readers can look for clue words such as those on the board. When clue words are not given, readers can determine the order of steps by inserting clue words themselves and by using their common sense.

- Invite students to read the passage on page 21 and study the diagrams. Remind them to look for clue words as they read.

- Have students complete the exercise. Check for understanding by asking what step is shown in each picture.

 ## Practice

Introducing Vocabulary

Before students read "Folding a Swan," introduce the vocabulary words *(behold, crease, elegant, opposite, original, thumbnail, unfold)* and discuss their meanings. Have students give a synonym for as many words as possible.

Reading the Passage

Ask students to read the title and preview the diagrams. Suggest that they think about the author's purpose as they predict what they will learn. How will the author try to clarify the steps for folding a swan?

Checking Comprehension

- Remind students that an author's main purpose for writing directions is to inform readers about how to do something. Point out that the author of "Folding a Swan" also wants to inform readers about the origins and popularity of origami.

- Tell students that they can understand a process by making comparisons and contrasts. They should think about how the steps in the new process are like, and unlike, the steps in a familiar process.

Practicing Comprehension Skills

Point out that diagrams or illustrations often accompany written directions. Ask students to look at each illustration in "Folding a Swan" and match it to the written step.

Practicing Vocabulary

- Review the vocabulary words. Have students identify the two words with the letter combination *old.*
  (behold, unfold)

- Ask students to complete the vocabulary exercise independently. Then go over the answers as a class.

Apply

Making the Reading and Writing Connection

Find out which students wrote directions for things that can be made easily with classroom materials. Volunteers can read their directions aloud, while classmates follow the directions.

You may want to use pages 136–138 in *The Write Direction,* Grade 5 for additional opportunities in writing directions and instructions.

MEETING INDIVIDUAL NEEDS

Phonics: Letter Combination *old*

On the board, write the vocabulary words with the letter combination *old: behold, unfold.* Say the words aloud and have students repeat them.

- Circle the letters *old* in each word. Ask a volunteer to explain what sound *o* makes. (the long *o* sound) Help students conclude that words ending in *-ld* preceded by *o* generally have the long vowel sound.

- Set a time limit, and have partners or trios list as many words as they can that end with *old* and rhyme with the two vocabulary words.

You may want to use pages 25–26 in *MCP Phonics,* Level E for additional practice with the letter combination *old.*

ESL Strategy

Make cards with sequence clue words: *begin, next, then, after that, finally.* As a volunteer follows the steps in a simple process, such as tying his shoes, hold up the cards in sequence for the group to read aloud and match with the appropriate action.

Multiple Intelligences: Bodily-Kinesthetic, Verbal-Linguistic, Interpersonal

Have groups of students work together to follow the directions on page 21 and make their own paper.

Home-School Connection

Suggest that students look through magazines or cookbooks to find a recipe. They can work with a family member to follow the directions and prepare a new main dish or snack.

Predicting Outcomes (pages 25–28)

Objective: Students can make and verify predictions about a text.

Teaching TIPS

- Students realize that a text progresses logically and that it has a recognizable structure when they make predictions.

- Students get more involved in a text when they make and verify predictions as they read.

Skills Reviewed and Maintained

Comprehension

Plot	See Checking Comprehension
Drawing Conclusions	See Checking Comprehension

Phonics

Syllabication	See Practicing Vocabulary, Phonics Mini-Lesson

Writing

Story	See Making the Reading and Writing Connection

Teach

Point out to students that they constantly make predictions in their daily activities. Predicting simply means using clues to tell what you think might happen next. Present the following scenarios or provide other examples drawn from students' own backgrounds:

- *While I was riding my bike, I ran over a sharp nail.*
- *The game's score was tied; then the visiting team sent out their star player.*
- *I borrowed my brother's skates without asking his permission.*

- Ask volunteers what might happen next in each case.

- Discuss how students used their own knowledge and experiences to make their predictions.

- Explain that readers use text and text cues (such as pictures and captions), as well as prior knowledge, to predict what might happen in fiction, or what might be learned in nonfiction.

- Review the directions on page 25. Then invite students to read the short article. Make sure they focus on predicting before and during reading.

- Have students complete the exercise. Check for understanding by discussing how they made their predictions.

On Your Own Practice

Introducing Vocabulary

Before students read the story, introduce the vocabulary words (*clawing, panic, pierced, pleaded, savagely, silent, wandered*) and discuss their meanings. Have students use the words in oral sentences.

Reading the Passage

Review the directions on page 26 to make sure students understand when and how they are to make predictions about story events. Have them use the title and picture to make an initial prediction about the story's subject and mood.

Checking Comprehension

- The author does not directly say that the boys are scared. Ask students what part in the plot can help them understand this.

- Have students evaluate the events in the story. Can they conclude that the boys had valid reasons for thinking Bigfoot was outside?

Practicing Comprehension Skills

Help students realize that a valid prediction, one that is sensibly based on information in the story, might turn out to be incorrect. Readers are expected to evaluate and revise their predictions as they read on and gather more information.

Practicing Vocabulary

- Review the vocabulary words. Have students identify the two words with one consonant between vowels. (*panic, silent*)

- Have students complete the vocabulary exercise independently. Review the answers with the group.

Apply

Making the Reading and Writing Connection

Have volunteers read their stories aloud. Listeners can point out clues that helped them predict each story's outcome.

You may want to use pages 50–51 in *The Write Direction*, Grade 5 for additional opportunities in writing stories.

MEETING INDIVIDUAL NEEDS

Phonics: Syllabication

On the board, write the vocabulary words that have one consonant between vowels: *panic, silent.*

- Say the words and have students repeat them. Divide the words into syllables. Ask students: In which word does the first syllable end with a long vowel sound *(si-lent)* and in which word does the first syllable end with a consonant after a short vowel sound? *(pan-ic)*

- Write and say the word *quivered*, from "Bigfoot." Ask whether the first syllable ends with a long vowel sound (like *silent*), or a consonant after a short vowel sound (like *panic*). (The first syllable of *quiv-ered* is like that in *panic.*)

- Explain how students can use long and short vowel sounds to help them divide words into syllables.

You may want to use pages 27–28 in *MCP Phonics*, Level E for additional practice with syllabication.

ESL Strategy

Have volunteers play the parts of Bobby, Hank, "Bigfoot," and Mother as you read aloud the story. Pause occasionally to let students make predictions.

Multiple Intelligences: Visual-Spatial

Have students design their own graphic organizer to show how the clues in the story help the reader predict "Bigfoot's" identity.

Home-School Connection

Suggest that students watch a television drama or comedy with family members. Members of the audience can write predictions during each commercial break. When the program is over, they can compare and discuss the predictions each person made.

Recognizing Cause and Effect (pages 29–32)

Objective: Students can understand relations of causality.

Teaching TIPS

- Students can use the knowledge of cause-and-effect relationships across content areas.

- Students better understand the motivations of characters when they recognize causes and effects.

Skills Reviewed and Maintained

Comprehension
Summarizing — See Checking Comprehension
Drawing Conclusions — See Checking Comprehension

Phonics
Vowel Digraph *ea* — See Practicing Vocabulary, Phonics Mini-Lesson

Writing
Eyewitness Account — See Making the Reading and Writing Connection

Teach

Make a statement about an everyday activity or event, such as, "I watered my plant." Ask a volunteer to expand the statement with a *because* clause. *(I watered my plant because the soil was dry.)* Challenge another volunteer to expand the new statement with another *because* clause. *(The soil was dry because the plant drank up the water.)*

- Copy and distribute the Graphic Organizer on page T107 of this Guide. Have students write the above statements in the appropriate boxes. Then generate more statements and repeat the process.

What happened: I watered the plant.	Why it happened: The soil was dry.

- Explain that an *effect* is what happens and a *cause* is why it happens. Sometimes a cause has more than one effect, and sometimes an effect has more than one cause.

- Tell students that when they read about a cause-and-effect relationship, they might find clue words in the text. Some clue words signal causes: *because, since, if.* Some clue words signal effects: *so, therefore, caused, as a result.* If there are no clue words, readers can insert them.

- Invite students to read the passage about asteroids and to think about the effects asteroids have had on Earth.

- Have students complete the exercise. Check to be sure that they can identify causes and effects.

 Practice

Introducing Vocabulary

Before students read the article about dinosaurs, introduce the vocabulary words *(collision, disappearance, increasing, nurture, preyed, species, vanished)* and discuss their meanings. Have students look up each word in the Glossary and create oral sentences with them.

Reading the Passage

Invite students to read the title, look at the picture, and then predict what the article will be about. Have them use the title to form a question beginning with *why. (Why did the dinosaurs die?)* Point out that the answer will present a cause-and-effect relationship.

Checking Comprehension

- Since information about scientific techniques is scattered throughout the article, students might find it helpful to summarize each paragraph before answering the question.

- To help draw conclusions, students can underline details in the text. They should pay particular attention to the second half of the article.

Practicing Comprehension Skills

To help students keep track of cause-and-effect relationships, suggest that they make charts or graphic organizers in which arrows show how cause(s) point to effect(s).

Practicing Vocabulary

Review the vocabulary words. Have students identify the two words with the vowel digraph *ea. (disappearance,*

increasing) Invite students to complete the vocabulary exercise independently. Review the answers with the group.

Apply

Making the Reading and Writing Connection

Have volunteers read their accounts aloud. Afterward, listeners can evaluate the cause-and-effect relationship.

You may want to use pages 130–131 in *The Write Direction,* Grade 5 for additional opportunities in writing eyewitness accounts.

MEETING INDIVIDUAL NEEDS

Phonics: Vowel Digraph *ea*

On the board, write the vocabulary words that contain the vowel digraph *ea: disappearance, increasing.*

- Say both words and have students repeat them. Be sure they hear that *ea* has a different sound in each word.

- Have partners scan the articles on asteroids and dinosaurs to find at least eight additional words in which *ea* represents a single vowel sound. *(each, Earth, years, dead, reveal, spread, really, creatures, reason, death)*

- The class can then classify the words by vowel sound.

You may want to use pages 41–42 in *MCP Phonics,* Level E for additional practice with the vowel digraph *ea.*

ESL Strategy

Students can draw a picture to show what might have caused the extinction of dinosaurs. Then ask them to write one or two sentences to explain the picture. Encourage them to use the word *because* in their explanations.

Multiple Intelligences: Verbal-Linguistic, Visual-Spatial, Interpersonal

Small groups can research current theories of why dinosaurs became extinct. Ask them to display their findings in a chart that shows cause-and-effect relationships.

Home-School Connection

Suggest that students and family members look for cause-and-effect relationships at home. Ask them to create a list of ideas to share with the class. (For example: *I earned a dollar since I cleaned the patio. The grass is tall because our lawnmower is broken.*)

LESSON 7

Using Context Clues (pages 33–36)

Objective: Students can use context clues to figure out word meanings.

Teaching TIPS

- Students understand even complex written material much more quickly when they know how to use context clues.
- Students become more independent readers when they know how to use context clues.

Skills Reviewed and Maintained

Comprehension

Making Judgments	See Checking Comprehension
Comparing and Contrasting	See Checking Comprehension

Phonics

Diphthong *ew*	See Practicing Vocabulary, Phonics Mini-Lesson

Writing

Description	See Making the Reading and Writing Connection

Teach

Tell students that even the best readers come across unfamiliar words from time to time. Explain that there are strategies to help a reader understand what a word means without having to stop and look it up in a dictionary. To figure out the meaning of a word, readers can use its context—the words in the sentence and paragraph surrounding the unfamiliar word.

- On the board, write the following sentence: *The stalactites hanging from the roof of the cave looked like big icicles.* Ask students to explain what a stalactite is *(an icicle-shaped form hanging from the roof of a cave)* and to explain how they were able to figure out the word's meaning.

- Invite students to look at the chart on page 33, and have volunteers read aloud the explanations of four kinds of context clues: definition or explanation, example, synonym, and description.

- Tell students to read the passage about flashlight batteries. Invite them to note the types of context clues they come across.

- Have students complete the exercise. Check to be sure they can distinguish between the different types of context clues.

On Your Own Practice

Introducing Vocabulary

Before students read the story, introduce the vocabulary words *(annual, panels, recipe, renewable, solar, strewn, submit)* and discuss their meanings. Have students look up the words in the Glossary.

Reading the Passage

Have students study the picture and read the directions to discover what kind of convention, or assembly, the title refers to. Ask them to predict what the story characters will do at an invention convention.

Checking Comprehension

- Remind students that a judgment is an informed opinion based on information in the text as well as their own knowledge and experience. Have students think about how they use their imaginations to help solve problems.

- To help students compare and contrast the two inventions, suggest that they list the features of the rolling rake and the solar window in order to identify their similarities.

Practicing Comprehension Skills

After students have figured out a word's meaning using its context, they should reread the text, inserting the meaning in place of the unknown word. Does the text make sense with the new meaning inserted? If not, students should use a dictionary.

Practicing Vocabulary

- Review the vocabulary words. Ask students to identify the two words with the diphthong *ew. (renewable, strewn)*

- Have students complete the vocabulary exercise independently. Review the answers with the group.

Apply

Making the Reading and Writing Connection

Have volunteers read aloud their descriptions. Listeners can take note of special terminology and unfamiliar words and tell whether context clues made those words clear.

You may want to use pages 98–99 in *The Write Direction,* Grade 5 for additional opportunities in writing a descriptive paragraph.

MEETING INDIVIDUAL NEEDS

Phonics: Diphthong *ew*

On the board, write the vocabulary words that contain the diphthong *ew: renewable, strewn.*

- Say both words and have students repeat them, noting the sound *ew* makes.

- Explain that a diphthong is two letters blended together as one vowel sound.

- Have partners identify the base word in *renewable.* (*new*) Then challenge them to list as many rhyming

words as they can in one minute that end in *ew.* Pairs can then compare lists. (Examples: *few, threw, stew*)

You may want to use pages 57–58 in *MCP Phonics,* Level E for additional practice with the diphthong *ew.*

ESL Strategy

Help students write sentences about their native countries or cultures. Sentences should be written in English but contain one word from the student's first language. The context should provide clues to the word's meaning.

Multiple Intelligences: Verbal-Linguistic

Have students write a sentence for each vocabulary word. The sentences should contain context clues to help a reader figure out the words' meanings. Challenge students to use all four types of context clues and to connect the sentences in a short narrative.

Home-School Connection

Suggest that students read aloud to a family member from a challenging book or article. They can list three unfamiliar words from the selection and decide whether there are helpful context clues. If not, they should use a dictionary.

LESSON 8 — Comparing and Contrasting (pages 37–40)

Objective: Students can identify comparisons and contrasts and make their own.

Teaching TIPS

- Students recognize that comparison and contrast can be used to organize a piece of writing.

- Students can better understand new material when they compare and contrast it with what they already know.

Skills Reviewed and Maintained

Comprehension
Drawing Conclusions	See Checking Comprehension
Character	See Checking Comprehension

Word Study
Word Root *spect*	See Practicing Vocabulary, Word Study Mini-Lesson

Writing
News Story	See Making the Reading and Writing Connection

Teach

Explain to students that making comparisons and contrasts is especially helpful when learning or explaining something new. For example, a description of soccer can be clearer if you compare that game to one you already know, like basketball.

- Have students choose two sports to compare and contrast.

- Copy and distribute the Graphic Organizer on page T110 of this Guide. Together, fill out the Venn diagram. Have students label each circle with the name of a sport. List shared characteristics in the overlapping section, and list differences in the separate sections.

- Explain that writers sometimes, but not always, use clue words to signal comparisons and contrasts. List comparison clue words *(like, same, both, also)* and contrast clue words *(unlike, different, but, however)* on the board.

- Model using a clue word with information from the Venn diagram. *(Example: Badminton and tennis are both played with racquets and nets.)* Have volunteers make statements using other clue words.

- As students read the article about the two sports, they should notice comparisons and contrasts.

- Have students complete the exercise. Make sure they notice that the first paragraph compares and the second contrasts.

 **On Your Own Practice**

Introducing Vocabulary
Before students read the story, introduce the vocabulary words *(prospect, protested, referees, signaled, spectators, technique, weight)* and discuss their meanings. Give a synonym and have students identify the vocabulary word.

Reading the Passage
Have students use the directions, title, and pictures to predict what could happen to a "double-duty" father. Ask how comparisons and contrasts might be used in the story.

Checking Comprehension
- To help students draw conclusions, suggest that they think about sports events they have played in or attended. How do the fans show their support for a team?

- Remind students that a character's words and actions reveal his or her personality. When describing Mr. Chapman, students should cite details in the story.

Practicing Comprehension Skills
Encourage students to make comparisons and contrasts themselves—between ideas within a text, between a new text and previously read texts, and between prior knowledge and new ideas.

Practicing Vocabulary
Review the vocabulary words. Have students identify the two words with the root *spect. (prospect, spectator)* Have students complete the vocabulary exercise independently. Go over the answers together.

Apply

Making the Reading and Writing Connection
Have volunteers read their news stories aloud. Ask listeners to identify similarities and differences that the writer included.

You may want to use pages 139–149 in *The Write Direction*, Grade 5 for additional opportunities in writing news stories.

MEETING INDIVIDUAL NEEDS

Word Study: Word Root *spect*
On the board, write the vocabulary words that contain the root *spect: prospect, spectator.* Say both words and have students repeat them.

- Explain that the root *spect* means "see, look, examine."

- Discuss how the root meaning relates to the definitions of *prospect* and *spectator.*

- Write these words containing the root *spect* on the board: *spectacle, spectacular, spectrum, inspect, perspective, aspect, retrospect.* Have students use dictionaries to find definitions and tell how each word relates to the root meaning.

You may want to use pages 99–100 in *MCP Phonics*, Level E for additional practice with the root *spect.*

ESL Strategy
Students can compare and contrast their native country or culture with American culture. They can either draw pictures or write a short paragraph. Students who are from the same country or culture can work together.

Multiple Intelligences: Verbal-Linguistic, Interpersonal
Students can challenge classmates to a comparison-contrast contest. Partners can take turns comparing two sports or games using this pattern: "In both of these sports, *(players wear helmets).* One sport *(is played mostly indoors),* but the other *(is played outdoors).* What are the sports?"

Home-School Connection
Suggest that students work with a family member to compare and contrast two movies they have seen, two books they have read, or two people they know.

LESSON 9

Summarizing (pages 41–46)

Objective: Students can summarize both fiction and nonfiction.

(pages 41–46)

Teaching **TIPS**

- Students organize information and evaluate the relative importance of ideas and events when they summarize.
- Students who summarize have improved comprehension.

Skills Reviewed and Maintained

Comprehension

Main Idea	See Checking Comprehension
Making Judgments	See Checking Comprehension

Word Study

Prefixes in-, un-	See Practicing Vocabulary, Word Study Mini-Lesson

Writing

Summary	See Making the Reading and Writing Connection

Teach

Tell students that they summarize information or events every day. They do so when they describe a movie to a friend or tell their parents what happened in school that day.

- Copy and distribute the Graphic Organizer on page T104 of this Guide. Select a movie that most students have seen. Then have the class tell what happened in the movie. Write their responses in the chart.

  Main Idea Woody, a stuffed cowboy, is Andy's favorite toy.

  Main Idea One Christmas, Andy receives a toy astronaut called Buzz. Buzz becomes Andy's new favorite. Woody is jealous and competitive.

  Main Idea Woody and Buzz fall into the hands of Sid, a vicious boy who lives next door. After several attempts, they finally escape. Buzz and Woody eventually become friends.

  Summary Andy has two toys, a cowboy and an astronaut, who compete for the boy's attention. The two toys become friends after they narrowly escape from the clutches of an evil neighbor.

- Together, use the main ideas and events to write a summary, as in this sample for the movie *Toy Story*.

- Invite students to read "The Visitor" and "A Friendly Mission" and complete the exercises. Check understanding by noting whether students have used their own words to summarize the main ideas.

On Your Own **Practice**

Introducing Vocabulary

Before students read the article, introduce the vocabulary words (*adapted, atmosphere, infrequently, ponder, researchers, telescopes, unknown*) and discuss their meanings. Use the words in questions and have students answer.

Reading the Passage

Have students look at the photograph and read the title. Ask them to predict what they will probably learn about in "Life Beyond Earth."

Checking Comprehension

- To clarify the main idea, have students reread the text for descriptions of life-supporting features on Earth.

- To help students make judgments about scientific evidence, discuss the details the text gives about life on other planets. Encourage students to use their prior knowledge of the subject.

Practicing Comprehension Skills

Show various methods of identifying the main ideas in a text: highlighting, underlining, or margin notes. Students should ask themselves, "Is this idea important enough to include in a summary?" Students can try the different methods and decide which they prefer.

Practicing Vocabulary

- Review the vocabulary words. Have students identify the words with the prefix *in-* or *un-*. (*infrequently, unknown*)

- Ask students to complete the vocabulary exercise independently. Talk about the answers as a class.

Apply

Making the Reading and Writing Connection

Have partners exchange their summaries. Readers should look for any trivial or repetitive material.

You may want to use pages 44–45 in *The Write Direction*, Grade 5 for additional opportunities in writing summaries.

MEETING INDIVIDUAL NEEDS

Word Study: Prefixes *in-*, *un-*

On the board, write the vocabulary words *infrequently* and *unknown*. Say the words and have students repeat them.

- Remind students that a prefix is a word part added to a base word that changes the word's meaning and sometimes its part of speech.

- Explain that the prefixes *in-* and *un-* both mean "not." Ask what *infrequently* and *unknown* mean.

- Write these base words on the board and have volunteers add *in-* or *un-* to make new words: *visible, aware,*

correct, complete, usual, steady. Discuss the meanings of the new words.

You may want to use pages 67–68 in *MCP Phonics*, Level E for additional practice with the prefixes *in-* and *un-*.

ESL Strategy

Have small groups of students read "The Visitor" aloud. On a story board, they can draw pictures of the three main events and write captions describing the events. Then they can combine the picture captions into a story summary.

Multiple Intelligences: Verbal-Linguistic, Interpersonal

Have small groups of students write a short narrative about discovering life on another planet. Afterward, they can write a summary of their story.

Home-School Connection

Students and a family member can watch a science or nature television program and then write a summary of it. Suggest that they compare their summary to the one in the television guide.

Paraphrasing (pages 47–50)

LESSON 10

Objective: Students can use their own words to restate written material.

Teaching TIPS

- Students check their comprehension when they paraphrase written material.

- Students can use paraphrasing to take notes, do research, and study for tests.

Skills Reviewed and Maintained

Comprehension

Cause and Effect	See Checking Comprehension
Comparing and Contrasting	See Checking Comprehension

Word Study

Prefix *post-*	See Practicing Vocabulary, Word Study Mini-Lesson

Writing

Descriptive Paragraph   See Making the Reading and Writing Connection

Teach

Name a familiar story and ask students to retell it to themselves silently. Then discuss what they had to think about in order to retell the story.

- Explain that retelling a story or restating information is called *paraphrasing*. A paraphrase is often as long as the original text and contains all the same events and ideas, but it is told in the reader's own words. Therefore, a paraphrase is simpler to read than the original.

- Read aloud a paragraph from students' science or history textbook. Tell students to listen to it carefully in order to paraphrase it. Reread the paragraph. Then have volunteers offer oral paraphrases.

- Discuss whether each paraphrase was told in the volunteer's own words. Make sure the meaning of the original text wasn't changed and no opinions were added.

- Tell students to read the passage about secret codes. They should think about how they would paraphrase the ideas if they were taking notes.

- Invite students to complete the exercise. Check for understanding by having them use their own words to tell what a paraphrase is.

Practice

Introducing Vocabulary
Before students read the article, introduce the vocabulary words (*decision, operated, numerous, patriotism, postpone, postwar, skillful*) and discuss their meanings. Have students offer a synonym or antonym for each word.

Reading the Passage
Tell students to read the title and preview the photograph. Ask them to predict how code talkers might be used as a secret weapon. Encourage students to pause after each paragraph and paraphrase the information to themselves.

Checking Comprehension
- Review cause and effect relationships by having students complete this statement with evidence from the article: *American soldiers would have been in danger if their codes were broken because _____.*

- To help students compare and contrast, invite them to reread paragraphs five and six, which explain the differences between Navajo and English.

Practicing Comprehension Skills
Help students see that a paraphrase contains all the ideas and important details of the original text. Stress that this information must be put in the reader's own words. Copying an author's exact words, unless quotation marks are used, is called plagiarizing, and it's wrong.

Practicing Vocabulary
- Review the vocabulary words. Have students identify the two words with the prefix *post-*. (*postpone, postwar*)

- Invite students to complete the vocabulary exercise independently. Review the answers with the group.

Apply

Making the Reading and Writing Connection
Display the descriptions and the paraphrases on the bulletin board. Have students match each paragraph with its paraphrase.

You may want to use pages **98–99** in *The Write Direction*, Grade 5 for additional opportunities in writing descriptive paragraphs.

MEETING INDIVIDUAL NEEDS

Word Study: Prefix *post-*
On the board, write the vocabulary words *postpone* and *postwar*. Circle the prefix *post-* in each word.

- Tell students that the prefix post- means "after." It can be added before a word root (*pone*) or a base word (*war*). Ask how the meaning "after" is used in the two vocabulary words. (*When you postpone something, you put it off until afterward; a postwar period comes after a war is over.*)

- Have students take turns looking up these words in a dictionary and reading aloud their definitions: *postdate, postgraduate, postscript, postseason, postmark.*

You may want to use pages **79–80** in *MCP Phonics*, Level E for additional practice with the prefix *post-*.

ESL Strategy
Have students acquiring English work with a peer tutor to paraphrase each sentence of a short magazine or newspaper article.

Multiple Intelligences: Verbal-Linguistic, Interpersonal
Divide the class into small groups. Assign each group one paragraph from "Code Talkers." Students should work together to write a paraphrase of the paragraph. Afterward, the class can listen to each paraphrase and decide which paragraph it corresponds to.

Home-School Connection
Have students ask a family member to tell about an interesting or funny childhood event. Then students can paraphrase the story and share it with the class.

Recognizing Author's Purpose (pages 51–56)

Objective: Students can identify four common purposes for writing.

Teaching TIPS

- Students better comprehend and appreciate what they read when they are able to identify the author's purpose.

- Students can adjust their reading strategies in response to the author's purpose.

Skills Reviewed and Maintained

Comprehension
Summarizing	See Checking Comprehension
Making Judgments	See Checking Comprehension

Word Study
Prefix *mis-*	See Practicing Vocabulary, Word Study Mini-Lesson

Writing
With a Purpose	See Making the Reading and Writing Connection

Teach

Ask students to think about different kinds of material they read every day. On the board make a list of students' suggestions. A wide range of texts should be included: magazine ads, comic strips, menus, street signs, encyclopedia articles, mysteries, adventure stories, folk tales, science articles, and TV and movie reviews.

- List and number the four common purposes that authors have for writing: (1) to persuade, (2) to inform, (3) to express, (4) to entertain. Use the brief definitions on page 51 to discuss each purpose.

- Have students tell which number or numbers belong next to each text in the list. Encourage discussion, making the point that an author often has more than one purpose for writing.

- Explain that knowing an author's purpose affects the way a reader approaches a text. It determines how slowly, quickly, carefully, or critically the material is read.

- Invite students to read the passages on pages 51 and 52. Tell them to think about how the author's language and style fits the purpose of each passage.

- After students complete the exercises, check that they can differentiate between the four purposes.

On Your Own Practice

Introducing Vocabulary
Before students read the article, introduce the vocabulary words *(complicated, marsupial, misguided, mistrust, nocturnal, offspring, promptly)* and discuss their meanings. For each word, have students give a synonym or an example.

Reading the Passage
Have students read the title and the author's name. Have them look at the drawing to predict who the "I" in the title is and what her purpose might be for writing the article.

Checking Comprehension

- Tell students that summarizing an article means retelling only the most important ideas and events. Guide them in choosing just two or three main points to include in their summaries.

- Clarify that a judgment must be based on evidence in the text as well as personal experiences. Have students look for details to support their judgment about the author's lifestyle.

Practicing Comprehension Skills
Have students point out examples of humor in both the article on page 53 and the poem on page 55. Explain that authors choose their style and language to fit their purpose(s)—in this case, to entertain.

Practicing Vocabulary
Review the vocabulary words with students.

- Have students identify the two words with the prefix *mis-*. *(misguided, mistrust)*

- Invite students to complete the vocabulary exercise independently. Review the answers with the group.

Apply

Making the Reading and Writing Connection

Have volunteers read their poems or stories aloud. Ask listeners to tell the author's purpose(s).

You may want to use pages 100–105 in *The Write Direction,* Grade 5 for additional opportunities in writing poetry or stories with a purpose.

MEETING INDIVIDUAL NEEDS

Word Study: Prefix *mis-*

On the board, write the vocabulary words with the prefix *mis-: misguided, mistrust.*

- Explain that the prefix adds the meaning "bad" or "badly." Have students use the word *bad* or *badly* to explain why a misguided person would end up lost and why mistrust is not good for friendships.

- List the following base words: *spell, pronounce, lead,*

direct, step, use. Have students add *mis-* and use *bad* or *badly* in a brief definition of the new word.

You may want to use pages 71–72 in *MCP Phonics,* Level E for additional practice with the prefix *mis-.*

ESL Strategy

Lead a small-group discussion about pets. Guide students in making statements that persuade, inform, express, and entertain.

Multiple Intelligences: Verbal-Linguistic, Interpersonal

Suggest that partners take turns reading the passages and the poem aloud. The listener should decide whether the reader's tone of voice matches the author's purpose(s).

Home-School Connection

Suggest that students and a family member read a movie review together. They should look for examples of language that persuades, informs, entertains, and/or expresses a feeling or opinion. Together, they can write a sentence explaining the reviewer's main purpose.

LESSON 12 Statements of Fact and Opinion (pages 57–60)

Objective: Students can distinguish between statements of fact and opinion.

Teaching TIPS

- Students think critically about what they read when they learn to distinguish between fact and opinion.

- Students realize that statements of fact are not always true, and that some opinions are better supported than others.

Skills Reviewed and Maintained

Comprehension
Drawing Conclusions   See Checking Comprehension
Summarizing   See Checking Comprehension

Word Study
Prefixes *pre-* and *pro-*   See Practicing Vocabulary, Word Study Mini-Lesson

Writing
Editorial   See Making the Reading and Writing Connection

Teach

Have students recount situations in which they have said or heard the expression, *"Prove it!"* Discuss ways people can prove that something is true.

- Tell students that statements of fact can be correct or incorrect. Write these statements of fact on the board and have students suggest ways of proving the accuracy of each:

  Archaeologists study how people lived in the distant past. (Check the definition of *archaeologist.*)

  The ancient Egyptians were the only people in the world to build pyramids. (Look up *pyramids* in an encyclopedia to see whether other cultures built them.)

- Tell students that statements of opinion can't be proved true or false. State the following opinions and discuss why each can't be proved and why someone might agree or disagree with it:

   Archaeology is a rewarding career.

   I think that the pyramids of Egypt are fascinating.

- Direct students to read the paragraph about archaeologists. Have them underline statements of fact and circle statements of opinion as they read.

- Tell students to complete the exercise. Then ask them what the writer's main opinion is and whether strong supporting reasons are given.

 **Practice**

Introducing Vocabulary

Before students read the article, introduce the vocabulary words *(erupting, molten, terrified, precautions, prolonged, rooftops, wealthy)* and discuss their meanings. Have students use each word in an oral sentence.

Reading the Passage

Have students read the title, look at the photo, and tell what kinds of facts they might learn in "Pompeii Buried!" Remind them that statements of fact are verifiable while statements of opinion express what the writer feels or believes.

Checking Comprehension

- Help students draw conclusions by reviewing relevant details, such as people's reactions to signs from Mount Vesuvius.

- Before students write their summaries, have them reread the paragraphs that tell about events on August 24 and 25 and identify the main idea of each.

Practicing Comprehension Skills

Students should realize that writers do not always mark their opinions with clue phrases such as *I think* or *I believe*. Words such as *most* and *best* may signal an opinion, as may adjectives such as *interesting* and *amazing*.

Practicing Vocabulary

Review the vocabulary words. Have students identify the words with the prefixes *pre-* and *pro-*. *(precautions, prolonged)* Have students complete the vocabulary exercise independently. Go over the answers together.

Apply

Making the Reading and Writing Connection

Ask volunteers to read their editorials aloud. Listeners can restate the writer's opinion and identify supporting facts.

You may want to use pages 186–188 in *The Write Direction*, Grade 5 for additional opportunities in writing editorials.

MEETING INDIVIDUAL NEEDS

Word Study: Prefixes *pre-* and *pro-*

On the board, write the vocabulary words *precautions* and *prolonged*. Say the words and have students repeat them.

- Circle the prefix *pre-* and tell students that it means "before." Ask a volunteer to define *precautions*. *(Precautions are safety measures you take beforehand.)*

- Circle the prefix *pro-* and tell students that it means "go forward." Ask how "going forward" relates to the meaning of *prolonged*. *(Something prolonged seems to be stretched forward.)*

- Write these base words and word roots on the board: *tend, test, motion, dict, mature, duct, ject*. Ask volunteers to make new words by adding the prefix *pre-* or *pro-* to each.

You may want to use pages 73–74 in *MCP Phonics*, Level E for additional practice with the prefixes *pre-* and *pro-*.

ESL Strategy

Help students write a statement of fact and a statement of opinion about the same topic; for example, today's weather. Let students share their sentences. Listeners can identify each statement as a *fact* or an *opinion*.

Multiple Intelligences: Verbal-Linguistic, Interpersonal

Let groups of students scan today's newspaper for examples of facts and opinions. Students can cut out the examples and use them to make a poster that explains the differences between statements of fact and opinion. They can display their posters on the bulletin board.

Home-School Connection

Have students read a magazine article with a family member. They should find one statement of fact and one statement of opinion. Then they can decide how the fact can be proved and if the opinion is well supported.

Making Judgments (pages 61–64)

Objective: Students can make and support judgments about a text.

Teaching **TIPS**

- Students monitor their own comprehension of a text when they make judgments.

- Students think critically about evidence in the text, as well as their own experiences and values, when they make judgments.

Skills Reviewed and Maintained

Comprehension

Cause and Effect   See Checking Comprehension

Main Idea and Details   See Reading the Passage, Checking Comprehension

Phonics

Vowel Digraph *oo*   See Practicing Vocabulary, Phonics Mini-Lesson

Writing

Character Sketch   See Making the Reading and Writing Connection

Teach

Choose an issue that students will probably have a strong opinion about, such as school uniforms. Start a discussion of the topic. Encourage students to consider both sides of the issue.

- Make a chart on the board listing reasons in support of and in opposition to school uniforms.

- Explain that a judgment is an opinion based on certain criteria. Stress the importance of logical reasons, factual evidence, and personal experiences and values when making judgments.

- Talk about how readers make judgments about characters or ideas in a text. Point out that making judgments is a two-way street. Aside from judging the actions of characters, ideas in articles, and so on, readers judge the accuracy of texts, the objectivity of writers, and the validity of writers' conclusions.

- Tell students to read the passage about Mother Teresa and to make judgments about her and her work.

- Have students complete the exercise. Then discuss how they made their judgments.

Practice

Introducing Vocabulary

Before students read the article, introduce the vocabulary words *(accessible, broaden, overlooked, pollute, afternoon, suitable, volunteering)* and discuss their meanings. Have students give at least one synonym, or description, for each word.

Reading the Passage

Have students look at the photograph and read the title. What do they think the main idea of "Kid Power" will be? Let students predict what they might be making judgments about in this passage.

Checking Comprehension

- Have students identify the cause-and-effect relationships in the fourth and fifth paragraphs before they decide whether kids can make a difference.

- Before students answer the question, they should identify the article's main idea and decide whether it is supported by enough details.

Practicing Comprehension Skills

Point out that an article may present a set of facts and then conclude with the author's judgment. To decide whether the author's conclusion is valid, students should establish criteria such as, *"Does the writer consider both sides of the issue?"*

Practicing Vocabulary

- Have students identify the two words with the vowel digraph *oo. (afternoon, overlooked)*

- Invite students to complete the vocabulary exercise independently. Review the answers with the class.

Apply

Making the Reading and Writing Connection

Have volunteers read their character sketches aloud. Ask the class to determine the writer's judgment and to identify two supporting reasons.

You may want to use pages 116–118 in *The Write Direction,* Grade 5 for additional opportunities in writing character sketches.

MEETING INDIVIDUAL NEEDS

Phonics: Vowel Digraph *oo*

On the board, write the vocabulary words with *oo: afternoon, overlooked.*

- Say the words, emphasizing the vowel sound in the last syllable of each word. Have students repeat the words.

- Underline *oo* and help students identify the sound the letters represent in each word. (/o͞o/, /o͝o/) Explain that the vowel digraph *oo* can represent either sound.

- Say the following words and have students tell which sound *oo* makes in each: *football, brook, root, goodbye, noodle, moonlight, poodle, textbook, neighborhood, toothbrush.*

You may want to use pages 49–50 in *MCP Phonics,* Level E for additional practice with vowel digraph *oo.*

ESL Strategy

Students can work with a peer tutor to read "Kid Power" aloud and to highlight statements that express the author's judgments.

Multiple Intelligences: Verbal-Linguistic

Have students research a particular volunteer job and then make a speech advocating it. Guide them in making judgments that are supported by evidence and logical reasons.

Home-School Connection

Have students interview a family member about his or her ideas on a subject such as the environment. Remind students to ask questions that prompt the family member to support judgments with facts and reasons.

Point of View (pages 65–70)

Objective: Students can identify first-person and third-person points of view.

Teaching TIPS

- Students learn that identifying point of view is vital to understanding a work of literature.

- Students learn that a story's point of view determines how much and what kind of information the reader is given.

Skills Reviewed and Maintained

Comprehension
Drawing Conclusions	See Checking Comprehension
Character	See Checking Comprehension

Word Study
Prefix *over-*	See Practicing Vocabulary, Word Study Mini-Lesson

Writing
Story	See Making the Reading and Writing Connection

Teach

Narrate a simple series of events, such as going to the store or the movies, from the first-person point of view. Then narrate the same events from the third-person point of view. Discuss the differences between the two versions.

- Make a two-column chart on the board titled *Point of View.* List *First-Person* pronouns in one column (*I, me, mine*) and *Third-Person* pronouns in the other column (*he, she, it, him, hers, its, they, them, theirs*).

- Ask students to differentiate between the narrator of a story and its author. Make sure they understand that when authors write a story, they create a narrator to tell the story from the first-person or third-person point of view.

- Explain that a narrator speaking from the first-person point of view might say, *"I had an adventure yesterday that scared me!"* This narrator is also a character in the story. A third-person narrator would express the same idea differently: *"Oscar had an adventure yesterday that scared him!"* This narrator is outside the story.

- Select sentences from stories that include pronouns from the chart. As you say each sentence, students should tell its point of view.

- Invite students to read the explanations and stories on pages 65 and 66, and complete the exercises.

- Check students' understanding by asking how they identified the narrator in each version of the story.

 **Practice**

Introducing Vocabulary
Before students read the story, introduce the vocabulary words *(blared, congratulate, expressed, overboard, overeager, satisfying, smudged)* and discuss their meanings. Ask students to use each word in an oral sentence.

Reading the Passages
Have students use the titles and pictures to predict what "Walking the Dog" and "The Ping-Pong Tournament" might be about. To decide on the narrator's point of view, they should notice which pronouns are used and if one or more characters' thoughts are given.

Checking Comprehension

- To draw conclusions, students should think about the following: what Kenny and Phillip say, what they think, and how they react.

- Discuss Jerome's actions, thoughts, and feelings to help students think about his character.

Practicing Comprehension Skills
Explain that point of view affects how the reader experiences a story's events. Ask students to think about how each story might change if told from a different point of view.

Practicing Vocabulary

- Have students identify the two words with the prefix *over-*. *(overboard, overeager)*

- Students can complete the vocabulary exercise independently. Review the answers with the class.

Apply

Making the Reading and Writing Connection
Have volunteers read their stories aloud. Ask listeners to tell at what point in the story they were able to identify the narrator and the point of view.

MEETING INDIVIDUAL NEEDS

Word Study: Prefix *over-*
On the board, write the vocabulary words *overeager* and *overboard.* Say both words and have students repeat them.

- Tell students that the prefix *over-* means "too much" or "too." Ask a volunteer to describe how an overeager person might act.

- Have students find the word *overboard* in "Walking the Dog." Discuss the figurative meaning of the idiom "to go overboard."

- Have students use a dictionary to find five words in which *over-* means "too much" or "too." (Possible answers: *overact, overcharge, overdo, overpaid, overtired, oversized*) Then let students compare their lists.

You may want to use pages 81–82 in *MCP Phonics,* Level E for additional practice with the prefix *over-*.

ESL Strategy
Read aloud sentences from "Walking the Dog." Guide students in restating the sentences with first-person pronouns.

Multiple Intelligences: Verbal-Linguistic, Interpersonal
Have small groups of students rewrite "The Ping-Pong Tournament" from the third-person point of view.

Home-School Connection
Tell students to observe their own or a neighbor's pet or some other animal. Then have them write a paragraph telling about an event from that animal's point of view. They can read the paragraph aloud to family members, who should try to guess the story's narrator.

Text Structure (pages 71–76)

Objective: Students can identify a text's structure and select a reading strategy.

Teaching TIPS

- Students read more efficiently when they identify a text structure.
- Students are better able to comprehend and summarize a text when they identify its structure.

Skills Reviewed and Maintained

Comprehension
Main Idea   See Checking Comprehension
Making Judgments   See Checking Comprehension

Word Study
Prefix *sub-*   See Practicing Vocabulary, Word Study Mini-Lesson

Writing
Nonfiction   See Making the Reading and Writing Connection

Teach

Clarify the distinction between the two major genres, fiction and nonfiction, by holding up various texts (such as a short story, a magazine article, a novel, a science textbook) and asking students to tell what genre each one is. Discuss the main features of each genre.

- Explain that because fiction tells what happens to story characters, events are usually arranged in chronological, or time, order.

- Tell students that nonfiction may also be organized chronologically. Talk about types of informational writing in which chronological order might be important. *(For example, histories, biographies, directions)*

- Emphasize that nonfiction texts can also be organized in other ways as well. Review the text structures listed on page 71. Explain how students can read more efficiently if they recognize these structures.

- Encourage students to give examples of each kind of text structure.

- Invite students to read the article and letter on page 72. After students complete the exercises, check that they can explain what text *structure* means.

On Your Own Practice

Introducing Vocabulary
Before students read the article, introduce the vocabulary words *(coincidence, subject, poverty, privileged, senseless, subsided, varied)* and discuss their meanings. Ask students to use each word in an oral sentence.

Reading the Passage
Have students identify the portraits of Lincoln and Kennedy and tell what they know about each president. After they read the title of this passage, ask them to predict a likely text structure.

Checking Comprehension

- Remind students that the main idea states what the article is mostly about. Suggest that they use the information in the title to compose a main idea statement.

- To help sudents make their judgments, suggest that they first look at text details and then think about their own responses to these details.

Practicing Comprehension Skills
After students have read the articles, ask them to think about how the information would be arranged if the author had chosen a different text structure.

Practicing Vocabulary

- Review the vocabulary words. Have students identify the two words with the prefix *sub-. (subject, subsided)*

- Have students complete the vocabulary exercise independently. Go over the answers together.

Apply

Making the Reading and Writing Connection
Have volunteers read their nonfiction passages aloud. Ask classmates to identify the text structure and identify any clue words that helped them figure it out.

You may want to use pages 134–135 in *The Write Direction*, Grade 5 for additional opportunities for writing nonfiction.

MEETING INDIVIDUAL NEEDS

Word Study: Prefix *sub-*

On the board, write the vocabulary words *subject* and *subsided*. Say the words and have students repeat them.

- Tell students that the prefix *sub-* means "under or below" or "not quite." Have students use one of those meanings to explain what "an article's subject" is *(the topic under consideration)* and what happened when "the storm subsided." *(it was not quite as strong)*

- Ask students to define these words: *submarine, suburb, submit, substitute, subway.* Encourage them to use a dictionary.

You may want to use pages 85–86 in *MCP Phonics*, Level E for additional practice with the prefix *sub-*.

ESL Strategy

Provide simple books or articles for small groups to read together. Guide students in identifying the text structure used in each.

Multiple Intelligences: Visual-Spatial, Interpersonal

Small groups can work together to draw an appropriate graphic organizer for each passage in the lesson.

Home-School Connection

Students and a family member can find a book, reference source, or on line site about U.S. presidents. Students should identify the text structure and explain how they figured it out.

LESSON 16 Understanding Author's Viewpoint (pages 77–80)

Objective: Students can identify and evaluate an author's viewpoint.

Teaching TIPS

- Students read more critically when they evaluate an author's viewpoint.
- Students can better analyze the validity of a text when they identify the author's viewpoint.

Skills Reviewed and Maintained

Comprehension

Comparing and Contrasting	See Checking Comprehension
Making Judgments	See Checking Comprehension

Word Study

Word Root *dict*	See Practicing Vocabulary, Word Study Mini-Lesson

Writing

Editorial	See Making the Reading and Writing Connection

Teach

Introduce the term *author's viewpoint* and explain that it refers to the way an author looks at the subject or ideas he or she is writing about. Balanced writing presents both sides of an issue while biased writing does not. It is up to the reader to figure out whether a piece of writing is balanced or biased.

- Read aloud the following statements and have students tell whether each one is balanced or biased:

  1. The smallest fifth-grade class at Endicott School has 35 students in it. *(balanced)*
  2. Students learn less in overcrowded classrooms. *(biased)*
  3. Town voters will decide on Tuesday whether to fund the building of a new school. *(balanced)*
  4. Citizens who care about our children's future will vote in favor of this tax bill. *(biased)*

- Reread statements 2 and 4 and have students note words that suggest bias. *(overcrowded, care, our children's future)* Explain how "loaded" words reveal the author's viewpoint and usually indicate bias.

- As students read the letter to the editor, they should think about the author's viewpoint and keep an eye out for loaded words.

- After students complete the exercise, check understanding by having them explain the difference between biased and balanced writing.

Practice

Introducing Vocabulary

Before students read the script, introduce the vocabulary words (*absences, adopt, conducted, dictate, districts, participate, predict*) and discuss their meanings. Have students use the words in oral sentences.

Reading the Passage

Invite students to look at the pictures and read the script title and cast list. Ask them why they think the TV program is called *News and Views*. Do students think that only one or both sides of an issue will be presented?

Checking Comprehension

- To help students compare and contrast school schedules, have them highlight details that explain Carver's schedule.

- Remind students that in order for a judgment to be valid, it should be supported by facts and logic, not just by personal feelings about the issue.

Practicing Comprehension Skills

Point out to students that a biased text must be consistently biased, not just contain quotes or views that are biased. Discuss how a text that cites biased views can still be balanced. Have students think about this point in relation to the script.

Practicing Vocabulary

- Have students identify the two words with the root *dict. (dictate, predict)*

- Invite students to complete the vocabulary exercise independently. Review the answers together.

Apply

Making the Reading and Writing Connection

Have volunteers read their editorial articles aloud. Ask listeners to tell whether the articles are balanced or biased and to explain how they arrived at their conclusions.

You may want to use pages 186–188 in *The Write Direction*, Grade 5 for additional opportunities in writing editorials.

MEETING INDIVIDUAL NEEDS

Word Study: Word Root *dict*

On the board, write the vocabulary words *dictate* and *predict*. Read the words aloud, prompting students to read them along with you.

- Tell students that the root *dict* means "tell" or "say." Ask which word means "to tell ahead of time" (*predict*) and which one means "to say or read aloud." (*dictate*)

- List these affixes on the board: *un-, -able, -or, -ship, -ion*. Work with the class to add the affixes to the two vocabulary words to create five longer words. (*unpredictable, prediction, dictation, dictator, dictatorship*)

- Have volunteers use the root meaning of *dict* to define each of these words: *contradict, diction, dictionary.*

You may want to use pages 97–98 in *MCP Phonics*, Level E for additional practice with the root *dict*.

ESL Strategy

Help students find sentences from the television script that contain loaded words. (*"This isn't fair," for example.*) Students can practice saying the sentences with the appropriate tone of voice and expression.

Multiple Intelligences: Verbal-Linguistic, Interpersonal

Small groups can research the subject of year-round schooling. They should then use the TV script, additional research, and their own knowledge to write a speech in favor of or in opposition to year-round schooling. Have them present their speeches to the class.

Home-School Connection

Have students and a family member read a magazine article together. They should decide if the writing is balanced or biased.

LESSON 17
Making Generalizations (pages 81–84)

Objective: Students can recognize, make, and evaluate generalizations.

Teaching TIPS

- Students think more critically about a text when they make generalizations about it.
- Students can better judge whether an author's argument is valid or biased when they recognize generalizations.

Skills Reviewed and Maintained

Comprehension

Main Idea	See Checking Comprehension
Summarizing	See Checking Comprehension

Word Study

Suffix -ward	See Practicing Vocabulary, Word Study Mini-Lesson

Writing

Biography	See Making the Reading and Writing Connection

Teach

Survey the class with one or two questions such as these: *What is your favorite TV show? What kinds of pets do you have? Where would you like to go on your next vacation?* Display students' responses in a list or chart.

- Use clue words such as *all, most, generally, usually,* and *never* to make valid and faulty generalizations based on the information gathered in the survey. (Example: *Most students have dogs.*) Have students tell whether each statement seems accurate, and explain why.

- Define a generalization as a broad statement or rule that applies to many examples. A generalization is valid if facts and logic support it. A generalization is faulty if it is not adequately supported.

- Explain that when students read, they should look for clue words that signal generalizations, such as *all, most, often, generally.* If there is no clue word, students can add one to test whether the statement is a generalization.

- Invite students to read the paragraph about barnstormers. Encourage them to pick out the author's examples in order to make generalizations.

- After students answer the questions, check to make sure their generalizations are valid.

On Your Own Practice

Introducing Vocabulary

Before students read the biographical article, introduce the vocabulary words *(afford, afterward, dazzled, downward, license, opportunities, stalled)* and discuss their meanings. Use the words in questions for students to answer. For example: *What are some items you can afford?*

Reading the Passage

Have students read the title and then tell who is shown in the photograph. Remind students to look for clue words that signal the author's generalizations as well as examples they can use to make their own generalizations.

Checking Comprehension

- Clarify the article's main idea by having students tell what they learned about barnstorming and Bessie's career.

- Have students summarize each of the first five paragraphs of the article. They can then combine these statements to answer the question.

Practicing Comprehension Skills

Have students use the words *in general* or *generally* to make valid generalizations based on examples in the article. Point out the mnemonic link between the clue words and the term generalization.

Practicing Vocabulary

- Review the vocabulary words. Have students identify the two words with the suffix *-ward. (afterward, downward)*

- Invite students to complete the vocabulary exercise independently. Review the answers with the class.

Apply

Making the Reading and Writing Connection

Let volunteers read their biographies aloud. Have listeners answer this question: What seems to be generally true about the person who is the subject of the biography?

You may want to use pages 55–67 in *The Write Direction,* Grade 5 for additional opportunities in writing biographies.

MEETING INDIVIDUAL NEEDS

Word Study: Suffix -ward

On the board, write the vocabulary words *afterward* and *downward.* Circle the suffix *-ward.*

- Invite volunteers to say the words and then use them in sentences.
- Tell students that the suffix *-ward* indicates a direction in time or space. Have volunteers tell which word shows direction in time *(afterward)* and which one shows direction in space. *(downward)*

- Say each of the following words: *upward, backward, skyward, forward, onward, toward, inward, homeward.* Have one volunteer write the word on the board while another explains its meaning.

You may want to use pages 115–116 in *MCP Phonics,* Level E for additional practice with the suffix *-ward.*

ESL Strategy

Students can draw a picture showing one thing that most barnstormers do. Help them write a sentence including the word *most* or *usually* to use as a caption.

Multiple Intelligences: Verbal-Linguistic, Interpersonal

Have small groups of students choose a topic and write three valid generalizations about it. Each generalization should use a different clue word.

Home-School Connection

Students can ask an older family member how children's lives many years ago were different than they are today. Students should write the responses as sentences that include *generally* or another clue word.

Outlining (pages 85–88)

Objective: Students can organize information in outline form.

Teaching TIPS

- Students focus on a text's main ideas and supporting details when they outline it.
- Students understand and remember the information found in a nonfictional text when they outline it.

Skills Reviewed and Maintained

Comprehension

Comparing and Contrasting	See Checking Comprehension
Cause and Effect	See Checking Comprehension

Phonics

Vowel Digraph *ui*	See Practicing Vocabulary, Phonics Mini-Lesson

Writing

Outline	See Making the Reading and Writing Connection

Teach

Have students name musical instruments and list them on the board. Make a partial outline using this model:

Musical Instruments

I. Strings
   A. Played with bow
      1. _____
      2. _____
   B. Plucked with fingers
      1. _____
      2. _____
II. Drums and other percussion instruments
   A. Hit with sticks
      1. _____
      2. _____
   B. _____

- With students, fill out the outline with names of instruments after each Arabic numeral, and with another subtopic after II B (Hit with hands). Add more categories to the outline, such as III. Wind instruments; A. Woodwinds, and so on.

- Explain that an outline helps readers see at a glance how ideas or things are related to each other.

- Review with students the parts of an outline.

- Invite students to read the article and use the information to fill in the outline. Check for understanding.

On Your Own Practice

Introducing Vocabulary

Before students read the article, introduce the vocabulary words *(acoustic, acquired, amplify, contraption, electrify, fad, guitar)*. Have students look up the definitions in the Glossary and create oral sentences with the words.

Reading the Passage

Invite students to read the title and look at the photograph. Have them predict what "Electrifying the Guitar" will teach them about electric guitars.

Checking Comprehension

- Before students compare and contrast the two types of guitars, have them look for clue words that signal contrasts *(difference, however)* and words with comparative endings *(-er, -est)*.

- Suggest that students think about cause-and-effect relationships by completing this sentence: *Solid-body, electric guitars became popular because* _____.

Practicing Comprehension Skills

Guide students in completing their outlines by pointing out that the article is about the development of electric guitars. The main topics of the outline reflect that process and are therefore ordered chronologically.

Practicing Vocabulary

- Have students identify the word with the vowel digraph *ui.* *(guitar)*

- Let students complete the vocabulary exercise independently. Review the answers together.

Apply

Making the Reading and Writing Connection

After partners outline each other's paragraphs, writers should check to be sure that all information in their papers is included in the outline.

You may want to use pages 46–48 in *The Write Direction,* Grade 5 for additional opportunities in writing outlines.

MEETING INDIVIDUAL NEEDS

Phonics: Vowel Digraph *ui*

On the board, start a two-column list. Write the vocabulary word with *ui: guitar* at the top of one column and the word *juice* at the top of the other column.

- Say the words, emphasizing the sound made by the vowel digraph, and have students repeat them.

- Explain that the vowel digraph *ui* can stand for the vowel sound they hear in *guitar* /ĭ/ or the vowel sound they hear in *juice* /o͞o/.

- Say other words with *ui (bruise, cruise, guilty, fruit, build, nuisance),* and have volunteers write them in the correct column on the board.

You may want to use pages 49–50 in *MCP Phonics,* Level E for additional practice with the vowel digraph *ui.*

ESL Strategy

Students acquiring English can work with peer tutors to make an outline with two main topics. Each main topic should focus on a type of music or on a particular sport. Students can use the outlines to tell others about the two types of music or two sports.

Multiple Intelligences: Visual-Spatial

Have students make a cluster diagram for a topic of their choice. The diagram should show how details grow from subtopics that grow from main topics. When finished, students can label each part with a Roman numeral *(main topic),* a capital letter *(subtopic),* or an Arabic numeral *(detail).*

Home-School Connection

Students and a family member can choose a goal, such as a home-improvement project. They can outline the main steps *(main topics)* needed to reach the goal, along with related tasks and necessary equipment *(subtopics and details).*

LESSON 19

Persuasive Devices and Propaganda (pages 89–94)

Objective: Students can recognize persuasive techniques often found in propaganda.

Teaching TIPS

- Students who recognize persuasive devices found in propaganda become more critical consumers.

- Students are better able to evaluate an author's argument when they recognize persuasive techniques.

Skills Reviewed and Maintained

Comprehension

Main Idea	See Checking Comprehension
Making Judgments	See Checking Comprehension

Word Study

Suffix -ful	See Practicing Vocabulary, Word Study Mini-Lesson

Writing

Poster	See Making the Reading and Writing Connection

Teach

Discuss different kinds of advertising that students have seen or heard: print ads, junk mail, billboards, radio and TV commercials, Web site banner ads. Ask what all these ads have in common. Students should realize that the purpose of all ads is to persuade people to buy or do something.

- Explain that the word *propaganda* is used to describe advertisements and other forms of biased writing, such as political speeches, that deliberately seeks to persuade.

- Have students read about the three kinds of propaganda listed in the chart on page 89. Volunteers can read aloud the examples with an appropriate tone of voice and expression.

- Discuss answers to these questions:

  Why does the ad for Save-Rite Market say "thousands of smart shoppers"?

  Has Muscle Mush helped Rock Ridges become an Olympic athlete? Why might someone think so?

  What loaded words are in the Health Nog ad?

- Emphasize that most ads are not intended to deceive. However, as with any persuasive writing, readers should think critically: Why is this statement being made? Is it always true? Are supporting facts given?

- Invite students to read pages 89 and 90 and complete the exercises. Check for understanding by asking them to summarize what they have learned.

On Your Own Practice

Introducing Vocabulary

Before students read the speech, introduce the vocabulary words (*energetic, fairness, flavorful, peer, popularity, representative, successful*) and discuss their meanings. Have students give a synonym or antonym for each word.

Reading the Passage

Have students read the first paragraph of the speech and tell who the speaker is and what his purpose is. Encourage students to highlight persuasive devices as they read.

Checking Comprehension

- First clarify the main idea of the speech: *Joseph wants voters to elect Beth.* To identify his supporting reasons, have students think about the main idea of each paragraph.

- To make judgments, students must decide whether Joseph's reasons are valid and whether they would like to have a student council president like Beth.

Practicing Comprehension Skills

Remind students that propaganda may sometimes be used for good purposes. Students must read carefully and critically so that they will be able to decide for themselves whether or not they wish to be influenced by it.

Practicing Vocabulary

- Review the vocabulary words. Have students identify the two words with the suffix -ful. (*successful, flavorful*)

- Invite students to complete the vocabulary exercise independently. Review the answers with the class.

Apply

Making the Reading and Writing Connection

Display students' posters. Have the class identify the persuasive devices used in each poster and decide whether they are effective.

You may want to use page 33 in *The Write Direction*, Grade 5 for additional opportunities in poster writing.

MEETING INDIVIDUAL NEEDS

Word Study: Suffix *-ful*

On the board, write the vocabulary words with *-ful: successful, flavorful.* Circle the suffix in each word.

- Say the words aloud, and have students repeat them.

- Explain that the suffix *-ful* means "full of." Ask students how that meaning relates to the two vocabulary words. (Something that is *successful* is full of success; something *flavorful* is full of flavor.)

- List other words with the suffix *-ful: careful, fearful, plentiful, thoughtful, graceful.* Have students create sentences that include both the base word and its suffixed form.

You may want to use pages 121–122 in *MCP Phonics*, Level E for additional practice with the suffix *-ful.*

ESL Strategy

Working with a peer tutor, students can find and list examples of loaded words used in newspaper ads.

Multiple Intelligences: Bodily-Kinesthetic, Musical, Interpersonal

Partners can create and perform a commercial song or jingle for an imaginary product or service. They should include at least two persuasive devices in their performance.

Home-School Connection

Have students and a family member analyze the commercials during a half-hour television program, noting the propaganda devices used in each.

LESSON 20 Literary Elements: Character (pages 95–98)

Objective: Students can identify and describe the traits of story characters.

Teaching TIPS

- Students better understand a story when they analyze its characters.

- Students practice making inferences when they use story details to determine a character's traits.

Skills Reviewed and Maintained

Comprehension

Setting	See Checking Comprehension
Main Idea	See Checking Comprehension

Word Study

Compound Words	See Practicing Vocabulary, Word Study Mini-Lesson

Writing

Character Sketch	See Making the Reading and Writing Connection

Teach

Write the following character types on the board: *brave heroine, greedy miser, neighborhood bully, best friend.*

- Divide the class into four groups and assign each group one of the character types. Tell each group to write down (a) what the character might do, (b) what the character might say, (c) what other characters might say about the character, and (d) how other characters might act toward the character.

- Have a volunteer from each group read the group's character descriptions. Afterward, have the class discuss whether the descriptions are consistent with the character types.

- Point out that readers can understand a character's motivations and actions by thinking about his or her traits. Readers can also predict what the character might do next.

- Invite students to read the story. Encourage them to notice how the character's traits are revealed.

- Have students complete the exercise. Then discuss how they knew Selah was brave when the author never used the word *brave* to describe her.

 **Practice**

Introducing Vocabulary

Before students read the article, introduce the vocabulary words *(clenched, haven, readying, recognized, runaway, swiped, underground)* and discuss their meanings. Offer synonyms *(grasped, shelter, preparing, identified, escapee, rubbed, hidden)* and have students identify the correct vocabulary word.

Reading the Passage

Have students tell what they know about the Underground Railroad. Ask them to predict what role the boy in the illustration might play in the story. Encourage students to think about the character traits of the boy as they read.

Checking Comprehension

- Have students identify details in the illustration and in the story that point to the setting—a farm in the past. Have them explain how their knowledge of history also helped them identify the story's setting.

- Clarify the story's main idea by having students explain its title.

Practicing Comprehension Skills

Remind students that authors don't always spell out a character's traits. The reader must think about the character's thoughts, words, and actions and make inferences about the kind of person the character is. Have students give examples from the story.

Practicing Vocabulary

- Review the vocabulary words. Have students identify the two compound words. *(runaway, underground)*

- Have students complete the vocabulary exercise independently. Review the answers with the class.

Apply

Making the Reading and Writing Connection

Have partners read their character sketches aloud to each other. The listener should jot down the character's traits and identify supporting evidence.

You may want to use pages 116–118 in *The Write Direction,* Grade 5 for additional opportunities in writing character sketches.

MEETING INDIVIDUAL NEEDS

Word Study: Compound Words

On the board, write the vocabulary words *runaway* and *underground.* Say the words and have students repeat them.

- Have a volunteer circle the smaller words in each compound word. Discuss how the meanings of the smaller words help students understand the meaning of the compound word.

- Write these compound words on the board: *runway, castaway, playground, underpaid.* Have students name the smaller words in each. Discuss the meanings of the compound words.

You may want to use pages 101–102 in *MCP Phonics,* Level E for additional practice with compound words.

ESL Strategy

Have students draw or find a picture of someone they admire. List character traits on the board *(brave, honest, kindhearted,* and so on) and have students choose a trait that describes that person. Have them write a sentence about the person using the word.

Multiple Intelligences: Verbal-Linguistic, Bodily-Kinesthetic, Interpersonal

Students can write a play based on "Onions to the Rescue." They can use dialogue from the story and add additional lines. Their performance should convey Jake and Louisa's character traits.

Home-School Connection

Have students ask a family member to name a favorite character from a book, a movie, or a television series. Together, they can make a web with the character's name in the center, and several traits and examples of those traits in the outer circles.

Literary Elements: Plot (pages 99–102)

LESSON 21

Objective: Students can identify the basic elements of plot structure.

Teaching TIPS

- Students are better able to make predictions about, summarize, and interpret stories when they understand plot structure.

- Students have more success writing their own stories when they understand plot structure.

Skills Reviewed and Maintained

Comprehension

Main Idea	See Checking Comprehension
Theme	See Checking Comprehension

Word Study

Suffix -ity	See Practicing Vocabulary, Word Study Mini-Lesson

Writing

Short Story Plan	See Making the Reading and Writing Connection

Teach

Display this passage on an overhead projector and read it aloud. Reread it and insert students' plot suggestions.

Once upon a time, a girl had a problem. The problem was (describe problem). The girl tried to solve her problem by (tell what she decided). She (tell what happened first, next, and after that). At last, (give the solution). The girl lived happily ever after.

- Explain that the girl, like most story characters, has a problem. A character's problem sets the story's action, or plot, in motion. Its solution ends the story.

- Review the chart on page 99. Discuss examples of each plot feature, using familiar stories.

- Review the devices of foreshadowing and flashback. Have students tell which device is shown in each of these sentences:

1. The prince thought back to his meeting with the queen, when she said, "Never climb the stairs in the west tower of the castle." *(flashback)*

2. The prince put one foot on the staircase and looked up. What danger lay at the top? *(foreshadowing)*

- Discuss how shifts in time order affect the plot.

- Have students read the story and answer the questions. Check for understanding by having them summarize the plot.

On Your Own Practice

Introducing Vocabulary

Before students read the story, introduce the vocabulary words *(ascend, enormity, galloped, labor, nudged, pasture, personality)* and discuss their meanings. Have students suggest a synonym for each word.

Reading the Passage

Have students use the title, illustration, and first paragraph of the story to predict the problem that will set the plot in motion.

Checking Comprehension

- Help students understand that the reason Meg's father changes his mind is one of the main ideas in the story. The reason isn't stated directly, however, so students must figure it out themselves.

- Remind students that a story's theme is the "big idea" that stands on its own outside the story. Discuss what the story reveals about ideas such as obedience, risks, and changes of mind.

Practicing Comprehension Skills

Discuss how and when the writer introduces the story's problem. Review the different types of problems: problems between characters, problems between a character and nature, and problems that characters have within themselves (such as having to make a big decision).

Practicing Vocabulary

Review the vocabulary words. Have students identify the two words with the suffix -ity. *(enormity, personality)* Invite students to complete the vocabulary exercise independently. Review the answers with the class.

Apply

Making the Reading and Writing Connection

Have partners take turns using their story maps to explain the plots of their planned stories. Encourage students to write the whole story.

You may want to use pages 49–96 in *The Write Direction,* Grade 5 for additional opportunities in writing a story.

MEETING INDIVIDUAL NEEDS

Word Study: Suffix *-ity*

On the board, write the vocabulary words *enormity* and *personality.* Circle the suffix *-ity.* Say each word and have students repeat it.

- Explain that the suffix *-ity* means "the quality or state of being." Have volunteers explain how the suffix relates to each word's meaning. *(The word* enormity *means "the quality of being enormous"; the word* personality *means "the quality of being a person.")*

- Write these words on the board: *real, active, formal, human, sincere, creative.* Have students copy the words, add the suffix *-ity,* and pronounce each new word. Explain that in some cases, the final *e* is dropped. *(sincere: sincerity)* Discuss the meanings.

You may want to use pages 129–130 in *MCP Phonics,* Level E for additional practice with the suffix *-ity.*

ESL Strategy

Have partners tell each other a favorite story from their native culture. Together, they can talk about the story's plot.

Multiple Intelligences: Visual-Spatial

Provide a standard plot-structure diagram: a rising line for rising action, a peak for the climax, and a falling line for outcome. Have students fill in the diagram using a favorite story.

Home-School Connection

After viewing a television program or movie, students and a family member can summarize and then evaluate the plot. Was the plot strong or weak? Was it suspenseful? Unclear? Believable?

LESSON 22 Setting (pages 103–106)

Objective: Students can identify a story's setting and explain its significance.

Teaching TIP

- Students understand that setting can affect story events and influence the actions and behavior of characters.

Skills Reviewed and Maintained

Comprehension

Character	See Checking Comprehension
Making Predictions	See Reading the Passage, Checking Comprehension

Word Study

Multi-Meaning Words	See Practicing Vocabulary, Word Study Mini-Lesson

Writing

Story	See Making the Reading and Writing Connection

Teach

List these three settings on the board: (1) the open ocean during a hurricane, (2) a secret passage in a house one hundred years ago, (3) a school cafeteria today. Ask students to imagine story situations for each setting.

- Discuss how a story's setting *(the time and place it occurs)* affects what happens in the story.

- Have students write descriptive phrases for each setting listed above. (Examples: *(1) roaring winds, wild waves, life-or-death struggle; (2) damp walls, sticky spiderwebs, trembling voices; (3) loud laughter, clattering trays, friendly chatter.)* Discuss how the details create a specific mood.

- Explain that in some types of stories—such as adventure stories, mysteries, and historical fiction—the setting plays an especially important part.

- Have students read the story about a hiking adventure and answer the question. Check for understanding by having them tell how the setting affects the main character.

 Practice

Introducing Vocabulary
Before students read the story, introduce the vocabulary words *(blur, kayak, replayed, shadowy, shimmered, strand, surface)* and discuss their meanings. Have students look up each word in the Glossary and create oral sentences with them. Invite students to look at the picture of the kayak on page 106 to help them understand better the concept of kayak.

Reading the Passage
Have students look at the illustration and make predictions about what type of summer school the characters are attending. Remind students to notice details about the setting as they read.

Checking Comprehension
- Review how readers make inferences about characters. Then have students find story details that give information about the character Andy.

- To make a prediction, students should consider what they know about Andy from the story. They should also consider how they would feel if they were in Andy's position.

Practicing Comprehension Skills
Encourage students to use the author's descriptive language to visualize the story's setting. Putting themselves "right there" in the action will enhance their experience of a story.

Practicing Vocabulary
- Review the vocabulary words. Have students identify the word that has more than one meaning. *(strand)*

- Direct students to complete the vocabulary exercise independently. Review the answers with the class.

Apply

Making the Reading and Writing Connection
Invite volunteers to read their stories aloud. Have listeners note details that help them identify the setting.

You may want to use pages 49–96 in *The Write Direction,* Grade 5 for additional opportunities in writing a story.

MEETING INDIVIDUAL NEEDS

Word Study: Multi-Meaning Words
On the board, write the vocabulary word *strand.* Say the word and have students repeat it.

- Explain that some words have several meanings. Have students look up *strand* in a dictionary, locate the word in the story, and decide which meaning fits the story's context.

- Have volunteers explain the difference between the italicized words in the following pairs of phrases.

1. squirmed *down* in his sleeping bag
   a *down*-filled sleeping bag

2. shadowy *figures*
   figures out the problem

3. the *row* of kayaks
   to *row* a boat

You may want to use pages 169–170 in *MCP Phonics,* Level E for additional practice with multi-meaning words.

ESL Strategy
Have students write a few sentences describing the setting shown in the illustration for "Kayaking School."

Multiple Intelligences: Verbal-Linguistic
Have students scan "Kayaking School" for especially vivid descriptions of the setting. They should choose one or more to expand into a poem or descriptive paragraph.

Home-School Connection
Have students write the opening of a story that takes place in a setting familiar to family members, such as the front porch, a relative's kitchen, or a vacation spot. Students can read aloud the description and ask family members to guess the setting.

Literary Elements: Theme (pages 107–110)

LESSON 23

Objective: Students can express the theme of a story.

Teaching TIPS

- Students gain greater understanding of a story when they think about its theme.
- Students practice making inferences and generalizations when they think about a story's theme.

Skills Reviewed and Maintained

Comprehension

Drawing Conclusions	See Checking Comprehension
Character	See Checking Comprehension

Word Study

Possessives	See Practicing Vocabulary, Word Study Mini-Lesson

Writing

Realistic Story	See Making the Reading and Writing Connection

Teach

Discuss familiar fables, such as "The Tortoise and the Hare" and "The Little Red Hen," and the lessons they teach. *(Slow and steady wins the race; if you don't help with the work, don't expect the reward.)*

- Explain that these kinds of lessons or "big ideas" also appear in other stories. A story's "big idea" is called its theme. A theme is a generalization about life, nature, or human behavior.

- Point out that a story's theme presents an idea or message that goes beyond the story itself. For example: *Friendships are valuable and need special attention.*

- Explain that usually a story's "big idea" or theme is not stated directly. Readers must figure it out on their own, using evidence from the story.

- Tell students to read the story on page 107 and think about its theme.

- Have students complete the exercise. Check understanding by having them compare their themes.

On Your Own Practice

Introducing Vocabulary

Before students read the story, introduce the vocabulary words *(attended, effortless, experimental, futile, friends', mother's, recited)* and discuss their meanings. Have students use the words in oral sentences.

Reading the Passage

Have students use the title and illustration to predict what "big idea" the characters might learn at an ice-skating party.

Checking Comprehension

- To draw conclusions about Betsy's actions, students should use what the author tells them along with what they know from their own experiences.

- To understand the character of Trevor, students should think about what he does and says and how other characters react to him.

Practicing Comprehension Skills

Help students understand that not all readers will see the theme of a story in exactly the same way. Explain that this is acceptable as long as readers can back up their statements of theme with evidence from the story.

Practicing Vocabulary

- Review the vocabulary words. Have students identify the two possessive nouns. *(friends', mother's)*

- Allow students to complete the vocabulary exercise independently. Review the answers together.

Apply

Making the Reading and Writing Connection

After partners have read each other's stories, they should decide whether the themes are clear or not. Students can then revise their stories.

You may want to use pages 49–96 in *The Write Direction,* Grade 5 for additional opportunities in writing a story.

MEETING INDIVIDUAL NEEDS

Word Study: Possessives
On the board, write *friends'* and *mother's.* Have volunteers read the words aloud.

- Invite students to find each word in the story and rewrite the phrase without the possessive to show the same meaning. *(the backpacks of her friends; the glint in the eye of her mother)*

- Explain that if a noun is singular, the apostrophe comes before the *s;* if a noun is plural, the apostrophe comes after the *s.*

- Write these words on the board: *mother's, mothers'; friend's, friends'; boy's, boys'; girl's, girls'.* Have volunteers explain the difference in meaning between the possessives in each pair.

You may want to use pages 103–104 in *MCP Phonics,* Level E for additional practice with possessives.

ESL Strategy
Write a common story theme on the board and discuss its meaning. (For example: *Hard work pays off; honesty is the best policy.)* Have students think of stories they know from their native cultures that present the same theme. Let them share the stories.

Multiple Intelligences: Verbal-Linguistic, Intrapersonal
Have students work in pairs to rewrite "Make New Friends ..." from the viewpoint of Trevor. Their stories should present a different theme.

Home-School Connection
Suggest that students and family members read a story together and talk about its theme.

Synonyms (pages 111–114)

Objective: Students can identify synonyms and distinguish shades of meaning.

Teaching TIPS

- Students can use synonyms as context clues.

- Students appreciate a writer's word choice when they recognize synonyms.

Skills Reviewed and Maintained

Comprehension
Plot	See Checking Comprehension
Making Judgments	See Checking Comprehension

Word Study
Suffix *-ment*	See Practicing Vocabulary, Word Study Mini-Lesson

Writing
Myth	See Making the Reading and Writing Connection

Teach
Ask students to imagine that they've been hired to write an ad for a new perfume. Have them think of vivid words to describe the scent. Write their words on the board.

- Identify words that have similar meanings as synonyms. Discuss the shades of difference between the synonyms. Explain that writers choose words to create a certain mood or tone.

- Have students tell which of these words is most likely to be in a perfume ad and why: *smelly, fragrant, strong-scented, odorous.*

- Write this sentence on the board and say it: *The odor of rotting meat is the sweetest aroma in the world to flies.* Have a volunteer identify the two synonyms. *(odor, aroma)* Point out that synonyms can help readers figure out unfamiliar words. For example, readers can figure out the meaning of *aroma* by recognizing that it is a synonym for *odor.*

- Tell students to read the story about Angela Appleseed and to pay attention to synonyms.

- After students complete the exercise, ask them to explain the difference between these three synonyms: *industrious*, *diligent*, and *hard-working*. Then ask why the author might have used all three words to describe Angela. (Possible reasons: *to add variety and to emphasize Angela's main character trait*)

 **Practice**

Introducing Vocabulary

Before students read the legend, introduce the vocabulary words *(bafflement, confronted, distinguished, overbearing, payment, shrieking, singed)* and discuss the meanings. Offer a synonym for each word and have students identify the matching vocabulary word. *(confusion, met, characterized, proud, fee, screeching, scorched)*

Reading the Passage

Have students read the title and identify the two animals in the illustration. Ask students to predict what they might learn by reading the legend. You might want to point out the country of Namibia on a map.

Checking Comprehension

- Clarify the problem that sets the plot in motion: *the scarcity of water*. Ask students how the problem is resolved.

- Remind students that a judgment is based on details in the story. Have students point out evidence that shows whether or not the baboon learned from his experience.

Practicing Comprehension Skills

Tell students that if they pay attention to synonyms as they read, they will increase their vocabulary. They can also analyze how the author creates a certain mood or tone.

Practicing Vocabulary

- Review the vocabulary words. Have students identify the two words with the suffix *-ment*. *(bafflement, payment)*

- Invite students to complete the vocabulary exercise independently. Review the answers with the group.

Apply

Making the Reading and Writing Connection

After students have suggested synonyms for each other's myths, have them evaluate their partner's word choice. Which synonyms work best, and why?

You may want to use pages 86–91 in *The Write Direction*, Grade 5 for additional opportunities in writing myths.

MEETING INDIVIDUAL NEEDS

Word Study: Suffix *-ment*

On the board, write *bafflement* and *payment* and circle the suffix *-ment*. Say the words and have students repeat.

- Tell students that the suffix *-ment* means "the state or condition of being" and turns a word into a noun. Ask students to define *bafflement* (*a feeling of being baffled or puzzled*) and *payment*. (*a way of being paid*)

- Write these words on the board: *apart, punish, treat, state, improve, amaze, excite*. Ask volunteers to add *-ment* to each word and explain the meaning of the new word.

- For each word, have students create sentences that include both the base word and its suffixed form.

You may want to use pages 123–124 in *MCP Phonics*, Level E for additional practice with the suffix *-ment*.

ESL Strategy

Students and peer tutors can select sentences from the legend and rewrite them, replacing words with synonyms. (Example: *"One of these rare* (unusual) *watering holes* (ponds) *in a great* (huge) *desert was guarded* (watched) *by a large* (big) *baboon."*)

Multiple Intelligences: Verbal-Linguistic, Interpersonal

Partners can practice using a thesaurus to find synonyms for a word *(big, for example)* and then list the synonyms to show some kind of order *(gradually increasing size or intensity, for example)*.

Home-School Connection

Students and a family member can take turns naming objects in their home for which the other person gives a synonym. (For example, *couch-sofa, pillow-cushion, rug-carpet.*)

Antonyms (pages 115–118)

Objective: Students can identify antonyms and use them to understand contrasts.

Teaching TIPS

- Students can recognize antonyms as context clues.
- When students identify antonyms, they understand contrasts that authors make.

Skills Reviewed and Maintained

Comprehension

Cause and Effect	See Checking Comprehension
Drawing Conclusions	See Checking Comprehension

Word Study

Doubled Final Consonants Before Suffixes	See Practicing Vocabulary, Word Study Mini-Lesson

Writing

Personal Essay	See Making the Reading and Writing Connection

Teach

Ask students to draw a sketch that fits this description: This is an *old* house with *huge* windows and a *tall* chimney. A *leafy* tree with a *fat* trunk is to the *left* of the house. Then read aloud the same description, substituting the words *new, tiny, short, leafless, skinny,* and *right.* Have students sketch this scene on the other side of the paper.

- Discuss the different settings and moods created by each description. Point out that the antonyms, words with opposite meanings, account for those contrasting moods.

- Explain that writers use antonyms to make contrasts, pointing out differences between people, places, objects, and ideas. Noticing antonyms helps readers understand those contrasts.

- Write this sentence on the board and say it: *Today the business owner is affluent, but she grew up poor.* Ask students to figure out the meaning of *affluent;* help them see that the word's context shows that it is an antonym for *poor.* Point out that antonyms can help readers figure out unfamiliar words.

- Tell students to read the article about Abigail Adams, paying close attention to contrasts.

- After completing the exercise, have students explain how they identified the antonyms in the article.

On Your Own Practice

Introducing Vocabulary

Before students read the article, introduce the vocabulary words *(sparkling, drabbest, hover, inadequate, mansion, public, stunned)* and discuss their meanings. Have volunteers use each word in an oral sentence.

Reading the Passage

Have students use the photograph and title to tell what the article will be about. Ask them to name antonyms for *house.* Remind students to notice contrasts revealed by antonyms as they read.

Checking Comprehension

- Clarify the cause-and-effect relationship by having students complete this sentence: *The White House was given its name because _____.*

- To draw conclusions, students should reread Abigail Adams's private and public statements about the mansion. They can also reread the article on page 115, which describes her character.

Practicing Comprehension Skills

Tell students that clue words such as *but, yet, not,* and *however* point to contrasts. By noticing those clue words, readers can figure out the meaning of an unfamiliar antonym.

Practicing Vocabulary

- Review the vocabulary words. Have students identify the two vocabulary words with the suffixes *-est* and *-ed. (drabbest, stunned)*

- Have students complete the vocabulary exercise independently. Go over the answers together.

Apply

Making the Reading and Writing Connection

Have volunteers read their essays aloud. Tell listeners to jot down the main difference that is pointed out and list antonym pairs.

You may want to use pages 119–129 in *The Write Direction,* Grade 5 for additional opportunities in writing compare-and-contrast essays.

MEETING INDIVIDUAL NEEDS

Word Study: Doubled Final Consonants Before Suffixes

On the board, write *drab + -est = drabbest* and *stun + -ed = stunned.*

- Explain that when a word with a short vowel sound ends in a single consonant, the final consonant is usually doubled before a suffix that begins with a vowel is added.

- Write these words on the board: *hopping, starred, flattest, winning, hotter.* Have volunteers take turns writing

an equation to show how the base word and suffix have been combined to make each word.

- Ask volunteers to create oral sentences for each suffixed word.

You may want to use pages 137–138 in *MCP Phonics,* Level E for additional practice with doubled consonants before suffixes.

ESL Strategy

Have partners read "The President's House" together and underline antonym pairs. Then they can make flashcards, with one word on each side.

Multiple Intelligences: Verbal-Linguistic

Have students list adjectives and adverbs used in the articles on pages 115 and 116. Then they can work in pairs to try to come up with an antonym for each word. Encourage them to use a thesaurus.

Home-School Connection

Have students write a paragraph describing someone in their family. They should then rewrite the paragraph using antonyms so that it describes that person's "opposite." Family members can read the second version and try to guess the person's identity.

LESSON 26 Understanding Homonyms (pages 119–122)

Objective: Students can distinguish between words that have the same spelling and pronunciation.

Teaching TIP

- Students' reading comprehension increases when they recognize homonyms, homographs, and homophones.

Skills Reviewed and Maintained

Comprehension

Main Idea	See Checking Comprehension
Drawing Conclusions	See Checking Comprehension

Word Study

Irregular Plurals	See Practicing Vocabulary, Word Study Mini-Lesson

Writing

Personal Narrative	See Making the Reading and Writing Connection

Teach

Present this riddle to students: What is the difference between a humorous story and the bulb on the back end of a car? *(One is a light tale, and the other is a tail light.)*

- Write *light tale* and *tail light* on the board. Explain that words that are spelled and pronounced the same, but have different meanings, are called homonyms. Have students identify the homonyms *(light, light)* and define each word. *("not serious"; "a bulb")*

- Explain that words that are pronounced alike, but are spelled differently and have different meanings, are called homophones. Have students identify the homophones *(tale, tail)* and define them. *("a story"; "the rear or back end")*

- Tell students that homographs are words that are spelled alike but have different pronunciations and meanings. Write this sentence on the board and read it aloud: *The nurse wound a bandage around the wound.* Have students identify the homographs. *(wound, wound)* Explain how the pronunciation of each word depends on its meaning.

- Tell students to read the story about the relay race and to look for homonyms, homographs, and homophones.

- Have students complete the exercise. Check that they have paid attention to spelling and context.

Practice

Introducing Vocabulary
Before students read the article, introduce the vocabulary words *(children, consumers, manufacturers, products, salespeople, styles, traditional)* and discuss their meanings. Have students group words into categories and explain their reasons.

Reading the Passage
Have students read the title and identify the corresponding homophones for "Sneak" and "Peak." Have them look for and highlight homophones, homographs, and homonyms as they read.

Checking Comprehension

- Clarify that the main idea of the article is the most important point the author makes.

- To help students draw conclusions about Goodyear's invention, have them reread and note details in the third paragraph.

Practicing Comprehension Skills
Explain that homographs, such as *content* or *perfect,* can cause confusion because their pronunciation is dependent on meaning. Tell students to first figure out the meaning of the word using its context, and then read the sentence aloud and experiment with the word's pronunciation.

Practicing Vocabulary

- Review the vocabulary words. Have students identify the vocabulary words that are plural forms of child and salesperson. *(children, salespeople)*

- Invite students to complete the vocabulary exercise independently. Review the answers with the group.

Apply

Making the Reading and Writing Connection
Have partners read each other's narrative and check that it is written from the point of view of the pair of sneakers and that the pronouns *I* or *we* are used. Partners can list the homonyms, homographs, and homophones they find.

You may want to use pages 50–51 in The Write Direction, *Grade 5 for additional opportunities in writing narrative paragraphs.*

MEETING INDIVIDUAL NEEDS

Word Study: Irregular Plurals
On the board, write *child/children* and *salesperson/salespeople.* Say each pair of words and have students repeat them.

- Describe the words as being either *singular* or *plural.* Have volunteers use each pair in a sentence.

- Tell students that regular plurals are formed by adding *-s* or *-es,* but some words, such as *child* and *person,* form irregular plurals.

- Write these words on the board: *foot/feet, tooth/teeth, woman/women, man/men, goose/geese, mouse/mice.* Encourage partners or small groups to write rhyming couplets that use both the singular and plural forms.

You may want to use pages 151–152 in MCP Phonics, *Level E for additional practice with irregular plurals.*

ESL Strategy
Review some commonly confused homophones. Have students use each word in an oral sentence. (Possible homophones: *too/two/to, their/there/they're.*)

Multiple Intelligences: Verbal-Linguistic, Visual-Spatial
Have students explain the author's play on words in the fifth paragraph of the article: *"They are the 'sole' of the company."* Then ask why a hair salon might be called Shear Beauty. Encourage students to come up with other product names that use homophones or homonyms.

Home-School Connection
Students and family members can look for magazine or newspaper ads that use clever wordplay. Have students copy or cut out examples that contain homophones or homonyms. They can share the examples with the class.

LESSON 27

Using Figurative Language (pages 123–126)

Objective: Students can interpret similes, metaphors, and personification.

Teaching TIPS

- Students appreciate an author's style when they recognize and interpret figurative language.
- Students who recognize figurative language understand that words can have meaning beyond their usual, everyday definitions.

Skills Reviewed and Maintained

Comprehension

Making Judgments   See Checking Comprehension
Comparing and Contrasting   See Checking Comprehension

Word Study

Words with More Than   See Practicing Vocabulary, Word Study
One Suffix   Mini-Lesson

Writing

Character Sketch   See Making the Reading and
Writing Connection

Teach

Tell students that they read, hear, and use figurative language every day. Write these sentences on the board:

    1. Anita looks like her mother.
    2. Anita looks like a cat about to pounce.

- Point out the comparison word *like* in both sentences. Help students see that the comparison in the first sentence is a literal one. The comparison in the second sentence is figurative—Anita doesn't really resemble a cat, but a tense face and body may suggest that she is about to attack someone or something.

- Write below sentence **2:** Anita is as tense as a cat about to pounce. Explain that both sentences are similes because they use *like* or *as* to make a comparison.

- Add this sentence: **3.** Anita is a cat about to pounce. Explain that this is a metaphor, a comparison that says one thing is something else without using *like* or *as*.

- Add this sentence: **4.** The sunny windowsill called out to the cat. Discuss how the sunny windowsill is com-

pared to a person. Explain that this is an example of personification, a figure of speech in which human traits are given to animals or inanimate objects.

- Add this sentence: **5.** Don't let the cat out of the bag. Explain that an idiom is a phrase or expression whose meaning cannot be understood from the ordinary meaning of the words that form it.

- Tell students to read the passage, complete the exercise, and explain each figurative expression.

On Your Own Practice

Introducing Vocabulary

Before students read "My Greatest Teachers," introduce the vocabulary words (*attractions, benefit, hopefully, infinite, resonant, reveal, uncertainty*) and discuss their meanings. Have volunteers read aloud their Glossary definitions.

Reading the Passage

Have students read the title and predict what they will learn about the people shown in the illustration. Remind them to look for examples of figurative language.

Checking Comprehension

- Have students support their judgments by identifying positive statements the author makes about his teachers.

- When students make comparisons and contrasts, they should concentrate on what the two teachers have in common as well as the differences the author points out.

Practicing Comprehension Skills

Explain that figurative language helps readers experience something in a new and sensory way. By comparing his teacher's face to the warm glow of a campfire, for example, Joseph Bruchac is helping readers feel his teacher's protective warmth. Encourage students to think of another figurative comparison to convey the same impression.

Practicing Vocabulary

Have students identify the vocabulary word with more than one suffix. *(hopefully)* Let students complete the vocabulary exercise independently. Review the answers as a class.

Apply

Making the Reading and Writing Connection

Have volunteers read aloud their character sketches. Listeners can tell what they pictured when they heard a figurative expression.

You may want to use pages 116–118 in *The Write Direction,* Grade 5 for additional opportunities in writing character sketches.

MEETING INDIVIDUAL NEEDS

Word Study: Words with More Than One Suffix

Write the vocabulary word *hopefully* on the board. Say the word and have students repeat it.

- Have students fill out an equation to show that base word + suffix + suffix = longer word. *(hope + ful + ly = hopefully)*

- Write these base words on the board: *care, thought, use, fear.* Then write these suffixes: *-ful, -ly, -ness, -less.* Ask

partners to form as many words as possible with at least two suffixes.

You may want to use pages 141–142 in *MCP Phonics,* Level E for additional practice with words with more than one suffix.

ESL Strategy

Have students identify an idiom from "My Greatest Teachers." They can then illustrate it with two cartoons, contrasting the literal and the figurative meanings of the expressions. (Idioms include *opened her heart, fell in love, looked forward, thought on his feet.*)

Multiple Intelligences: Verbal-Linguistic

Ask students to reread the author's figurative descriptions of Mrs. Monthony and Mr. Swick. They should then think of a person they know and describe him or her using figurative language.

Home-School Connection

Students and a family member can brainstorm a list of similes that have become clichés, such as *raining like cats and dogs, as cool as a cucumber.* They can then choose one to rewrite using an original figurative comparison.

Connotation and Denotation (pages 127–130)

Objective: Students can distinguish between the literal and suggested meanings of a word.

Teaching TIPS

- Students better understand an author's creative choices when they think about the connotations of words.

- Students read persuasive texts more critically when they pay attention to connotations.

Skills Reviewed and Maintained

Comprehension

Summarizing	See Checking Comprehension
Making Judgments	See Checking Comprehension

Word Study

Prefix *dis-*	See Practicing Vocabulary, Word Study Mini-Lesson

Writing

Friendly Letter	See Making the Reading and Writing Connection

Teach

Write on the board: *The temperature today reached 90 degrees Fahrenheit and humidity was high.* Divide the class into two groups. One group should imagine they love hot weather; and the other group hates hot weather. Have each group write a descriptive paragraph about the weather that reflects their positive or negative emotional associations.

- Invite the groups to read aloud their paragraphs. Have the class identify word choices that reveal attitude.

- Offer these additional examples and have students tell whether positive or negative feelings are suggested by each: *like a warm bun fresh from the oven* (positive); *broiling air, skin as sticky as a melted lollipop* (negative).

- Present the term *denotation,* explaining that it refers to the literal, dictionary meaning of a word. Explain that words can also have *connotations.* The connotation of a word includes the various emotional, imaginative, cultural, or traditional associations that surround it.

- Point out that writers use words with certain connotations so that readers will respond with particular feelings or attitudes.

- Tell students to read the letter and notice the connotations of words. Have students complete the exercise.

- Check understanding by having students explain what associations each listed word suggests to them.

 ## Practice

Introducing Vocabulary
Before students read the story, introduce the vocabulary words *(discharged, disentangle, gullible, publicity, shambles, transfixed, volumes)* and discuss their meanings. Have students offer a synonym or an example for each word.

Reading the Passage
Have students read the title, look at the illustration, and give ideas about what a sock hop is. Explain that a committee is a group of people organized to investigate and report on some cause. Remind students to think about the author's word choice as they read the story.

Checking Comprehension
- Guide students in summarizing the actions each member of the committee took. Remind them that a summary is brief, so they should substitute a general term for a list of specific actions.

- Clarify that a judgment is an opinion based on details in the story as well as personal experiences. Have students cite examples of both.

Practicing Comprehension Skills
Tell students that the language of advertising depends on connotative meanings. Have students examine advertisements and substitute neutral statements for the ones given, as a way to appreciate the power of connotation.

Practicing Vocabulary
Review the vocabulary words. Have students identify the words with the prefix *dis-. (discharged, disentangle)* Have

students complete the vocabulary exercise independently. Review the answers with the group.

Apply

Making the Reading and Writing Connection
Have volunteers read aloud their friendly letters. Listeners can jot down words that have positive and negative connotations.

MEETING INDIVIDUAL NEEDS

Word Study: Prefix *dis-*
Write the two vocabulary words with the prefix *dis-* on the board: *discharged* and *disentangle.* Say the words.

- Point out that the prefix *dis-* means "not" or "the opposite or reverse of." Ask students how that meaning is reflected in the two vocabulary words.

- Write *agree, connect, honest, infect, please, respect* on the board. Have students add the prefix *dis-* to each word and define it.

- Students can use a dictionary to find and list at least six more words with the prefix *dis-.*

You may want to use pages 67–68 in *MCP Phonics,* Level E for additional practice with the prefix *dis-.*

ESL Strategy
Review idioms and figurative expressions used in the story: *"get moving," "two seconds flat," "take ages," "museum pieces," "it will be a snap," "being in shambles," "coming together," "stuck in the past," "having a blast."* Help students to see how the expressions create an informal, lighthearted tone.

Multiple Intelligences: Verbal-Linguistic
Students can choose sentences from the story in which words have positive or negative connotations, then rewrite the sentences to show the opposite connotation.

Home-School Connection
Have students and a family member look at magazine advertisements together. Have them note words with positive connotations. They can then substitute the words' denotative meanings to see what the ads are really saying.

LESSON 29

Using Maps (pages 131–134)

Objective: Students can recognize the purposes of a map and interpret its features.

Teaching TIPS

- Students can use maps to support or add to information in a text.
- Students can use their knowledge of map reading in real-life situations.

Skills Reviewed and Maintained

Comprehension

Cause and Effect	See Checking Comprehension
Drawing Conclusions	See Checking Comprehension

Word Study

Prefix *mid-*	See Practicing Vocabulary, Word Study Mini-Lesson

Writing

Directions	See Making the Reading and Writing Connection

Teach

Name a familiar local destination. Then have students imagine that a visitor has asked them for directions from your school to that place. As volunteers give directions, sketch a simple map on the board.

- Discuss the purposes of maps by having students decide what type of map you drew: road, political, physical, or special-purpose.

- Tell students that to interpret maps, readers need to know how to use a compass rose, a key, and a scale.

- Explain that a compass rose shows how left, right, top, and bottom on the map correspond to directions on the Earth's surface. Add a compass rose to the map on the board, showing north, south, east, west.

- Add the label *Key* and insert two items on the map: a triangle symbolizing "You Are Here" and a star symbolizing the name of the destination.

- Tell students that printed maps are drawn to scale—1 inch on the map might stand for 1 mile, 10 miles, or 100 miles, for example. If possible, display an actual

map and point out its scale of distance. Have volunteers measure the distance between two map points.

- Have students use the map to understand the information in the passage. After students answer the questions, have them demonstrate how to use the key, the compass rose, and the scale.

On Your Own Practice

Introducing Vocabulary

Before students read the article, introduce the vocabulary words *(cycle, delicate, fascinating, midair, midweek, migrate, tourists)* and discuss their meanings. Have students read aloud their definitions from the Glossary.

Reading the Passage

Ask students to use the photograph to tell what kind of monarchs the title refers to. Have them preview the map to tell what information about monarchs it gives.

Checking Comprehension

- Review cause-and-effect relationships by having students complete this statement: *The eastern monarchs fly to Mexico each year because _____.*

- Help students draw conclusions by asking them to consider details, in the article and on the map, about the monarchs' flight.

Practicing Comprehension Skills

Suggest that students pause after reading the names of places and directions in order to check the map. Have them tell what they gained from looking at the maps while reading the passage on page 131 and the article on page 132.

Practicing Vocabulary

- Review the vocabulary words. Have students identify the words with the prefix *mid-. (midair, midweek)*

- Have students complete the vocabulary exercise independently. Review the answers with the group.

Apply

Making the Reading and Writing Connection

After partners have reviewed each other's maps and directions, each writer may revise and refine their product for a bulletin-board display.

You may want to use pages 136–138 in *The Write Direction*, Grade 5 for additional opportunities in writing directions.

MEETING INDIVIDUAL NEEDS

Word Study: Prefix *mid-*

On the board, write the vocabulary words with the prefix *mid-*: *midair* and *midweek*. Say the words and have students repeat them.

- Circle the prefixes. Tell students that *mid-* means "in the middle of." Have them tell how that meaning is reflected in the words *midair* ("in the middle of the air")* and *midweek. ("in the middle of the week")*

- List these other words: *midday, midsummer, midwinter, midmorning, midlife, midnight, midterm.* Have students define each word.

You may want to use pages 85–86 in *MCP Phonics*, Level E for additional practice with the prefix *mid-*.

ESL Strategy

Ask questions about either map in the lesson, using the words *north, south, east, west, left, right,* and *straight.* Encourage students to repeat the words as they point out answers on the map.

Multiple Intelligences: Visual-Spatial, Interpersonal

A small group of students can draw a mural depicting the monarch's migration route.

Home-School Connection

With a family member, students can use a highway map, street map, subway or bus map, museum floor plan, or other kind of map to plan a family outing.

LESSON 30 Understanding Charts and Tables (pages 135–138)

Objective: Students can interpret information presented in a chart or table.

Teaching TIPS

- Students learn how charts and tables can support or add to information in a text.
- Students learn to synthesize and organize information when they create their own charts and tables.

Skills Reviewed and Maintained

Comprehension

Character	See Checking Comprehension
Drawing Conclusions	See Checking Comprehension

Word Study

Root *port*	See Practicing Vocabulary, Word Study Mini-Lesson

Writing

News Story	See Making the Reading and Writing Connection

Teach

Have three volunteers tell what their after-school activities are Monday through Friday. Write the information in a chart like the one below.

After-School Activities

Student	M	T	W	Th	F
Malik	soccer			chess club	
Karen			swimming	Scouts	violin
Sonja		piano/—— walk dog ——			dance

- Explain that organizing data in a chart or table can make it easier to understand and compare.

- Ask questions that can be answered by looking at the table, such as: *How many afternoons does Sonja have activities? What does Karen do on Tuesday afternoons?*

- Display familiar examples of charts and tables, such as bus, train, and class schedules. Discuss the information presented in each one.

- Tell students to read the pet-day announcement and table. After they answer the questions, have them demonstrate how they found the correct data.

 **Practice**

Introducing Vocabulary
Before students read "A Day at the Races," introduce the vocabulary words *(category, feisty, loft, precisely, support, transported, veteran)* and discuss their meanings. Have students suggest a synonym for each word.

Reading the Passage
Have students read the title, look at the two tables, and predict what the story will be about. Ask them to think about why the tables accompany this story.

Checking Comprehension
- Make sure students recognize that the main character in this story is also the narrator. Remind students that they can understand a character by thinking about what he or she says, thinks, and does.

- Help students draw conclusions by having them identify story details that describe Phoebe's special qualities.

Practicing Comprehension Skills
Model how to skim a table to get a general sense of its content and how to scan a table to find specific data. Encourage students to skim and scan when they encounter tables in their reading.

Practicing Vocabulary
- Review the vocabulary words. Have students identify the two words with the root *port. (support, transported)*

- Allow students to complete the vocabulary exercise independently. Go over the correct answers as a group.

Apply
Making the Reading and Writing Connection
Students can display their news stories and tables on the bulletin board. Have them add a couple of questions for readers to answer by looking at the table.

You may want to use pages 139–149 in *The Write Direction*, Grade 5 for additional opportunities in writing news stories.

MEETING INDIVIDUAL NEEDS

Word Study: Root *port*
On the board, write the vocabulary words *support* and *transported.* Say both words and have students repeat.

- Explain that the root *port* means "to carry."

- Have students tell which word means "to carry the weight of" *(support)* and which one means "carried from one place to another." *(transported)*

- List these affixes: *im-, ex-, com-, de-, trans-, -ment, -ation, -able.* Have partners or small groups work together to build words by adding one or more affix to the root *port.* Encourage dictionary use. Have students compare their lists.

You may want to use pages 95–96 in *MCP Phonics,* Level E for additional practice with the root *port.*

ESL Strategy
Have partners find an example of a chart or a table in a book, magazine, or newspaper. They can study the chart or table and then share it with the class, describing the information it presents.

Multiple Intelligences: Logical-Mathematical, Interpersonal
Have partners create math problems based on the information in the tables on racing pigeons. Suggest that students focus on comparing two or more pigeons. Pairs can exchange their problems to solve.

Home-School Connection
Have students locate a local transportation schedule in their homes, at the library, on the Internet, or at train or bus stations. Students and family members can use the timetable to quiz each other. (Example: *What time does the 11:40 bus from Springfield arrive in Layton?*)

Using Graphs (pages 139–142)

LESSON 31

Objective: Students can interpret data presented in circle graphs.

Teaching TIPS

- Students are better able to compare and contrast information when they can interpret circle graphs.

- Students see how fractions, percentages, and other mathematical elements have practical applications when they use graphs.

Skills Reviewed and Maintained

Comprehension
Plot	See Checking Comprehension
Drawing Conclusions	See Checking Comprehension

Word Study
Suffixes -able, -ible	See Practicing Vocabulary, Word Study Mini-Lesson

Writing
Descriptive Paragraph	See Making the Reading and Writing Connection

Teach

Ask students to think about the career they dream of having. Then list these categories on the board: Sports, Computers, Military, Arts, Education, Medicine, Business, Law, Construction, Other. Ask for a show of hands for each type of job and write the number beside the appropriate category. Each student should raise a hand only once.

- Explain that numerical data is often shown graphically, which makes it easier to compare the information. Explain that the data listed on the board can be converted into a circle graph, also called a pie chart.

- Have students help you convert the list on the board into a circle graph. (1) Turn each number into the numerator of a fraction that has as its denominator the total number of responses/respondents. (2) Change fractions to percentages (divide numerator by denominator). (3) Divide a circle into pie sections. (4) Add labels to the graph.

- Explain that the pie shows a whole, or 100% of the data. Each slice of the pie shows a part of the whole.

- Tell students to read the story about school lunches and study the graph. After they answer the questions, have them explain how they found the data.

 ## Practice

Introducing Vocabulary
Before students read "Fifth-Grade Free Time," introduce the vocabulary words *(blurted, brainstorming, collectibles, individual, interrupt, memorable, merits)* and discuss their meanings. Have volunteers use the words in oral sentences.

Reading the Passage
Ask students to read the title of the story, look at the circle graph, and then predict what the story will be about. As students read the story, they should think about how the information might be converted into graphic form.

Checking Comprehension

- Help students clarify the plot by having them identify the fifth graders' goal.

- To draw a conclusion about Patrick's response to the survey, students should consider both his initial suggestion and his final comment.

Practicing Comprehension Skills
Tell students that as they look at circle graphs, they should draw conclusions about the patterns they find. Why might one section be twice as large as another, for example?

Practicing Vocabulary

- Review the vocabulary words. Have students identify the two words with the suffix *-able* or *-ible*. *(collectibles, memorable)*

- Have students complete the vocabulary exercise independently. Review the answers with the group.

Apply

Making the Reading and Writing Connection

After students develop the circle graph, work with them to write a paragraph summarizing the information and drawing conclusions from it.

You may want to use pages 98–99 in *The Write Direction*, Grade 5 for additional opportunities in writing descriptive paragraphs.

MEETING INDIVIDUAL NEEDS

Word Study: Suffixes -*able*, -*ible*

On the board, write the vocabulary words *collectibles* and *memorable* and circle the suffixes -*able* and -*ible*.

- Say both words and have students repeat them.

- Tell students that both suffixes mean "able to be." Ask students what people are able to do with collectibles *(collect them)* and what people are able to do if an event is memorable. *(remember it)*

- List these base words on the board: *comfort, sense, reverse, depend, value*. Ask volunteers to add the suffix -*able* or -*ible* to each one. Have students define each new word and then check its spelling in a dictionary.

You may want to use pages 125–126 in *MCP Phonics*, Level E for additional practice with the suffixes -*able*, -*ible*.

ESL Strategy

Help students write and read aloud a one-sentence summary for each graph in the lesson.

Multiple Intelligences: Logical-Mathematical, Visual-Spatial

Have students think of a question and then survey their classmates. (For example: *"What is your favorite color?"* or *"How many hours a week do you spend watching television?"*) Students can then use word-processing or spreadsheet software to create a pie chart.

Home-School Connection

Suggest that students and a family member look through newspapers and magazines for a graph. Together, they can analyze the graph and draw conclusions from it.

LESSON 32 Using a Dictionary (pages 143–146)

Objective: Students can use a dictionary to learn new words.

Teaching TIPS

- Students build their vocabulary when they use a dictionary to find the meanings of unfamiliar words.

- Students realize that dictionaries contain more than just word meanings.

Skills Reviewed and Maintained

Comprehension

Summarizing	See Checking Comprehension
Drawing Conclusions	See Checking Comprehension

Word Study

Suffix -*hood*	See Practicing Vocabulary, Word Study Mini-Lesson

Writing

Dictionary Page	See Making the Reading and Writing Connection

Teach

Write this sentence on the board: *The geyser shot high into the air.* Ask students to pronounce *geyser* and tell what it means. Challenge them to prove they are correct. Prompt students to realize that a dictionary is the place to look for such "proof."

- Model looking up the word *geyser*. Explain the various parts of a dictionary entry: the pronunciation, the part of speech, the definition, and the example sentences or illustrations.

- Point out the guide words that indicate the first and last entry words on the page. Ask why dictionary users need to understand alphabetical order. *(Entries are arranged in alphabetical order and fall between the guide words.)*

- Demonstrate how to use the pronunciation key to interpret the pronunciation symbols used in the dictionary.

- Have students look at the sample dictionary entry for *residence* on page 143 and identify each labeled feature.

- Have students read the passage about Buckingham Palace. After students complete the exercise, check for understanding by having them explain their answers.

 **Practice**

Introducing Vocabulary

Before students read "Touring the Tower," introduce the vocabulary words *(conqueror, entertain, exceedingly, historic, likelihood, neighborhood, prisoners)* and discuss their meanings. Have students read aloud each definition from the Glossary.

Reading the Passage

After students read the directions and look at the photograph, ask them why they think the article is called "Touring the Tower."

Checking Comprehension

- Review summarizing by having students reread the second paragraph and restate the most important information in just one or two sentences.

- To help students draw conclusions, have them identify facts and details about the Tower of London that might explain its appeal to visitors.

Practicing Comprehension Skills

Tell students that experienced readers often keep a dictionary nearby as they read. Instead of interrupting their reading for every unfamiliar word, they check to see whether they can understand the word from its context. If not, they use the dictionary.

Practicing Vocabulary

- Review the vocabulary words. Have students identify the words with the suffix *-hood*. *(likelihood, neighborhood)*

- Have students complete the vocabulary exercise independently. Go over the answers together.

Apply

Making the Reading and Writing Connection

After students create their dictionary entries, discuss the challenges real-life dictionary writers might face.

MEETING INDIVIDUAL NEEDS

Word Study: Suffix *-hood*

On the board, write the vocabulary words *likelihood* and *neighborhood*. Circle the suffix *-hood*. Say each word and have students repeat it.

- Ask what word *-hood* was added to to form *likelihood*. *(likely)* Then ask how the spelling of *likely* changed when the suffix was added. *(y was changed to i)*

- Explain that the suffix *-hood* means "state, condition, or quality of being." Ask students to use the word *likely* as they tell what a *likelihood* is *("the condition of being likely")* and to use the word *neighbors* as they tell what a neighborhood is. *("a place where neighbors live")*

- Have volunteers read aloud dictionary definitions of these words: *childhood, brotherhood, falsehood, parenthood, livelihood, knighthood.*

You may want to use pages 123–124 in *MCP Phonics,* Level E for additional practice with the suffix *-hood.*

ESL Strategy

Pair students who have the same native language. Partners can use a bilingual dictionary to take turns finding and pronouncing words in both languages.

Multiple Intelligences: Verbal-Linguistic, Interpersonal

Students can invent, describe, and play a dictionary game. Possibilities include timed searches, guessing an entry word after hearing its definition, and trying to spell a word after seeing its pronunciation.

Home-School Connection

Students can read aloud from a book while a family member listens for and jots down challenging words. Students should try to define each word and then check their guesses by consulting a dictionary.

Using an Encyclopedia (pages 147–150)

Objective: Students can find information in print and electronic encyclopedias.

- Students understand how an encyclopedia can help them research a topic.

- Students learn how information is organized when they review the parts of an encyclopedia entry.

Skills Reviewed and Maintained

Comprehension

Cause and Effect	See Checking Comprehension
Drawing Conclusions	See Checking Comprehension

Word Study

Prefixes *bi-, tri-*	See Practicing Vocabulary, Word Study Mini-Lesson

Writing

Summary	See Making the Reading and Writing Connection

Teach

Write these research questions on the board:
Who were the Aztecs?
Where are the Himalayas?
How do you do the backstroke?

- Ask students where they might find the answers to these questions. When someone suggests an encyclopedia, ask why this might be the first place to look. Explain that an encyclopedia contains general information about many topics.

- Guide students in identifying key words to look up in order to answer each question. (*Aztec, Himalayas, backstroke* or *swimming*).

- Use either a print, CD-ROM, or an Internet encyclopedia to model finding answers to the questions.

- Point out the various features of one of the entries: entry word, section headings, and cross-references (or hyperlinks).

- Tell students to read the encyclopedia article about the Olympics and to note its special features.

- After students answer the questions, be sure they can tell the purpose of each special feature.

 **Practice**

Introducing Vocabulary

Before students read the article about the Special Olympics, introduce the vocabulary words *(bicycling, excelled, handicapped, marathon, oath, physically, triathlon)* and discuss their meanings. Have students put the words in categories according to part of speech: noun, verb, adjective, and adverb.

Reading the Passage

Have students read the entry term and section headings. Then ask them to predict what they might learn about the woman shown in the photograph.

Checking Comprehension

- Review cause-and-effect relationships by having students use details from the article to complete this statement: *The Special Olympics program was created because _____.*

- Before students draw conclusions, have them think about the oath that the Special Olympics is based on.

Practicing Comprehension Skills

Discuss how an encyclopedia entry answers a specific question and also provides a broad overview of a topic. Let students practice using section headings and cross-references.

Practicing Vocabulary

- Review vocabulary words with students. Have students identify the words with the prefix *bi-* or *tri-*. (*bicycling, triathlon*)

- Have students complete the vocabulary exercise independently. Review the answers together.

Apply

Making the Reading and Writing Connection

Have students share and then display their summaries.

You may want to use pages 44–45 in *The Write Direction,* Grade 5 for additional opportunities in writing summaries.

MEETING INDIVIDUAL NEEDS

Word Study: Prefixes *bi-, tri-*

On the board, write the vocabulary words *bicycling* and *triathlon.* Circle the prefixes.

- Tell students that these prefixes refer to numbers: *bi-* means "two," and *tri-* means "three." A bicycle has two wheels, and a triathlon is a three-event sporting contest. Ask students to define *tricycle* and *biathlon.*

- Have volunteers use a dictionary to find and read aloud definitions of other words beginning with *bi-* and *tri-.* Classmates can try to guess the words.

You may want to use pages 87–88 in *MCP Phonics,* Level E for additional practice with the prefixes *bi-* and *tri-.*

ESL Strategy

Have students name a topic of interest and, working with a peer tutor, find and read an encyclopedia article about it. Partners should note important features they notice in the article, such as illustrations, photographs, diagrams, captions, section headings, and cross-references.

Multiple Intelligences: Verbal-Linguistic, Interpersonal

Have small groups look up either the Olympic Games or Special Olympics in both a print and an electronic encyclopedia. Group members can compare and contrast the encyclopedias. Which one is easier to use?

Home-School Connection

With a family member, students can write down three questions that might be answered in an encyclopedia. Students should identify key words and then look them up. After finding the answers to their questions, students can share the information with the class.

 LESSON 34

Using a Library Card Catalog/ the Internet (pages 151–156)

Objective: Students can search library catalogs and databases efficiently.

Teaching TIPS

- Students develop a strong foundation for doing research when they learn how to use library catalogs and databases.

- Students learn how to choose and refine search terms.

Skills Reviewed and Maintained

Comprehension

Drawing Conclusions	See Checking Comprehension
Predicting Outcomes	See Checking Comprehension

Phonics

Vowel Digraph *ie*	See Practicing Vocabulary, Phonics Mini-Lesson

Writing

Nonfiction	See Making the Reading and Writing Connection

Teach

Hold up a nonfiction book and ask students how they would find the book in the library. Prompt them to suggest the following terms and write them on the board: *title, author, subject, on-line catalog, call number, Dewey decimal system.*

- Tell students that some school and public libraries still use a card catalog to list books. Review the material on page 151 and have students answer the questions.

- Explain that most libraries list books, videos, recordings, and magazines in a computerized catalog. You type in a title, author, or subject to find out if and where the library has what you are looking for.

- Review the explanation of the Dewey decimal system on page 152 and direct students to fill out the chart. Then have students tell the exact search terms they would use to find each book listed.

- Explain that most libraries provide access to the Internet. Libraries also subscribe to on-line Web sites and computerized databases that describe articles from magazines. The articles may be available as well.

- Have students read the information about the Internet and the passage on page 153 and answer the question.

On Your Own Practice

Introducing Vocabulary

Before students read the story, introduce the vocabulary words (*admired, autobiographies, grasping, menu, namesake, related, spied*) and discuss their meanings. Have students give an example or synonym for each.

Reading the Passage

Have students read the directions, the title, and the first paragraph of the story. Ask them to predict what J. R. Williams might want to look up in the library's on-line catalog.

Checking Comprehension

- To help draw conclusions, students should look for text details that describe the similarities between J. R. Williams and Jackie Robinson.

- Encourage students to tell how their predictions changed as they read the story. At what point did they predict the actual outcome?

Practicing Study Skills

Because on-line sources and methods for searching the Internet are continually updated, encourage students to use the Help feature that accompanies search engines.

Practicing Vocabulary

Review the vocabulary words with students. Have them identify the words with the letters *ie. (autobiographies, spied)* Have students complete the vocabulary exercise independently. Review the answers with the group.

Apply

Making the Reading and Writing Connection

Ask volunteers to read aloud their nonfiction passages. Have students discuss sources they found useful and interesting.

MEETING INDIVIDUAL NEEDS

Phonics: Vowel Digraph *ie*

On the board, write the words *autobiographies* and *spied*.

- Say both words and have students repeat them. Explain that the final *y* of each base word (*autobiography, spy*) was changed to *i* before the ending was added, resulting in the vowel digraph *ie*. Point out that the vowel digraph *ie* can also be found in base words, such as *field* and *tie*.

- Have partners write as many words with the vowel digraph *ie* as they can think of. They can sort the words into long *e* and long *i* lists. (Possible answers: *chief, relief, shield, tried, relied, pie, die, lie*)

You may want to use pages 61–62 in *MCP Phonics*, Level E for additional practice with vowel digraph *ie*.

ESL Strategy

Ask students simple research questions. (For example, *"What are the rules for soccer?"*) Work with them to identify the keyword or search term they would use to find the answers.

Multiple Intelligences: Visual-Spatial, Verbal-Linguistic, Interpersonal

Partners or small groups can create a step-by-step guide to using the library catalog. Suggest that they write and illustrate their guide so that a younger student can understand exactly how to find a book or other item.

Home-School Connection

Students and a family member can explore the home page of the local public library to learn about available on-line sources targeted to young learners.

LESSON ______________

Name ____

Story Sequence Chart

Read the story. Answer the questions in each box. Retell the story using what you wrote.

Who?

When?

Where?

What happened? List events in order.

How did it end?

GRAPHIC ORGANIZER **LESSON** ____________

Name ____

Summarizing Chart

Use the title of the story as a clue to the main idea given in the story. Write two or three main ideas. Then write a paragraph that summarizes these ideas.

Main Idea

Main Idea

Main Idea

Summary

LESSON ____________

Name ____

Prediction Chart

What I predict will happen

____

____

____

____

Why I think this will happen—these are the clues that I used

____

____

____

____

What did happen

____

____

____

LESSON ____________

Name ____

Main Idea and Details Chart

Read the story. Write in the first box the idea that tells what the whole story is about. Then in the other boxes write details that support the main idea.

Main Idea

Detail

Detail

Detail

LESSON ____________

Name ____

Cause and Effect Chart

1. What happened

Why it happened

2. What happened

Why it happened

3. What happened

Why it happened

Name _____

Fact and Opinion Chart

Read the story. Identify three statements of fact or opinion from the story. Write why they are statements of fact or opinion.

Fact	Opinion
Why?	

Fact	Opinion
Why?	

Fact	Opinion
Why?	

LESSON ____________

Name ______________________________

Story Elements

Title ______________________________

Setting

Characters

Plot / Conflict

Solution

Name _____

Venn Diagram for Comparing and Contrasting

Read the selection. Compare and contrast the two main items of the selection by writing the differentiating features in the outside circles. Write the common features in the middle part.

_____   _____

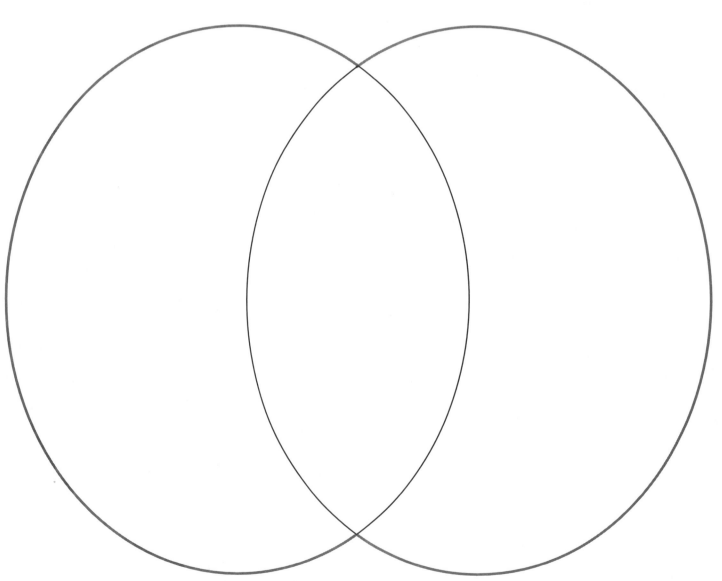

Comprehension PLUS

LEVEL E

Dr. Diane Lapp
Dr. James Flood

Modern Curriculum Press

Ping Pong® is a registered trademark of Parker Brothers, a division of Hasbro, Inc. *Converse* ®, *Keds*®, *All Star*®, *Cons*®, and *Chucks*® are registered trademarks of Converse Inc. Use of these trademarks implies no relationship, sponsorship, endorsement, sale, or promotion on the part of Modern Curriculum Press, Inc.

All photos ©Pearson Learning unless otherwise noted.

Photographs:

5: SuperStock, Inc. 6: ©W. Bacon/Science Source/Photo Researchers, Inc. 7: Courtesy of Erik Weihenmayer. 11: Erich Lessing/Musée d'Orsay Paris, France/Art Resource. 25: UPI/Corbis-Bettman. 43: NASA. 47: Jerry Proc. 48: Corbis. 57: ©Joel S. Fishman/Science Source/Photo Researchers, Inc. 58: Bruce Coleman Inc. 61: Susan Greenwood/Liaison International. 62: James Shaffer/PhotoEdit. 72, 123: Culver Pictures Inc. 75: Unknown. 81: Bettman-Corbis. 82: Underwood & Underwood/Corbis. 85: PhotoDisc, Inc. 86: Chris Sorensen/The Stock Market. 115: Brown Brothers. 116: John Elk III/Bruce Coleman Inc. 136: PhotoDisc. Inc. 138: Roger Wilmshurst/Bruce Coleman Inc. 144: ©Marcello Bertinetti/Photo Researchers, Inc. 147: Duomo/Corbis. 148: Courtesy of Pennsylvania Special Olympics.

Illustrations:

17: Charles Shaw. 21-22, 33: P.T. Pie. 26: David Wenzel. 29-30: Gary Torrisi. 34: Meg Aubrey. 38: Gershom Griffith. 41-42: Antonio Castro. 51-53: Pam Tanzey. 67, 69: Anni Matsik. 78, 119: Roberta Collier Morales. 89, 90-91: Diana Thewlis. 95-96: Diana Magnuson. 99, 100, 102: Laurie Harden. 103-104, 106: Denny Bond. 107-108: Deborah White. 111, 112, 114: Dennis Hockerman. 124: Jane Kendall. 127-128: Anni Matsick. 131: David E. Myers/Stone. 132: Don Larson. 139: Jane McCreary. 152-154: Gary Lippincott.

Cover art: photo montage: Wendy Wax. background: Doug Bowles.

Design development: MKR Design, New York: Manuela Paul, Deirdre Newman, Marta K. Ruliffson.

Design: Jim O'Shea

ISBN: 0-7652-2184-5
Printed in the United States of America

8 9 10   09 08 07 06 05

Modern Curriculum Press

Pearson Learning Group

1-800-321-3106
www.pearsonlearning.com

Table of Contents

Comprehending Text

Story Structure

Word Study

Document Reading

Main Idea and Details

Every paragraph, story, or article that you read has a **topic**—what the piece of writing is about. The **main idea** is the most important idea that the writer wants you to remember about the topic. Recognizing the main idea can help you understand and remember what you read. Writers sometimes state the main idea in a topic sentence. A topic sentence can appear at the beginning, middle, or end of a piece of writing.

Supporting details are smaller pieces of information that tell more about the main idea. As you read, use supporting details to help you identify the main idea.

Read this passage about mountain climbing. As you read, look for the main idea and supporting details.

Over the last hundred years, mountain climbing gear has changed a lot. In the 1800s, climbers wore heavy clothes and boots with spikes. Today companies have created clothes that are both warm and light, so climbers can move more freely.

Modern climbers also use nylon rope and pitons. Pitons are large nails with a ring in one end. Rope is attached to the ring. Climbers pull themselves up a few feet at a time. They pound pitons into rock as they go. In the past these nails were made of iron. Climbers found, however, that the heavy nails damaged the surface of the mountain. Climbers now use soft metal nails. These do much less damage.

Is the main idea of this passage stated or unstated? _____stated_____

Fill in the circle next to the sentence that best expresses the main idea of the passage.

○ Mountain climbing equipment used to be heavy.

○ Today, mountain climbing equipment is lighter than in the past.

○ Modern equipment causes less damage to mountains.

● Over the last 100 years mountain climbing gear has changed a lot.

Write one detail that supports the main idea.

Possible answer: Lighter clothing lets climbers move more freely.

An author does not always state the main idea of a paragraph or an article directly. Sometimes as you read you will need to figure out what the main idea is. You can do this by thinking about the supporting details. Ask yourself, "What idea do these details all tell about?" Then you can create a topic sentence that summarizes the most important information in the details.

Read the following passage. As you read, think about the main idea.

An experienced climbing party gathers at the foot of a mountain. Recent storms have put layers of snow on the rocks and trees. The climbers know that the snow layers may be unstable. Because each heavy layer of snow may not stick well to the next, avalanche danger is high.

During an avalanche, snow can slide down a mountain slope at speeds from 20 to 100 miles an hour. Avalanches can catch climbers by surprise and carry them miles down the mountain.

The climbers study the conditions. They are judging the chances of a snow slide. Then the careful group turns back. They decide that the danger of an avalanche is too high to climb that day.

Is the main idea of this passage stated or unstated? _____unstated_____

One way to figure out the main idea of a passage is to look for an important word that is repeated in many of the sentences. List some of the words that are repeated throughout the passage: _____snow, climbers, avalanche_____

Reread the supporting details. Then fill in the circle next to the best main idea for this passage.

○ The climbers are starting up the mountain and notice the heavy snow.

○ An avalanche can slide down a mountain slope at speeds from 20 to 100 miles an hour.

● Experienced mountain climbers must be aware of the danger of avalanches.

○ Mountain climbing is an extremely dangerous sport.

Tip

When the main idea of a piece of writing is not stated, you can figure it out by thinking about the supporting details. Ask yourself, "What idea do all these details tell about?"

Write two supporting details that helped you figure out the main idea.

Possible answers: The climbers know that the snow layers may be

unstable. Avalanches can catch climbers by surprise and carry them

miles down the mountain.

Read the following article about a mountain climber named Erik Weihenmayer. As you read, look for the main idea and supporting details.

Erik Weihenmayer: Climbing to Meet Every Challenge

by Lou Ann Walker

Erik Weihenmayer's dream is to climb the Seven Summits, the highest mountain on each of the world's continents. Many climbers have scaled the Lucky Seven—but none of them has been blind. Erik was born with a rare disease that caused his sight to deteriorate as he grew.

Erik loved sports and wouldn't let anything stop him from being an athlete. At age 8 he could see the basketball backboard but not the basket. With his father's help, he devised a system of planning shots by spotting marks on the court.

By age 13, Erik was totally blind. At first, he worried that it wasn't cool to read Braille and use canes. Then one day when he was 13, Erik fell off a dock. He realized he would have to accept himself as he was. "Blindness is a nuisance, but it's not the reason you can't do something," he says.

In high school, Erik became captain of his wrestling team. He also began hiking with his family. When he took on rock climbing, he was always attached to climbing partners by a system of safety ropes and clips. Erik admits he left a lot of skin on the rocks! Soon he learned to search for handholds and footholds.

As his confidence grew, Erik took on the challenge of mountain climbing. In time he climbed South America's highest peak, Aconcagua (ah-kan-KAH-gwuh), in fierce winds. Erik used the mountaineer's standard system of safety ropes. His partner attached sleigh bells to

his ice ax to help guide Erik. Still, winds were so strong that his partner had to whistle loudly so Erik would know which way to climb.

To train for climbs, Erik wears a 70-pound backpack to run up all the stairs in a 50-story building. He is so strong he can do pull-ups with his fingertips. As part of his work-out, Erik anchors cords to a bicycle and jogs along while someone else rides. That someone is often his wife, Ellen Weihenmayer. Erik proposed to Ellen, who is also a mountaineer, while on a climb. They were married on a mountain.

Erik began a teaching career, but later left teaching to spend more time climbing. He has written a book called *Touch the Top of the World.* He also travels the country giving motivational speeches.

His words encourage others not to give up. "When I start something, I know I'm going to flop on my face," Erik explains, "but failure is a valid way of learning." For Erik, life is all about character. It's not just about achievement. It's about reaching to be the best he can be.

Checking Comprehension

1. How does Erik Weihenmayer meet the challenge of blindness? [Summarizing/Inferential]

   Erik is willing to learn by failing. He does not let his blindness prevent him from setting

   and reaching goals.

2. Do you think it is likely that Erik will eventually climb the Seven
   Summits? Explain your response. [Making Predictions/Critical]

   Possible answer: Yes. Erik's great determination has helped him achieve other difficult goals

   and will likely help him reach this one, too.

Practicing Comprehension Skills

Write the answer on the lines.

3. Was the main idea of "Erik Weihenmayer: Climbing to Meet Every
   Challenge" stated or unstated? _____unstated_____

4. What is the main idea of the article?

   Possible answer: Erik Weihenmayer hasn't let blindness stop him from following his dream

   of climbing the Seven Summits.

Fill in the circle next to the correct answer.

5. Which sentence is NOT a supporting detail for the main idea?

   ○ Erik is determined to climb the
     Seven Summits.

   ● Erik's wife, Ellen, is also a mountaineer and
     his training partner.

   ○ Erik has found ways to tackle different
     sports, despite his blindness.

   ○ For Erik, life is about reaching to be the best
     he can be.

6. Which sentence gives the main idea of paragraph 3?

   ○ Blindness is a nuisance.

   ● Erik had to learn to accept himself the way
     he was.

   ○ At first, Erik didn't think it was cool
     to read Braille.

   ○ By age 13, Erik was totally blind.

Read the following passage. Think about the main idea.

Mount Everest is the highest mountain in the world. It is part of a large Asian mountain range called the Himalayas. Over the years, mountaineers have braved fierce winds and thin air to take on the challenge of climbing Mount Everest. In 1921 a group of English climbers made it to 22,900 feet. A year later another group made it to 27,000 feet. Still, no one had reached the peak at 29,028 feet.

In 1952, Edmund Hillary and his guide, Tenzing Norgay of Nepal, climbed to more than 28,000 feet. Determined to reach the top of the world, Hillary and Norgay tried again the next year. On May 29, 1953, after 80 days of climbing, the two men became the first humans to conquer Everest's peak. Since then, there have been more climbs. In 1975 the first woman, Junko Tabei of Japan, reached the top. The first solo climb to the peak, made by Reinhold Messner of Italy, came in 1980. Many have tried to reach the top of Everest. Some have died trying. Only a few have been able to say, "I stood on top of the world!"

7. Is the main idea of the paragraph stated or unstated? _____stated_____

Write the main idea of the passage in the top box. In each of the smaller boxes, write a supporting detail that tells more about the main idea.

8. Over the years, mountaineers have braved fierce winds and thin air to take on the challenge of climbing Everest.				
9. In 1921, English climbers reached 22,900 feet.	**10.** In 1922, climbers got to 27,000 feet.	**11.** In 1953, Hillary and Norgay reached Everest's peak.	**12.** In 1975 the first woman, Junko Tabei, reached the top of Everest.	**13.** In 1980 the first solo climb was made by Reinhold Messner.

14. What if the following statement had been the main idea of the passage? "Changes in mountaineering clothing and equipment have made today's Everest climbs very different from Hillary and Norgay's climb to the top of Mount Everest." What kinds of details would the author have needed to include to support this main idea?

Possible answer: The author would have needed to include details about the clothing

and equipment that were used in the 1950s and those used today.

15. Fill in the circle next to the best title for the passage.

○ The Life of Edmund Hillary   ● Reaching the Top of the World

○ A Dangerous Sport   ○ Mountains of the World

Practicing Vocabulary

Write the word from the box that belongs in each group.

16. created, designed, _____devised_____

17. secures, fastens, _____anchors_____

18. stimulating, inspirational, _____motivational_____

19. accomplishment, attainment, _____achievement_____

20. bother, trouble, _____nuisance_____

21. convincing, solid, _____valid_____

22. decline, weaken, _____deteriorate_____

| achievement |
| anchors |
| deteriorate |
| devised |
| motivational |
| nuisance |
| valid |

Writing a Character Sketch
On a separate sheet of paper, write a paragraph about a person you admire. Be sure to tell what you respect about the person. Your main idea can be stated or unstated. Provide details that support your main idea.

Drawing Conclusions

As you read a story or an article, you draw conclusions about characters, events, ideas, and other details. Your **conclusion** is the opinion or decision you reach after thinking about what you have read. To draw conclusions, think about details from your reading. Combine those facts with what you know from your own experiences. Ask yourself questions such as, "What is the author's point? What do I know about this character or the subject of this article? What can I infer from these details?"

Read the following passage. As you read, look for facts and details that will help you draw conclusions.

A famous painting by Georges Seurat

Have you ever noticed that you can see more detail when you get closer to an object? An artist named Georges Seurat who lived in the late 1800s used this fact to create a special effect in his paintings called pointillism. In pointillism, a painter uses thousands of tiny colored dots to create an image.

Seurat studied light and color. He used what he learned to apply colors that contrasted with each other. When the points of color in a Seurat painting are viewed from a distance, the eye is unable to tell them apart. The colors blur together to form a solid picture. You can see this technique today if you look very closely at a TV screen or a newspaper photograph.

What do you think you would see if you looked very closely at a television screen or a newspaper photograph?

You would see that the picture is made up of many small colored

dots.

Tip

When you draw a conclusion, think about the facts and what you already know. Make sure you can back up your conclusion with information from the selection or reasons of your own.

Fill in the circle next to the best answer.

You can conclude that a pointillist painter would

○ mix the colors first and then paint lines.

○ use a few, large dots to create an image.

● apply small dots of color that contrast with each other.

○ use large, sweeping brushstrokes.

Read the article about optical illusions. As you read, draw conclusions about why you see certain things.

Fooling the Eye

What your eye really sees and what your brain thinks it sees are not always the same. The brain tends to see what it expects to see. Sometimes there are not enough clues in an image. Then the brain fills in the missing pieces. Other times there is too much stimulation in an image. Then the brain becomes tired. It continues to act even when the stimulation stops. When either of these things happen, you will usually see an optical illusion.

The invention of motion pictures relied on an optical illusion. Think about the pictures you see in a movie theater. The pictures are not really moving. What you see is really a series of still pictures that are shown to you very quickly. Your brain cannot process the still pictures as fast as they are shown. As a result, it fills in the motion that it expects to see between pictures.

The colors you perceive on a computer screen are also optical illusions. Actually, there are only three colors of dots on your computer screen: red, green, and blue. When you see many different combinations of dots, your brain is fooled into thinking it sees a variety of colors on the screen.

There are also many other kinds of optical illusions that trick your brain. Look at the drawings below. Do you see a star shape in the middle of design A? Do you see a circle in the middle of Design B?

Neither of these shapes is really there. Your brain has just filled them in. Now look at Design C, where dark squares are aligned in rows. Do you see many gray dots, some brighter than others, in the white spaces? The dots are caused by light receptors in your eyes that help you see strong light and dark patterns. In the places where you see dots, the receptors are not doing their job!

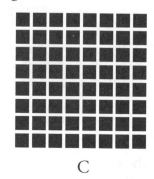

C

Cartoonist W. E. Hill created the following famous eye trick.

Look at the drawing. What is the first thing you see? Some people see a young woman looking over her right shoulder. Other people see a gnarled, older woman gazing downward. If you have trouble seeing both, here are some hints: The young woman's chin and jaw are the older woman's nose. The young woman's left ear is the old woman's left eye. The young woman's necklace is the old woman's mouth. Now what do you see?

A   B

Checking Comprehension

1. If the image on a computer screen could be enlarged a hundred times, what would you see? Why? [Making Predictions/Inferential]

   <u>You would see a collection of dots in three different colors, because that is what makes</u>

   <u>up the color on the screen.</u>

2. What is one cause of an optical illusion? [Cause and Effect/Inferential]

   <u>Possible answer: There are not enough clues in an image, so the brain</u>

   <u>fills in the missing pieces.</u>

Practicing Comprehension Skills

Fill in the circle next to the correct answer.

3. Which conclusion can you draw about cartoonist W. E. Hill?

   ○ He drew a picture of an old woman.   ○ He drew many optical illusions.

   ○ He drew a picture of a young woman.   ● He created the optical illusion on purpose.

4. Which conclusion can you draw about optical illusions?

   ○ All optical illusions are the same.   ● They are tricks created by your brain.

   ○ Most people see the same thing when   ○ They are cartoonists' mistakes.
     they see W. E. Hill's optical illusion.

5. Do you agree or disagree with this conclusion? Write your answer on the lines. Explain your reasoning:

   Your brain is not working efficiently if it is tricked by an optical illusion.

   <u>Possible answer: I disagree. Your brain fills in the gaps when there is not enough</u>

   <u>information. It also becomes tired when there is too much stimulation. This is why you</u>

   <u>see optical illusions.</u>

6. In the top box is a conclusion you might draw after reading "Fooling the Eye." In the three boxes below, write facts you know and details from the article that support this conclusion. Write one fact or detail in each box.

Conclusion:
Animated cartoons rely on the brain's ability to see optical illusions.

The brain cannot process still pictures shown very quickly.

Cartoons are created as a series of still pictures, like movies.

The brain fills in the motion it expects to see between the still pictures.

Practicing Vocabulary

Choose the word from the box that best completes the analogy. Write the word on the line.

optical   7. *speaking* is to *oral* as *vision* is to _____

aligned   8. *broke* is to *fixed* as *bent* is to _____

stimulation   9. *bored* is to *sameness* as *excited* is to _____

gnarled   10. *even* is to *straight* as *twisted* is to _____

illusion   11. *true* is to *false* as *reality* is to _____

cartoonist   12. *joking* is to *comedian* as *drawing* is to _____

shoulder   13. *foot* is to *ankle* as *arm* is to _____

aligned
cartoonist
gnarled
illusion
optical
shoulder
stimulation

Writing About a Conclusion
Write a paragraph describing a conclusion you drew about a person or place that later turned out to be incorrect. Tell why your conclusion was incorrect and what you learned from that experience. Write your paragraph on another sheet of paper.

Sequence: Order of Events

When you read a story or an article, it's easier to understand what is happening if you can identify the **sequence,** or order, in which events take place. In some pieces of writing, the events follow a normal time order—one event follows another. In other stories, authors refer to actions that happened in the past, actions that are happening now, or actions that will happen in the future.

As you read, try to keep track of the order of events. Look for clue words such as *first, next, then, later, finally, meanwhile, yesterday, today,* and *afterward* to determine the order of events.

Read the following passage. As you read, picture the order in which the events occur.

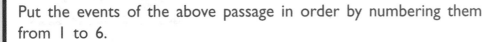

Students at Markham School have their share of problems, like students at most schools. However, Markham's students work together to solve problems through a peer mediation program.

First, students volunteer to be peer mediators. This means they are willing to help their peers, or fellow students, to solve problems. Next, a group of teachers and student leaders interviews the volunteers. They look for people who respect other students and can keep talks private. After the peer helpers are chosen, they go to several training sessions. There they role-play listening to problems and practice helping to solve them. Finally, they are ready to serve as peer mediators.

Put the events of the above passage in order by numbering them from 1 to 6.

2	A group interviews the volunteers.
6	Helpers are ready to serve as peer mediators.
4	Peer helpers go to training sessions.
1	Students volunteer to be mediators.
3	The peer helpers are chosen.
5	Peer helpers role-play and practice.

As you read the next passage about peer mediation, you will find a change in the order of events. By using a **flashback,** the author interrupts the normal sequence of events to describe an event or events that happened in the past. Flashbacks can help the reader to learn more about the people and details in a story or article. Then the author returns to the present and continues presenting events in sequence. When you read, look for phrases such as "A year before . . . ." or "She remembered when . . . ." They can be clues that the author is beginning a flashback.

Robert and Hannah were waiting in line to check out their books at the school library. Suddenly an older student pushed past them in line. Robert complained, "I can't believe it! Those older kids think they own this library!"

A year before, students with complaints like this might have felt they didn't have many options. Now Robert and Hannah have a way to take action. They arranged to meet with a trained peer helper.

First the mediator asked the girl who had cut in front of Robert and Hannah to join their discussion. "I know I cut in on them," the student admitted. "The younger kids are getting books just for fun. I need books for projects and assignments!"

"Wait a minute," Hannah said. "We check out books for projects, too!" The discussion continued. Then the mediator suggested ways to approach the other students who were part of the problem. The three students also talked to the librarian. In the end, the problem was solved.

Find four clue words or phrases in the passage that tell the order of time. Write them on the line.

Possible answers: A year before, now, first, then, in the end
_____

Find a sentence in the passage that signals a flashback. Write it on the line.

A year before, students with complaints like this might have felt they

didn't have many options.
_____

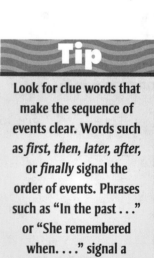

Tip

Look for clue words that make the sequence of events clear. Words such as *first, then, later, after,* or *finally* signal the order of events. Phrases such as "In the past . . ." or "She remembered when. . . ." signal a flashback.

As you read the following play, try to figure out the order in which the events occur. Look for clue words.

A Long Walk Home

by Joyce Annette Barnes

Setting: After school on an icy winter day. From the school door, Brooke waves frantically to her sister Brianna down the hall.

BROOKE: Brianna, hurry up! We'll miss the bus.

BRIANNA: Just a second!

BROOKE: Never mind—there it goes! Come on, let's call Mom to pick us up.

BRIANNA: No! We'll walk home.

BROOKE: Are you kidding? It's freezing out there. We live more than a mile away!

BRIANNA *(pointing first to her feet, then her sister's):* That's what these are for! *(She pushes the school door open and drags her sister outside.)*

BROOKE: I'm calling Mom.

BRIANNA: You can't! She told us last time: If she has to leave work once more because we missed the bus, we'll be grounded for a month. That means we can't go ice-skating this Friday. Is that what you want?

Brianna walks on; Brooke hurries to catch up.

BROOKE: My nose is freezing. *(Brianna doesn't respond.)* Brianna! You're walking too fast.

Brianna sighs, stops walking, and wraps her scarf around Brooke's face.

BRIANNA: There! Now are you happy? *(She continues walking.)*

BROOKE *(following):* No. Now my feet are soaking wet!

BRIANNA *(grabbing her sister's arm):* Wiggle your toes and keep walking! We have to get home before Mom calls, or she'll worry about us.

BROOKE: I can't! *(Dodging from Brianna's grasp, Brooke slips and falls into a puddle.)* Now look what you've done! It's your fault we missed the bus! Now I'm going to catch pneumonia and end up in the hospital. But that's OK! As long as you get to your precious skating rink!

BRIANNA: Don't exaggerate—oh, look at that icy hill up ahead!

Both girls fall silent as they contemplate the hill. Then Brianna helps her sister up.

BRIANNA *(reassuringly):* Come on, it's just up the hill and around the corner.

BROOKE *(shivering):* I c-can't d-do it.

BRIANNA: You have to, Sis. We need to hurry. Here, give me your arm.

Holding onto each other, they start up the incline and exit the stage.

Seconds later, they reappear onstage, huddled together, creeping along as if frozen. Brianna produces a key and, with stiff fingers, turns the lock just as a phone starts ringing offstage. The two girls look at each other with relief and exit the stage. From offstage, we hear:

BROOKE: Oh, hi, Mom! . . . Cold out? We hardly noticed!

Checking Comprehension

1. Why do the two sisters decide to walk home on an icy day?   [Summarizing/Inferential]

    Possible answer: They missed the bus, and their mother has told them she'll ground them

    for a month if she has to leave work again to pick them up.

2. Why do the two girls stop quarreling and work together instead? [Cause and Effect/Critical]

    When they see an icy hill up ahead, Brianna offers to help Brooke so they can hurry.

Practicing Comprehension Skills

Think about the sequence of events in "The Long Walk Home." Write one
or two sentences in each box to tell what happened at the beginning,
middle, and end of the play.

3. **Beginning:** Brooke and Brianna miss the bus and decide to walk home from school.

4. **Middle:** Brooke complains about the cold and falls in a puddle. When the two girls see an icy

    hill up ahead, they have to work together instead of quarreling.

5. **End:** The girls make it home just as their mother calls to check on them.

Fill in the circle before the correct answer.

6. Which of these events has happened before the play starts?

- ○ Brooke and Brianna decided to walk home.
- ● The girls missed the bus at least once before.
- ○ Brooke complained that her nose was freezing.
- ○ Brianna wrapped her scarf around Brooke.

Write the following events in order on the time line from earliest to latest.

Brooke and Brianna start to walk home.

Brooke complains about her nose freezing.

Brooke and Brianna get home as Mom calls.

The girls face an icy hill.

Brianna wraps a scarf around Brooke's face.

Mom threatens to ground them if they miss the bus again.

Time Line: A Long Walk Home

Earliest

7. Mom threatens to ground them if they miss the bus again.

8. Brooke and Brianna start to walk home.

9. Brooke complains about her nose freezing.

10. Brianna wraps a scarf around Brooke's face.

11. The girls face an icy hill.

Latest

12. The girls get home as Mom calls.

The following scene could have been in a longer version of "A Long Walk Home." As you read it, think about how it fits into the sequence of events.

BRIANNA: We can't call Mom to pick us up. Remember what happened last time she had to leave work because we missed the bus?

Brianna and Brooke both frown as they recall their mother's words.

MOTHER *(heard distantly from offstage):* Girls, I thought I could count on you, and you've disappointed me. We all have jobs to do. Mine is to work in my office. Yours is to get on that bus on time. I've warned you about this time and time again. You've got to learn to take responsibility, so the next time this happens . . . you're grounded for a month!

BRIANNA: If we're grounded, we can't go ice-skating this Friday. Is that what you want?

13. Fill in the circle next to the words that best describe how this passage fits into the sequence of events. The passage

- ○ happens much later than all the other events of the play.
- ● is a flashback that happened long before all the other events of the play.
- ○ makes a good ending for the play and explains how the problem is solved.
- ○ has nothing to do with the story and would not make sense in the play.

Read each of the following direction lines from the play. Underline clue words that suggest the sequence of events.

14. Brianna <u>continues</u> walking around the stage.

15. <u>Then</u> Brianna helps her sister up.

16. <u>Seconds later</u>, they reappear onstage.

17. Brianna turns the lock <u>just as</u> a phone starts ringing offstage.

Practicing Vocabulary

Choose the word from the box that best matches each definition. Write the word on the line.

		contemplate
		exaggerate
		frantically
		incline
		precious
		reappear
		reassuringly

<u>precious</u>   **18.** highly valued

<u>reassuringly</u>   **19.** in a way that restores confidence

<u>incline</u>   **20.** a slope or a hill

<u>exaggerate</u>   **21.** to say that something is much better or worse than it really is

<u>contemplate</u>   **22.** to think about something for a long time

<u>reappear</u>   **23.** to appear again

<u>frantically</u>   **24.** in a panicked way

Writing a Play
On a separate sheet of paper, write a play about students who solve a problem by working together. In your play, include words that signal the order of events.

Sequence: Steps in a Process

The **steps in a process** can help you follow directions to a place, use a recipe, or put a bicycle together. Steps in a process follow a certain sequence, or order. If the steps are not numbered, look for clue words and phrases such as *first, next, then, after, finally,* and *when you have finished.* Be sure to look at any pictures included with the directions.

Read the steps for making paper. As you read, look for clue words that tell you the order of the steps.

 First, tear paper into small scraps. Place four cups of water

and 35 scraps in a blender and blend for 90 seconds.

 Pour the mixture into a baking pan and stir it. Then submerge

a square of window screen in the pan until it is evenly covered with pulp.

Pull up the screen and place it on an opened newspaper. Fold the newspaper

and press down, using a rolling pin to squeeze out any moisture.

 Next, fold back the newspaper and let the pulp dry overnight.

Finally, after the pulp dries, peel up the new sheet of paper.

Write these steps in order from 1 to 7.

_____6_____ Next, let the pulp dry overnight.

_____3_____ Pour the mixture into a pan and stir it.

_____1_____ First tear the paper into scraps.

_____5_____ Place the screen on an opened newspaper, fold the paper over, and press down.

_____7_____ Finally, peel up the new sheet of paper.

_____2_____ Put water and scraps into a blender and blend.

_____4_____ Then submerge a square of window screen in the pan until it is evenly covered with pulp.

Tip

Before you follow the steps in a process, read each step to be sure you understand it. Try to picture each step in your mind. Use clue words and pictures to help you visualize the process.

STRATEGY: Identifying Sequence: Steps in a Process

21

The directions below tell how to make a paper swan. Use the diagrams to help you picture the sequence.

Folding a Swan

Origami is the art of paper folding. Almost as soon as paper was invented, people began folding it to create things. Paper folding traveled from eastern Asia to the Middle East and then on to Europe and the rest of the world.

The following steps will turn a sheet of paper into a simple but beautiful swan.

Begin with a square sheet of paper. Work on a hard table. Match up two of the opposite corners. Make a crease down the center. Make your folds sharp and exact, especially at the tips of the corners.

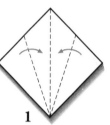

Unfold the paper and place it in front of you. One of the points on a fold should point toward you. Next, fold the sides into the center fold to make a kite shape. Then flip the kite shape over. Be sure to keep the top and bottom points in the same place. Now fold the opposite sides into the center fold. The shape will look like a paper airplane.

Bring the bottom point that is nearest you up to the top point and make a crease.

Then fold down the narrow point. This will form the swan's head on its long neck.

Fold the shape in half, following the original fold. This forms the swan's back. It also brings the fold of its wings down on either side.

Finally, pull up the head and neck until it forms about a 60-degree angle to the body. If you wish, you can use your thumbnail to make a sharp crease along the length of the swan. Behold your elegant swan!

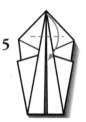

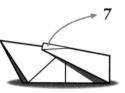

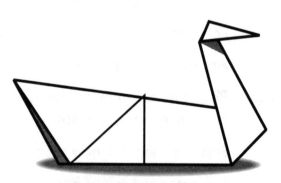

origami swan

Checking Comprehension

1. How does the author show the popularity of origami?   [Author's Purpose/Inferential]

    The author says that as soon as paper was invented, people began making shapes with it.

    The author also describes how origami spread from eastern Asia to the rest of the world.
                                                        [Comparing and Contrasting/Critical]
2. How does making an origami swan compare with the process of making
    other shapes out of paper, such as a paper hat or a paper airplane?

    Answers will vary. Students will probably say that making an origami swan is more difficult

    than making a paper hat or paper airplane because there are more steps.

Practicing Comprehension Skills

3. Number the steps below in the correct order from 1 to 7. Write the
    number of each step on the line.

    ___4___   Bring the bottom point up to the top point and crease it.

    ___6___   Fold the shape in half, following the original fold, to make
               the swan's back and wings.

    ___5___   Then fold down the narrow tip to form the swan's head.

    ___1___   Begin with a square of paper. Match up two opposite corners,
               make a crease down the center, and unfold the paper.

    ___2___   Next, fold the sides into the center to make a kite shape,
               then flip it over.

    ___7___   Finally, pull up the head and neck and crease it at a 60° angle
               to the body. You can use your nail to make a sharp crease.

    ___3___   Now fold the opposite sides into the center fold to make
               a shape like a paper airplane.

4. What clue words in the article tell you the order in which to follow the steps?

    Begin, next, then, now, finally

Fill in the circle next to the correct answer.

5. What do you do after you have made the kite shape and flipped it over?

  ○ Pull up the neck and crease it.

  ○ Fold down the tip to create the wing.

  ● Fold the opposite sides in to make an airplane shape.

  ○ Fold the shape in half along the crease.

6. Can any steps in the process of making an origami swan be skipped or eliminated? Explain your answer.

Yes. The words "if you wish" show that you don't have to crease the swan at the end.

Practicing Vocabulary

Write the word from the box that belongs in each group.

7. unwrap, uncover, _____ unfold _____

8. exquisite, graceful, _____ elegant _____

9. toenail, fingernail, _____ thumbnail _____

10. first, basic, _____ original _____

11. view, observe, _____ behold _____

12. wrinkle, pleat, _____ crease _____

13. different, unlike, _____ opposite _____

> behold
>
> crease
>
> elegant
>
> opposite
>
> original
>
> thumbnail
>
> unfold

Writing Directions

On a separate sheet of paper, write directions that tell how to make something, such as a paper airplane or a craft. Include at least six steps. If possible, ask a partner to follow the directions and tell why the directions were easy or difficult to follow.

Predicting Outcomes

Have you ever tried to figure out what will happen next in a story? If you have, you have made a **prediction**. Making predictions gets you involved in your reading. When you predict what will happen next, you want to read on to see whether or not your prediction is correct. To make predictions, use the facts and details of a selection together with what you already know.

Before you begin to read the article below, look at the title and photo to predict what you will be reading about. Stop after reading the first paragraph to make a prediction about what you will read next.

Does Bigfoot Really Exist?

Thousands of people, especially those in the Pacific Northwest, say they have seen Bigfoot, a giant, humanlike animal. Bigfoot is said to be six to ten feet tall, covered with hair, and shaped like an ape. This creature is supposed to weigh about 500 pounds.

Most scientists doubt people who say they have seen Bigfoot. Nor do they believe that photos and footprint casts of the creature are real. Scientists want proof. They want to see bones or bodies. That is the only way scientists will be convinced that Bigfoot really exists.

What did you predict that the article would be about?

<u>Students will probably say that they predicted that the article would</u>

<u>be about whether or not Bigfoot was real.</u>

After reading the first paragraph, what did you think you would read next?

<u>Answers will vary. Students might have predicted that the article</u>

<u>would try to prove Bigfoot's existence. Others might say that</u>

<u>because of the title of the article, they thought the passage would</u>

<u>say there is no scientific proof that Bigfoot exists.</u>

Tip

Before you read, look at the title and any art to help you make a prediction. Pause from time to time as you read to see whether your prediction was correct. Use details with what you already know.

On Your Own Before you read the following story, predict what it will be about. Stop at the places marked in the story to make predictions about what will happen next. Write your answers on page 27.

Bigfoot

by Trinka Hakes Noble

The night swiftly turned black as a damp mist began creeping through the trees. Hank and Bobby were silent as they crawled inside their tent for the night. It was the brothers' first campout. From a dark clump of bushes came a rustling noise. Then a twig snapped.

"It's probably Bigfoot," Bobby whispered.

"You mean that nine-foot-tall hairy creature that lives in the wilderness? The one with the big feet?" Hank asked, trembling.

"That's the one." Bobby nodded seriously.

Prediction #1: Predict what will happen next.

The noise grew louder as Bigfoot loped toward the tent, breathing hard. Hank scrambled for the flashlight, but it was nowhere to be found.

Bigfoot slowly circled the tent. A hairy aroma seeped in.

"What do you think it wants?" Hank quivered.

Prediction #2: What do you think is outside the boys' tent?

"Our feet!" Bobby screeched.

"Quick, let's put on our sneakers. It might not like how they taste."

"Uh, Hank, we can't," Bobby stuttered. "I put them outside. They were smelling up the tent."

Bigfoot snarled low, then began clawing savagely at the tent with its sharp nails.

"Well, at least the flap is zipped," Hank said, trying not to panic. "That'll slow it down."

"I forgot to zip it," Bobby whimpered.

"Oh, no, we're doomed!" shrieked the soon-to-be-footless brothers.

Suddenly, a shrill whistle pierced the foggy night. Then a stern voice shouted, "Boy, you come home *now!*" Bigfoot crouched down, whining.

"Yikes! It's Mother of Bigfoot!" yelled Bobby. "She's even worse!"

Prediction #3: Predict what will happen next. Are the boys in any danger?

Before Bigfoot's mother could get there, Bigfoot burst into the tent.

"Aaaah—help!" screamed the boys as Bigfoot's wet tongue licked their feet, then their faces.

"Boomer, come here," Mom scolded as she grabbed the happy dog's collar.

Prediction #4: Predict how the story ends.

"I'm sorry, boys. He's been whining at the back door ever since you came out in the yard. I'll take him inside."

"No, Mom. Bigfoot . . . uh . . . I mean Boomer . . . can stay," stammered Bobby.

"Please, Mom?" pleaded Hank.

"All right," Mom agreed.

The boys smiled with relief. "Thanks, Mom."

Gratefully, Hank and Bobby rubbed their bare feet through Boomer's warm fur. That night Boomer slept with his nose sticking out of the tent—just in case any Bigfoots wandered by, but mostly because he loved the smell of Hank and Bobby's sneakers.

Checking Comprehension

1. Why were the boys scared during their campout?   [Plot/Critical]

   Possible answer: It was their first campout. It was dark, and they heard strange noises.

2. Why did the boys think that Bigfoot was outside the tent? [Drawing Conclusions/Inferential]

   Possible answer: The boys thought Bigfoot was outside because the animal was noisy and

   smelly, just the way they imagined Bigfoot to be.

Practicing Comprehension Skills

Write your own answers to Predictions 1–4 here.

Prediction #1: Possible answer: The boys will encounter some animal that might be Bigfoot. They will get really scared.

Prediction #2: Possible answer: There's an animal outside the tent, possibly a bear or a dog.

Prediction #3: Possible answer: Someone is looking for a stray dog. I don't think the boys are in danger, because the language of the story is humorous.

Prediction #4: Possible answer: The boys find out that Bigfoot is really Boomer, a dog. Boomer will stay with them and protect them.

On the lines provided, tell whether your answer to each of the predictions was correct or not and explain your answer. Be sure to tell what clues might have led you to make a correct prediction.

3. Was the prediction you made before you began reading the story correct or incorrect? Explain your response.

   Answers will vary. Students might say they thought the story would be about kids who

   encounter a Bigfoot, but in a humorous way. They might recognize author Trinka Hakes

   Noble as a writer of funny stories, or point out the humorous tone of the illustration.

4. Was your answer to Prediction #1 correct? Explain your response.

   Answers will vary. If students correctly predicted the creature would not be Bigfoot, they

   might point to their prior knowledge that there is no proof Bigfoot exists.

5. Was your answer to Prediction #2 correct? Explain your response.

Answers will vary. Students might have correctly predicted there was a real animal outside the tent. They might not have guessed the animal was the boys' own dog.

6. Was your answer to Prediction #3 correct? Explain your response.

Answers will vary. At this point, the exaggerated and humorous tone of the story will probably have led students to correctly predict that the boys are not in danger.

7. Was your answer to Prediction #4 correct? Explain your response.

Answers will vary. Students might have predicted Hank and Bobby would want the dog to stay with them because it is the boys' first campout and they were frightened.

Practicing Vocabulary

Choose the word from the box that is a synonym for each listed word or words below. Write the word on the line.

		clawing
pierced	**8.** cut	panic
silent	**9.** noiseless	pierced
clawing	**10.** scratching	pleaded
panic	**11.** show fright	savagely
pleaded	**12.** begged	silent
wandered	**13.** strayed	wandered
savagely	**14.** wildly	

Writing a Story
On a separate sheet of paper, write a story about an adventure. Your story can be funny or scary. Trade stories with a partner. Have your partner read the story, stopping at two points in the story to make predictions about what will happen next.

Recognizing Cause and Effect

What happens when you flick a light switch up? The light goes on, and you can see cause and effect in action. An **effect** is something that happens. A cause is the reason it happened. A **cause** may have more than one effect. For example, if you flick a light switch, the light will go on, but the light might also help you do your homework. Similarly, an effect may have more than one cause. The lights come on because you flick the switch, but also because of the power of electricity.

Sometimes you can use clue words to help you figure out cause-and-effect relationships. Words and phrases such as *because, the reason for,* and *since* signal a cause. Words such as *so, consequently, as a result,* and *thus* signal an effect. When a cause is not stated directly, ask yourself, "What happened?" and "Why did it happen?"

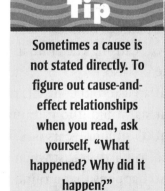

As you read the following paragraphs on asteroids, think about cause-and-effect relationships.

Cause Asteroids crash.	→	Effect Asteroids spin out of asteroid belt.

Between Mars and Jupiter is a ring, or belt, of rocky chunks made of stone or metal. These chunks are called *asteroids.* Sometimes, two asteroids crash into each other. The crash can send them spinning wildly into space. When a rock from space hits Earth, it's called a *meteorite.*

Each day, meteorites land on Earth. Scientists believe that about 50,000 years ago, a meteorite crashed in what is now Arizona and formed a huge crater. The Meteor Crater, as it is called, is 4,150 feet wide and 600 feet deep. Fortunately, most meteorites are small.

Read the following sentence. Identify the cause and the effect.

A meteorite formed Meteor Crater in Arizona 50,000 years ago.

Cause <u>A meteorite hit Arizona.</u>

Effect <u>It formed Meteor Crater.</u>

> ## Tip
>
> Sometimes a cause is not stated directly. To figure out cause-and-effect relationships when you read, ask yourself, "What happened? Why did it happen?"

As you read the article about dinosaurs, think about causes and effects.

The Death of the Dinosaurs

by J. Lynett Gillette

The dinosaurs are dead. They ruled the world for millions of years—but once the last one died, that was it. There were no more Maiasaura (mye uh SAWR uh) to nurture reptile babies, no more fierce Tyrannosaurus (tuh ran uh SAWR us), no more spiked Ankylosaurus (ang kye loh SAWR us).

Dinosaurs are just one of many groups of animals that no longer exist. Scientists don't always know why animals become extinct. They try to look at different kinds of evidence for answers. The first place scientists look is rocks. Rocks reveal the unusual conditions that might have taken place while the animals lived.

One popular explanation for the disappearance of dinosaurs is that a large asteroid hit Earth 65 million years ago. Dust from the impact could have spread over the whole planet. The dust would have dimmed the sun and killed many plants. Animals that ate plants would have starved, causing the animals that preyed on them to die off also.

If an asteroid collision really happened, scientists would find iridium in rocks that are about 65 million years old. This rare element is added to Earth's crust when asteroids hit Earth. It just so happens that around the world, many rocks created at that time do have high amounts of iridium. An asteroid impact would have blown a huge hole in Earth's surface. In fact, a giant crater was found just off the coast of Mexico. Scientists believe it is about 65 million years old.

Scientists know that dinosaurs vanished around the same time as this asteroid collision. Are the two events related? To find out, scientists need to study the bones of animals that lived then.

Dinosaurs were not the only animals alive when the asteroid struck Earth. What happened to other groups of creatures? Most frogs, for example, were not affected by the disaster. Most fish were fine too, as were lizards and mammals. Why did these animals go on living, when dinosaurs did not? Is it possible that the dinosaurs disappeared for a different reason?

Scientists have found fewer and fewer species of dinosaur fossils from the years before dinosaurs vanished altogether. This suggests that dinosaurs disappeared slowly, over thousands and millions of years, not in one crash of an asteroid. It's possible that dinosaurs did not compete well with the clever, warm-blooded mammals that were increasing in numbers on Earth.

Right now no one can say for sure what caused the death of the dinosaurs. There's a lot more work to do—in many areas of science.

Checking Comprehension

1. What kinds of clues help scientists draw conclusions about the death [Summarizing/Inferential] of the dinosaurs?

   Scientists look at rocks to find iridium. They examine bones and fossils, and they look for

   a crater that might have been caused by an asteroid.

2. Why might the most popular explanation for the death of the dinosaurs not be true? [Drawing Conclusions/Critical]

   Possible answer: Dinosaurs seem to have died out gradually, and plenty of animals were

   not affected by the asteroid collision.

Practicing Comprehension Skills

Fill in the circle next to the correct answer.

3. According to the passage, what would have been an effect of dust from a large meteorite?

   ○ Maiasaura would care for their babies.　　○ Frogs and fish would be killed.

   ○ Earth's crust would lose its iridium.　　● The sun's light would be dimmed.

4. A giant crater was found off the coast of Mexico. What do scientists believe was the cause of the crater?

   ○ dust spread over the planet　　○ large amounts of iridium

   ● an asteroid collided with the earth　　○ the sun's energy

Write your answer on the lines.

5. If dust from an asteroid impact dimmed the sun, what might be the effect or effects?

   Many plants would die. The animals that ate plants would starve, and so would the animals

   that preyed on the plant eaters.

Complete the cause and effect chart with information from "The Death of the Dinosaurs."

Possible Effects

Cause

An asteroid hit Earth.

6. Iridium was left on Earth.

7. A crater was formed off the coast of Mexico.

8. Sunlight was dimmed.
   Many plants and animals died

Practicing Vocabulary

Write the word from the box that belongs with each group of words.

9. passing from existence, departure, _____disappearance_____

10. impact, crash,_____collision_____

11. attacked, seized, _____preyed_____

12. category, type, _____species_____

13. growing larger, getting bigger, _____increasing_____

14. became invisible, went away suddenly, _____vanished_____

15. take care of, raise, _____nurture_____

collision
disappearance
increasing
nurture
preyed
species
vanished

Writing an Eyewitness Account
Imagine that you witnessed the crash of an asteroid today. On a separate sheet of paper, describe what you see happening. Use clue words to discuss causes and effects.

Using Context Clues

Sometimes when you read, you may come across a word that is not familiar. You can use the words before or after the unfamiliar word, or words in nearby sentences, to help you figure out the word's meaning. These clues to a word's meaning are called **context clues**. This chart gives examples of types of context clues.

Definition or Explanation	Example	Synonym	Description
A definition or explanation directly states or explains a word's meaning. "A *battery* is a container that holds the materials to produce electricity."	An example provides samples in the same category. "*Camping gear* typically includes a flashlight, a first aid kit, matches, water, and a knife."	A synonym gives alternate, often simpler, words with the same meaning. "An *electric current* passes from one battery to another. This flow of electricity powers the flashlight."	Context clues may describe the unknown word. "We set up camp under a shady *canopy* of trees that hung overhead like a roof."

Read the paragraph about how batteries work. Use context clues to help you understand the information.

   When you check your camping gear, always check your flashlight. If it doesn't light, make sure the cap is on tight. Also check to see that the cells have been put in correctly. The cells are the batteries inside the flashlight. They must be loaded in the right order. Look for the positive (+) and negative (-) terminals, or ends, of the cells. Match the symbols with those on the flashlight. Replace the cap.

What context clues in the paragraph help you figure out the meaning of the word *cells*? What type of clue is this?

Cells are the batteries inside the flashlight; definition/explanation

What context clues in the paragraph help you figure out the meaning of the word *terminals*? What type of clue is this?

Terminals means "ends"; synonym

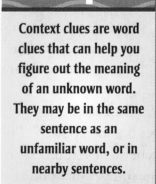

Tip

Context clues are word clues that can help you figure out the meaning of an unknown word. They may be in the same sentence as an unfamiliar word, or in nearby sentences.

STRATEGY: Using Context Clues   33

This story tells about students at a special kind of science fair called an invention convention. As you read, look for context clues that help you understand unfamiliar words and phrases.

The Invention Convention

Two students from Mr. Shaw's class were chosen to showcase their ideas at the annual invention convention. It was the fourth year that Mr. Shaw's students would present their work at the convention. The class's projects had included models, drawings, and even a recipe for a new way to make ice cream.

Kat invented a rolling rake to help her with yard work. "We have a huge yard," said Kat. "In the fall, the wind blows the leaves around till they're strewn everywhere. I took apart four rakes to make my invention. I then attached the heads to a pole. The pole hooks onto the back of my bike. I ride around on the lawn, dragging the rakes behind me. I get plenty of exercise, and I don't get blisters on my hands!"

A judge raised her hand. "Don't the wheels of your bicycle leave tread marks on the lawn?"

"I thought about that," Kat said. "I fitted the bike with extra wide tires that don't have any tread. In other words, there's no pattern of ridges cut into them that could make holes in the lawn."

Eric invented a design for windows that collect the sun's power. "I think we should try to use renewable resources," said Eric. "These are energy sources that don't run out or can be replaced. When you heat your home with fossil fuels, such as natural gas, coal, or oil heat, you use energy sources that are limited. When you heat a room with large, south-facing windows, you use solar energy. These windows collect the sun's energy and direct it to special tiles. The tiles absorb, or soak up, heat during the day and then release it at night."

One of the judges had a question. "How do you block the sun's heat during the summer?"

Eric pointed to his drawing. "You plant deciduous trees, such as maple, oak, beech, or ash trees, outside the windows. Their leaves block the sunshine in the summer, but when they lose their leaves in the winter, the sun comes in. You also design your house with special panels called overhangs above the south windows. They block out the sun when it's high in the sky, as it is in the summertime. In the winter, when the sun is lower in the sky, the overhangs let the sun in."

Eric received a second-place ribbon for his design. Kat was invited to submit her idea to a gardening magazine. Mr. Shaw was proud of his students.

"Let's see," he joked. "What if we used Kat's invention to rake the leaves from Eric's trees?"

"I know," Kat said, laughing. "We'd have a solar roller no-holer!"

Checking Comprehension

1. Why is imagination just as important as knowledge when it comes to creating an invention? [Making Judgments/Critical]

    Inventors need to be able to look at ordinary things in everyday situations and see them

    in new and different ways.

2. What do Kat's and Eric's inventions have in common?   [Comparing and Contrasting/Critical]

    Possible answers: Both inventions solve a problem. Both have something to do with trees

    and leaves. Neither invention depends on electricity or fuel.

Practicing Comprehension Skills

Find the words or phrases below in the passage. On the line provided, write the meaning of the word or phrase. Then write **definition, example, synonym,** or **description** to name the type of context clue given in the passage.

3. showcase _____ present; synonym _____

4. renewable _____ doesn't run out; definition _____

5. fossil fuels _____ fuels such as natural gas, coal, or oil heat; example _____

6. strewn _____ scattered widely; description _____

Find each word or phrase in the passage. Use context clues to figure out the meaning. Then fill in the circle before the correct meaning.

7. absorb

    ○ during the day   ○ release at night   ○ south-facing   ● soak up

8. solar energy

    ○ a fossil fuel   ○ deciduous   ● the sun's energy   ○ natural gas

9. overhangs

    ○ south windows   ○ resources   ● special panels   ○ leaves

Circle the correct answer.

10. Which of these phrases gives you example context clues for the meaning of the word *deciduous*?

    (a) trees such as maple, oak, beech, or ash   c) natural gas, coal, or oil heat

    b) windows, sun, and tile   d) a solar roller no-holer

11. Look back at the beginning of the passage to find the word *tread*. Which of the following dictionary definitions matches the context clues given?

    a) to step or walk

    b) the upper part of a step in a staircase

    (c) the pattern of ridges made or cut in the face of a tire

    d) to move your arms and hands in the water in a way that keeps your body upright

Practicing Vocabulary

Choose a word from the box that best matches each clue. Write the word on the line.

annual
panels
recipe
renewable
solar
strewn
submit

_____submit_____ 12. send in to be considered for publication

_____panels_____ 13. flat pieces of construction material, usually rectangular

_____renewable_____ 14. able to be used over and over

_____annual_____ 15. happening once every year

_____recipe_____ 16. set of directions for making something to eat

_____strewn_____ 17. scattered over an area

_____solar_____ 18. having to do with the sun

Writing a Description
Think about inventing a machine or device that would be helpful to you, such as a room cleaner, a trash compactor, or a homework machine. On a separate sheet of paper, write a description of the invention and how it would work. Use context clues to help explain the meanings of words that may be unfamiliar to others.

Comparing and Contrasting

Writers use **comparisons** and **contrasts** to tell how things are alike and how they are different. Often, something unusual is compared and contrasted with something familiar. For example, a writer may describe the game of rugby by comparing it with football. Writers sometimes, but not always, use clue words to signal comparisons and contrasts. Words such as *like* and *also* show comparisons. Words such as *but* and *unlike* signal contrasts.

You can make comparisons during and after reading. When you read fiction, you might ask yourself how a story or character is similar to another story or character. When you read nonfiction, you can compare the facts and details with things you already know.

As you read the article about two sports, look for comparisons and contrasts.

The games of lacrosse and field hockey are alike in many ways. Lacrosse comes from a game that Native Americans have played for centuries. Field hockey is also an old game. It can be traced back to the ancient Greeks and Romans. In both games, players hit a ball into a net with sticks. Also, both games are usually played outdoors.

However, the sticks used are different. A lacrosse stick has a net on one end. In contrast, a field hockey stick ends in a head. A field hockey team has 11 players, but a lacrosse team has 10 or 12 players. A field hockey game may end in a tie. Unlike field hockey, lacrosse is played until one team or the other wins.

Fill in the chart to show how lacrosse and field hockey are alike and how they are different.

Lacrosse and Field Hockey

Alike	Different
1. Both are very old games.	1. Lacrosse stick has a net. Hockey stick has a head.
2. Players hit a ball into a net with sticks.	2. Number of players on each team is different.
3. Usually played outdoors.	3. Field hockey can end in a tie. Lacrosse can't.

Tip

Comparisons show how two things are alike. Contrasts show how they are different. Clue words such as *like* or *also* can signal comparisons. Clue words such as *but* or *unlike* can signal contrasts.

Read the story about a father who tries to be at two different sporting events at once. Notice how the author makes comparisons and contrasts.

Double-Duty Dad

As the Chapman car arrived at the high school, Emily grabbed her bag. "See you, Dad," she said. She turned to Matt. "Good luck, squirt!"

Matt protested, "Who are you calling a squirt? You're three years older than I am and I'm nearly as tall as you!" Both Chapman children were thin and wiry, small for their age, and very interested in sports.

"Emily has it made!" Matt thought as they drove off. "She'll be on a basketball court with teammates. They can help her. At my match, it's just me against the other guy on the mat. If I make a mistake, we lose!"

As Matt worried, his father thought about his own concerns. Matt's wrestling team took the mat at 7:30. Emily's basketball team would also tip off at 7:30. How could he be in two places at once? The prospect made him a little nervous, but he decided to try his best to see both events.

Mr. Chapman began at Matt's school. He had worn his red "Lions Middle School Wrestling Fan" T-shirt. Since the lightest wrestlers were first, he could watch Matt. Then he could drive across town to watch Emily in her game.

Matt was first. Because wrestlers are divided into weight groups, he faced someone near his own size. "Get the pin!" fans yelled. Matt tried hard to hold the other boy's shoulders to the mat. After six minutes, there was no pin. Matt won,

though. The referees awarded Matt points for skillful holds.

Mr. Chapman had little time to enjoy Matt's win. He headed for the high school. There he changed to a gold shirt that said, "Bridgemore High School Bears Basketball Fan." Emily was playing as he came into the gym. She was the shortest girl on the court, but one of the fastest.

"Make that hoop!" shouted the spectators. Unlike Matt's sport, basketball gave no points for technique. Only a basket got a score.

Soon after Mr. Chapman arrived, Emily shot and scored!

"Foul!" signaled the whistle. Someone's elbow had hit Emily's cheek. Mr. Chapman was glad that in both sports unfair play was not allowed.

At the end, Emily's team won. Emily hurried toward Mr. Chapman, smiling. "Wrestling matches last longer than basketball games," she cried. "We can catch the end of Matt's match."

Still wearing his Bears' gold, Mr. Chapman made it back to hear Matt named winner in his weight group. Matt grinned. In wrestling and basketball, winners wore the same happy faces.

For Mr. Chapman, it had been a night of cheering "Take him down!" to Matt and "Put it up!" to Emily. In all ways, it had been a great night!

Checking Comprehension

1. Why did Mr. Chapman wear two shirts in one night?   [Drawing Conclusions/Inferential]

   He wore the shirts of the different school teams to support each of his children.

   _____

2. How would you describe Mr. Chapman? Explain your answer.   [Character/Inferential]

   Most students will say he is a good dad because he supported his children. Even though it

   was difficult, he figured out a way to share his time with both of them.

Practicing Comprehension Skills

3. Use what you have read and your own knowledge to compare and
   contrast wrestling and basketball. In the outside circles of the
   Venn diagram, write three things that are different for each sport.
   In the middle, write three things the two sports share.

Wrestling

- one-on-one
- points for a pin or
  technique
- players matched by size

Both

- played in gym
- unfair play is not
  allowed
- use referees
- spectators watch
  and cheer

Basketball

- team sport
- only get points for a
  basket
- players of all sizes
  compete

The author compares and contrasts Matt and Emily. Think about each character as you answer the questions.

4. What are two ways in which Emily and Matt are similar?

Possible answers: Both are athletes, both are small and thin, both are victorious.

_____

5. What are two ways Emily and Matt are different?

Possible answers: Emily is a girl and Matt is a boy; Emily is older; Emily plays basketball while

Matt wrestles; Emily goes to high school, while Matt goes to middle school.

Practicing Vocabulary

Write a word from the box to complete each sentence.

6. He _____protested_____ loudly over the referee's decision.

7. She was excited at the _____prospect_____ of being named team captain.

8. The _____spectators_____ root for their favorite team.

9. To ensure that athletes play by the rules, _____referees_____ watch the action carefully.

10. In wrestling, you face wrestlers whose _____weight_____ is close to yours.

11. The whistle _____signaled_____ that a foul had been made.

12. Winning wrestlers show a good _____technique_____ and use skillful holds.

> **prospect**
> **protested**
> **referees**
> **signaled**
> **spectators**
> **technique**
> **weight**

Writing a News Story
Think about a real sports event or invent a fictional one. On a separate sheet of paper, write a news story reporting the event. In your story, compare and contrast two of the players or two teams.

Summarizing

How would you describe a movie to a friend? Would you tell the whole story, or would you just tell the important parts of the plot? If you said you would just tell the most important parts, you already know about summarizing. A **summary** is a short statement, usually one or two sentences, that tells the main ideas and most important details of a story or an article. A summary can help you to understand and remember what you read.

To summarize a story, ask yourself, "What are the most important events? What does the main character learn?" For nonfiction, ask, "What is the main idea?" Look for topic sentences, and choose only the most important information. Leave out unnecessary details.

As you read the following story about a visiting alien, think about a summary of the story.

The Visitor

It was Thursday afternoon. Charlie was sitting in math class watching his teacher writing on the board when something flew past the window. Charlie looked out, expecting to see a bird. He saw a small silver rocket ship land behind the playground slides.

When the lunch bell rang, Charlie hurried out to the playground to examine the rocket ship. The ship looked like a dented soda can. Nearby sat a creature with blinking gold eyes and three arms. Over and over, it held up three fingers, five fingers, and seven fingers.

"Sorry, little guy," Charlie said. "We talk in words here, not numbers. Let's see—my uncle is a computer programmer. Maybe he can speak your language!"

What is the most important event in the first paragraph?

Charlie sees a spaceship land behind the slides.

Fill in the circle next to the best summary of this story.

○ A silver spaceship that looked like a dented soda can landed at Charlie's school.

○ An alien did Charlie's homework for him.

● Charlie saw a spaceship land but couldn't communicate with the alien he met.

○ On Thursday, Charlie's teacher was teaching math when a rocket ship landed.

You can keep your summaries short by including only the most important material. When you see a list of actions, try to think of one action that names the whole list. For example, if a story tells of an alien who "squealed, squeaked, and babbled," you might summarize by saying "the alien made strange sounds." When you see a list of items, try to think of a word or two that names the whole list.

Read the following selection about a spacecraft bound for Earth. As you read, underline main ideas that you would include in a summary. The main ideas in the first paragraph have been underlined for you.

A Friendly Mission

    <u>As commander of the mission to Earth, Zaneeta had carefully planned the food, tools, and other items that the spaceship would carry.</u> Now she watched as the last container moved through the entryway. She brushed a claw across her forehead. At last the ship was loaded and ready to go.
    <u>Zaneeta's most important task had been to find a way to show the Earthlings that the visitors from the planet Zalenthia meant no harm and came in peace.</u> What could Zalenthia offer that Earthlings would value? Zaneeta smiled as she looked at the precious containers. <u>Each one held the resource that Zalenthians valued above all else—ten gallons of water.</u>

Think of a shorter word or phrase that you could use in a summary to substitute for the italicized words.

She planned the *food, tools, and other items*.

supplies _____

On the lines below, summarize "A Friendly Mission." Include the main ideas you underlined, writing them in your own words.

Possible answer: As commander in chief of a mission from her

planet, Zalenthia, to Earth, Zaneeta had carefully planned the

supplies. Because her most important task was to show that the

Zalenthians were friendly, Zaneeta decided to bring water, their
most valuable resource, as a gift.

On Your Own

Read this article about the search for life in outer space.

Life Beyond Earth

Is there life anywhere in the universe other than on Earth? To answer that question, scientists look at outer space through telescopes. They send up rockets and satellites and study the information that comes back. Scientists also study life forms on Earth. They think about the features on Earth that support life. Every answer helps them to know what to look for in outer space.

Researchers have learned that two things are required to keep life going on Earth. These things are energy and flowing water. All life forms need water during some part of their lives. It takes energy to keep water in its liquid state, however. Earth's energy comes from the sun. Our source for water is rain and snow. These are collected by oceans, lakes, rivers, and streams.

What places in our solar system are likely to have water and the energy to keep it in a liquid state? The answer to that question is unknown, but scientists have some ideas. They are looking very closely at the planet Mars. Although the atmosphere of Mars is very different from Earth's atmosphere, it does have water. Martian air holds only about 1/1000 as much water as Earth's air. Even that small amount can produce clouds, fog, and frost—all filled with water. The greatest problem with keeping water in a liquid state on Mars is the planet's extreme cold. The average

temperature on Mars is –81 degrees Fahrenheit. The warmest it gets is 68 degrees Fahrenheit, and the coldest recorded temperature is –220 degrees Fahrenheit!

Life may also be possible on Europa (yoo ROH puh), one of the moons of the planet Jupiter. Scientists believe Europa may have liquid water and volcanoes. The heat from volcanoes may keep oceans from freezing. Scientists are planning missions to Jupiter and Europa to bring back samples of surface ice. They suspect that if there is life on Europa, it may exist in an ice-covered ocean. They believe that deep below the ice, hot springs in the ocean floor heat the water.

Scientists also look at life on Earth to ponder questions about life in outer space. Life forms have adapted to some remarkably harsh conditions. Creatures too tiny to be seen with the human eye live in ice-covered Antarctic lakes and in steaming hot springs. Infrequently, small creatures can even be found in the dry centers of rocks. The existence of these life forms suggests that some very harsh places can support life. As scientists unlock the secrets of how living things survive on this planet, they come closer to answering questions about life forms elsewhere in our solar system and beyond.

Checking Comprehension

1. How does studying life on Earth help scientists investigate life in other   [Main Idea/Inferential]
   parts of the universe?

   <u>Understanding what living things need and where they can and cannot survive on Earth</u>

   <u>helps scientists know what to look for on other planets and moons.</u>

2. Think about the ideas in the article. Do you think the details prove that
   there is life on other planets? Explain your answer.   [Making Judgments/Critical]

   <u>Possible answer: No, the article doesn't prove that life exists on other planets. It says that</u>

   <u>Mars and Europa might have the things that life forms need to survive.</u>

Practicing Comprehension Skills

3. Reread "Life Beyond Earth." Use the information to fill in the chart with
   the main idea of each paragraph.

Paragraph	Main Point
1	[Scientists study Earth and outer space to determine if there could be life on other planets.]
2	[Energy and liquid water are the two things required to support life.]
3	[Scientists believe Mars may have enough water to support life.]
4	[Europa, a moon of Jupiter, may have water and volcanoes.]
5	[Life forms on Earth can adapt to very harsh conditions.]

4. Which statement would belong in a summary of the article? Fill in the
   circle next to the correct answer.

   ○ The average temperature on Mars is
      −81 degrees Fahrenheit.

   ● Energy and water are needed to support
      life.

   ○ Tiny creatures live in ice-covered
      Antarctic lakes.

   ○ Scientists use telescopes to get answers
      to their questions about other planets.

5. Read each of the following summaries of "Life Beyond Earth." On the lines provided, explain which is a better summary of the article.

A. Scientists study Earth and outer space to determine if there is life beyond Earth. After looking at life on Earth, they believe that living things need liquid water and energy. The planet Mars has water, while Jupiter's moon Europa may have energy and water. Scientists continue to look closely at extreme conditions that support life on Earth for clues to where life may exist in other parts of the universe.

B. Telescopes and space missions help scientists study Earth and outer space to determine if there is life beyond Earth. Even though the planet Mars gets very cold, it appears to have water. Scientists think that one of Jupiter's moons, Europa, has volcanoes that could melt ice to make water. It's amazing that life exists on Earth in places as frozen as Antarctica. Scientists continue to look closely at conditions that support life on Earth.

Choice A is the better summary because it includes only the main ideas. Choice B leaves out

important information and includes unnecessary details.

Read the following paragraph. Think about the main ideas you would use in a summary.

No Signs of Life

Some information encourages the belief that life may exist on Mars. However, other facts discourage the idea. In 1976 the United States sent the spacecraft *Viking* to Mars. Landers 1 and 2 took soil samples near the landing spots. These samples showed no evidence of life in the soil. By contrast, samples taken from Earth soil would certainly show living matter. Scientists believe that the extremely dry ground and the chemicals in it prevent life from forming in the soil on Mars.

Fill in the outer circles of the following web. Write key phrases that suggest main ideas of the paragraph titled "No Signs of Life."

6. Information both encourages and discourages idea of life on Mars

8. Brought back soil samples with no evidence of life

No Signs of Life

7. In 1976, *Viking* landers visited Mars.

9. Scientists believe soil prevents life from forming there.

10. On the lines below, write a three-sentence summary of "No Signs of Life."

   Possible answer: Scientific information both encourages and discourages the idea of life on

   Mars. In 1976, the spacecraft *Viking* took soil samples from Mars that had no signs of life.

   Scientists believe the soil on Mars prevents life from forming there.

Practicing Vocabulary

Choose a word from the box that best matches each definition. Write the word on the line.

telescopes	**11.**	optical instruments for looking at faraway objects
ponder	**12.**	to think about carefully
atmosphere	**13.**	the air and other gases around any planet or star
infrequently	**14.**	not often; seldom
adapted	**15.**	changed to suit or fit a certain situation
unknown	**16.**	not known
researchers	**17.**	people who do research or investigations

adapted
atmosphere
infrequently
ponder
researchers
telescopes
unknown

Writing a Summary

Think about a story, television show, or movie you read or saw recently. On another sheet of paper, write the title of the story, a five-sentence summary of the plot, and whether or not you would recommend it to others. Be sure to include only the most important information in your summary.

Paraphrasing

Explaining something in your own words is called **paraphrasing.** To paraphrase the sentence "All her life, Marie has been fascinated by the subject of codes," you could say, "Marie has always been interested in codes." Paraphrasing is different from summarizing. A summary includes the most important ideas in a piece of writing. A paraphrase restates *all* the information, but it is simpler to read. You do not add your own ideas or opinions. You use only the information the author has written.

Read the article about secret codes. Think about how you might paraphrase the information.

To keep information secret, people use secret forms of communication called codes. The people who invent codes make them very difficult to understand. In World War II, for example, Japan used Purple Code to report on war news. A machine changed each message into something no one else could read. The coded message was received by a similar machine. It decoded the message.

American code breakers spent months looking at messages in Purple Code. Eventually, the Americans solved the code and built their own Purple Code machine. With it, they read secret Japanese messages.

PARAPHRASE A	PARAPHRASE B
People use codes to keep information secret. In World War II, Japan used Purple Code. Only a machine could send or read messages in this code. The Americans tried to break the Purple Code. It took months, but finally they built a machine just like the Japanese one. Then they could decode Japanese messages.	To keep information secret, people use secret forms of communication called codes. They are very interesting. In World War II, Japan used Purple Code to report on war news. The code seemed unbreakable, but eventually the Americans figured it out.

Tip

Check your paraphrasing by asking yourself, "Did I use my own words? Am I telling all of the information? Is the paraphrase simpler to read than the author's original words?"

Look at the two paraphrases for the article. Which is better, A or B? Explain your answer on the lines below.

A is better. It restates all the information in different words and is

simpler to read. It doesn't add any opinions.

Read the following article about Navajo Code Talkers of World War II. After reading it, think about how you would paraphrase the information.

Code Talkers: America's Secret Weapon

In December 1941, the United States faced a tough decision. Japan's forces had stormed through the Pacific. They had taken over the Philippines and other important islands. On December 7, 1941, Japan bombed the U.S. Navy's battleships in Hawaii's Pearl Harbor. America was not fully ready, yet it could not postpone war with Japan.

The Japanese were skillful code breakers. They listened to all secret U.S. war messages. They broke every code the Americans came up with. When an American ship sailed, the Japanese usually knew where it was going.

In 1942, Japanese radio operators began hearing a new American code. Japan's best code breakers went to work on it. They never broke it, however. This new code was not even based on English: it was based on Navajo!

The U.S. Marine Corps had recruited more than 400 Navajos to become "code talkers." In the worst battles of the war, these Native Americans faced numerous challenges as they operated the phones and radios. They sent and received orders. They called in air strikes. They described troop movements. Their brave work saved many lives.

Why couldn't the Japanese crack the code? For one thing, Navajo is not a written language. It has no alphabet. It is spoken only by Navajo people and those who wish to communicate in Navajo. The language is also hard to learn. No one in Japan knew Navajo. In fact, fewer than 30 non-Navajos around the world could speak Navajo!

The Navajo code talkers didn't speak ordinary Navajo, either. They created their own code talk. Some code words were colorful. A dive bomber was called a *gini,* Navajo for "sparrow hawk." The Navajo word for *turtle* was used for tanks. The words for *iron fish* were used for submarines. A special alphabet also was part of the code. For the letter A, the Navajos used their word for *ant.* B was their word for *bear,* and so on. The alphabet let them spell out any name in code.

The Navajo code talkers helped win many battles. In one important battle the code talkers worked around the clock. In two days they sent and received 800 messages without one mistake.

In the postwar years the code talkers could not talk about their work. The Navy thought it might need the Navajo code again. Today, anyone can learn the Navajo code. The fine work of the Navajo code talkers has been recognized publicly. They have been honored for their bravery and patriotism.

Checking Comprehension

[Cause and Effect/Inferential]

1. Why would American soldiers have been in danger if their codes were broken?

   Possible answer: The Japanese might have known where and when the Americans would

   attack.

2. In what ways is Navajo different from English?   [Comparing and Contrasting/Inferential]

   Navajo has no alphabet. It is not a written language, only spoken. It is mainly spoken by

   Navajos.

Practicing Comprehension Skills

3. Which is the best paraphrase of these sentences? Fill in the circle next
   to the correct answer. Explain your choice in item 4.

   In 1942, Japanese radio operators began hearing a new American code. Japan's best
   code breakers went to work on it. They never broke it, however. This new code was
   not even based on English: it was based on Navajo!

   ○ The new code used by the Americans wasn't even based on English.

   ● Beginning in 1942 the Japanese tried to break the new American code. They never cracked it, though. The code was based on Navajo.

   ○ Japanese code breakers didn't speak Navajo, so the new code was the best yet.

   ○ Since the new code was only heard, not written, Japanese code breakers had no luck with it.

4. This is the best paraphrase because

   Possible answer: it restates the meaning of the original sentences in different words. It

   does not give opinions and presents only the most important information.

5. Read this paraphrase of the second paragraph of "Code Talkers."
   Tell why it is or is not a good paraphrase.

   The Japanese were skillful code breakers. They knew beforehand
   everything the Americans were planning.

   This is not a good paraphrase. It uses one of the writer's original sentences. It does not

   include all the ideas in the original. Also, the writer adds ideas.

6. Write a paraphrase of the last paragraph of "Code Talkers."

Possible paraphrase: After the war, the Navajos and the Navy kept the code secret. They

thought they might use the code again. Now the code is public, and the code talkers have

been honored for their work.

Practicing Vocabulary

Fill in the circle next to the word or phrase that means about the same as the underlined word.

<table>
<tr><td>decision</td></tr>
<tr><td>numerous</td></tr>
<tr><td>operated</td></tr>
<tr><td>patriotism</td></tr>
<tr><td>postpone</td></tr>
<tr><td>postwar</td></tr>
<tr><td>skillful</td></tr>
</table>

7. The United States could not <u>postpone</u> its entry into World War II.

○ communicate   ● delay   ○ gain   ○ hurry

8. The U.S. Marine Corps made an important <u>decision</u> to recruit Navajos.

● careful conclusion   ○ comparison between two things

○ familiar name   ○ gift from a government

9. By serving their country, the code talkers showed great <u>patriotism</u>.

○ happiness   ● devotion to their country   ○ love of languages   ○ skill

10. The code talkers helped save lives in <u>numerous</u> ways.

○ usual   ● many   ○ written   ○ excellent

11. They used the code as they <u>operated</u> phones and radios.

○ saved   ● put to use   ○ avoided   ○ destroyed

12. The code talkers' work was careful and <u>skillful</u>.

○ lovely   ○ sad   ○ personal   ● expert

13. The Navajo code was kept secret in the early <u>postwar</u> years.

○ before the war   ○ during the war   ● after the war   ○ like the war

Writing a Descriptive Paragraph
Think of a code that you might invent. What would make it easy or hard to break? Describe your code on a sheet of paper. Then trade papers with a partner. Paraphrase your partner's description of a code.

Recognizing Author's Purpose

Authors usually have a purpose in mind when they write. The author's language and style of writing can help you figure out his or her reasons for writing. Four common reasons for writing are:

- To **persuade:** to convince readers to think or act a certain way
- To **inform:** to explain or give information about something
- To **express:** to create a mood, or feeling, through description
- To **entertain:** to amuse, interest, or scare readers, or make them feel sadness or joy

Sometimes authors have more than one purpose in mind when they write. Thinking about the author's purpose will help you understand what you read.

Read the following article about skunks. As you read, think about the author's purpose or purposes for writing.

Is a skunk the pet for you? Skunks are one of the unusual pets that have recently become popular. Many people are afraid of skunks because of their odor. The spray glands of skunks are removed, though, before the animals are sold as pets. Skunks are considered wild animals. Because of that, keeping a skunk as a pet may not be legal in your state.

Pet skunks need love and attention. Because they are very curious, you will need to "skunk-proof" your home. They are clean animals and can be trained to use a litter box. Before you decide to get a pet skunk, talk to an animal doctor and ask other skunk owners about their experiences.

What do you think was the author's purpose for writing this article? Explain your answer.

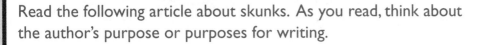

Possible answer: The author's purpose was to inform readers about keeping skunks as pets.

Think about the way you read this article. Which of the following would you be likely to read in a similar way? Fill in the circle next to the best answer.

- ● an article in a magazine
- ○ a poem in a poetry book
- ○ a description in a catalog
- ○ a joke in a joke book

Knowing the author's purpose for writing can also affect the way you read. You may quickly scan some material meant to persuade, such as an advertisement. If you are reading a science article meant to inform, you will probably want to read slowly and carefully.

Read the following sign posted on a community bulletin board. As you read, think about the author's purpose for writing.

Would you like to have one of the most unusual and interesting pets around? Then get a skunk! With this curious and friendly pet in the house, your life will never be the same.

My pet skunk, Cindersmella, just had a litter of five babies. Five lucky owners can adopt one of these lovely kittens—for *free*! We will have each baby de-scented. You'll have no trouble with housebreaking. Skunks are naturally clean.

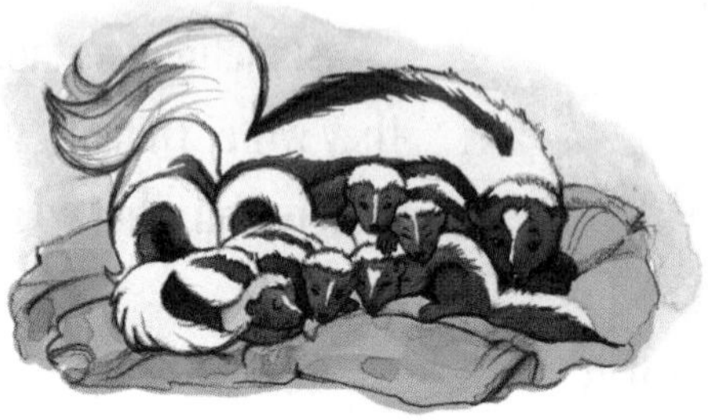

Do you know how a skunk calls home? On his smell phone! That's just a joke, because a de-scented skunk doesn't smell. Remember, if you want a great pet, adopt one of my fine skunks. You will gain a loyal friend.

Fill in the blanks in the chart below. In the blank lines on the left, write a purpose that the author had for writing the sign. In the blank lines on the right, write a sentence that could show the purpose.

Author's Purpose	Sentence That Shows the Purpose
to persuade	Remember, if you want a great pet, adopt one of my skunks
to entertain	Possible answer: Do you know how a skunk calls home? On his smell phone!
to inform	Skunks are naturally clean.

Which of the following selections would you be likely to read in the same way?

- ● a poster offering free puppies
- ○ an article about wild skunks
- ○ a biography of a skunk owner
- ○ a poem about a talking skunk

Read the article about pets. As you read, decide what the author's purpose or purposes are.

Pets I Have Known

by Ann Hodgman

A great thing about being a grown-up is that your parents can't stop you from owning all the pets you want. Want a hedgehog, two dogs, three cats, a prairie dog, two rabbits, a turtle that lives in the bathtub, two sugar gliders, seven birds, two hamsters, and six African pygmy mice? Go ahead! Just don't forget that since you are a grown-up, your parents won't be there to help you out.

As you may have guessed, I am the owner of all the pets I just listed. A while ago, I bought a hamster. Then I got worried that she was lonely, so I bought another hamster, who promptly had thirteen babies. We kept the babies in a big cage on our kitchen table. Life got pretty complicated, but at least the first hamster wasn't lonely anymore. I've found good homes for all the hamster offspring, and for several baby sugar gliders. A sugar glider is a marsupial that looks like a flying squirrel, in case you were wondering.

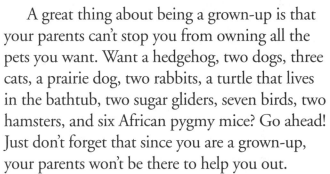

My big pets—the dogs and cats—live upstairs. My little pets live in cages in my basement in a special "pet nook" my husband built for them. My poor, misguided husband! He originally expected that we'd own a dog and a cat. Now, of course, he knows better. He has never gotten used to the noise. Whenever our front door opens, the dogs start barking. This makes the birds start screaming. This makes the prairie dog utter her special "someone's at the door" noise, which sounds like a shrill "Wacka! Wacka!"

All night, every night, the exercise wheels squeak. Most of my caged animals are nocturnal, which means they sleep during the day and run on their wheels during the night. Luckily, I'm nocturnal, too. Every night, after the dogs, cats, and humans in my house are asleep, I head down to the basement for a couple of hours. I move the rabbits into their exercise pen. I whistle to the birds. (I'm trying to teach my cockatiel, Japan, to sing "Here Comes the Bride." He's learned the first four notes, but it's taken him eight years.) I take out Daisy, the prairie dog, and scratch her ears. I watch the hedgehog—that's about all you can do with a hedgehog. I also clean cages.

My children are starting to mistrust me. "Are you sure you can handle this, Mom?" they ask me whenever I buy an animal magazine, because they know a real-life animal will soon follow. Of course I can handle it, I tell them. After all, the night is eight hours long. When I'm done with all the cages, I might even have time to sleep for a couple of hours before breakfast.

Checking Comprehension

1. Summarize the article.   [Summarizing/Inferential]

   <u>Possible answer: The author and her family own a wide variety of pets that range from</u>

   <u>dogs and cats to sugar gliders and a prairie dog. The big pets live upstairs with the family,</u>

   <u>while the small pets live downstairs. The author cares for the small pets at night.</u>

2. Think about the details in the article. Would you like to live in the
   home the author describes? Explain why or why not. [Making Judgments/Critical]

   <u>Answers will vary. Some students may say that they love animals and it sounds fun. Other</u>

   <u>students may say that the author's home sounds too noisy and hectic.</u>

Practicing Comprehension Skills

Fill in the blanks in the chart below. In the blank line on the left, write a
purpose that could be described with the sentence provided. In the blank
lines on the right, write a sentence that could show the purpose "to inform."

Author's Purpose	Sentence That Shows the Purpose
3. <u>to entertain</u>	This makes the prairie dog utter her special "someone's at the door" noise, which sounds like a shrill "Wacka! Wacka!"
to inform	4. <u>Possible answer: A sugar glider is a marsupial that looks like</u> <u>a flying squirrel, in case you were wondering.</u>

5. Ann Hodgman could have just given information about her pets, but
   instead she uses humor to show how the pets have affected her life
   and her family's life. Why do you think she does that?

   <u>Possible answer: By using humor, she changes the story from an informative one to a story</u>

   <u>that both entertains and informs.</u>

Below are the titles of some articles and stories about pets. For each title, predict the author's purpose or purposes for writing. Write each title in one or more circles.

Stop Pet Skunks!

Great Dog Jokes

Encyclopedia article: "Snakes"

My Beautiful Parrot

Cat Poems

Gerbils Make Great Pets

365 Hamster Riddles

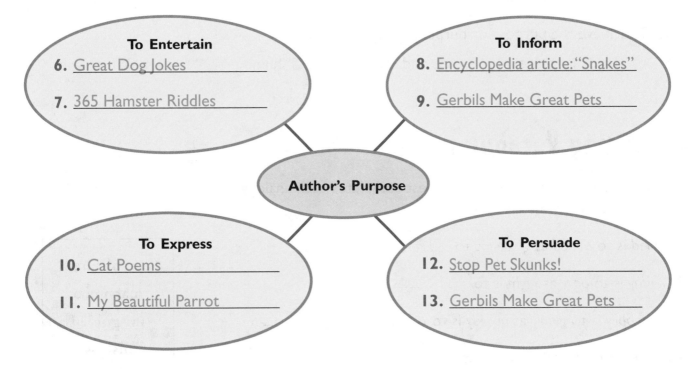

To Entertain
6. Great Dog Jokes

7. 365 Hamster Riddles

To Inform
8. Encyclopedia article: "Snakes"

9. Gerbils Make Great Pets

Author's Purpose

To Express
10. Cat Poems

11. My Beautiful Parrot

To Persuade
12. Stop Pet Skunks!

13. Gerbils Make Great Pets

Read the following poem and think about the author's purpose or purposes for writing.

The Oldest Excuse in the Book!
Teacher, sir, I know you've heard
This lame excuse before.
I'm sure you'll shake your head and state
That zero is my score.

But it's no falsehood when I say
My life is complicated.
I can't hand in my science project —
My thirteen hamsters ate it!

Fill in the circle next to the answer or answers that will complete each statement.

14. The author's purpose or purposes for writing the poem might have been
    ○ to persuade readers to get a hamster
    ○ to present facts about hamsters
    ● to entertain
    ○ to create a mood

15. To achieve the purpose or purposes, the writer uses
    ○ poetic language   ○ facts and statistics   ● humor   ○ scientific language

Practicing Vocabulary

Choose the word from the box that best completes each analogy. Write the word on the line.

16. *led* is to *misled* as *guided* is to _____misguided_____

17. *day* is to *daily* as *night* is to _____nocturnal_____

18. *happily* is to *gladly* as *quickly* is to _____promptly_____

19. *easy* is to *difficult* as *simple* is to _____complicated_____

20. *hen* is to *chick* as *parent* is to _____offspring_____

21. *dog* is to *mammal* as *kangaroo* is to _____marsupial_____

22. *believe* is to *trust* as *doubt* is to _____mistrust_____

complicated
marsupial
misguided
mistrust
nocturnal
offspring
promptly

Writing for a Purpose
On a separate sheet of paper, write a poem, a story, or an article about pets. Decide whether the purpose of your writing is to inform, persuade, entertain, express, or a combination of these purposes. Make sure your purpose or purposes are clear in your writing.

Statements of Fact and Opinion

As you read stories and articles, you will find statements of fact and statements of opinion. A **statement of fact** tells something that can be proven to be true or false. You can make sure that a statement is a fact by looking it up in a reference source or by checking it yourself. Even if it is proven false, it is still a statement of fact. *Volcanoes on Mars explode all the time* is a statement of fact, even though it is not true.

A **statement of opinion** tells ideas, feelings, or beliefs. It cannot be proven true or false. For example, *Volcanoes are really exciting* is a statement of opinion because it cannot be proven or checked. Sometimes statements of opinion begin with clue words such as *I believe, I think,* or *in my opinion.*

Read the following paragraph. Look for statements of fact and statements of opinion.

Archaeologists dig in historic places called sites. They want to learn how people lived through the ages. Archaeologists sometimes dig in areas where ancient people lived. They might also dig in places that were inhabited just a century ago. People have different ideas about what sites should be explored. I think it's wrong to disturb a site that could give us interesting clues about the past just to construct a building or a highway. Destroying a site is like erasing a piece of history.

Write one sentence from the paragraph that is a statement of fact. Explain why it is a fact.

Possible answer: "Archaeologists sometimes dig in areas where ancient people lived." It can be proven to be true or false.

Write one sentence from the paragraph that is a statement of opinion. Explain why it is an opinion.

Possible answer: "I think it's wrong to disturb a site that could give us interesting clues about the past just to construct a building or a highway." This is a statement of opinion because it tells about beliefs and cannot be proven.

Tip

To figure out whether a statement is an opinion or a fact that can be proved true or false, ask yourself: "Can I look it up or check it myself? If not, can I find clue words that show an opinion?"

On Your Own

Read the following article about the ancient city of Pompeii.
As you read, look for statements of fact and statements of opinion.

Pompeii Buried!

In the year A.D. 79, Pompeii was a wealthy city on the west coast of Italy. In August that year, the people of Pompeii began to see signs that the nearby volcano Mount Vesuvius was "waking up." Vesuvius was often active. These prolonged signals did not scare most people. They went about their daily lives, sure that the mountain would soon quiet down again. I believe they should not have been so certain.

On the morning of August 24, the top of the mountain split apart in a huge blast. Smoke shot up into the sky, blocking out the sun. Birds fell dead from the sky. Terrified animals ran and tried to hide. Even then, many people took no precautions to protect themselves.

At first a light layer of ash began to cover the city. People simply brushed the powder off their clothes and hair. Before long, though, small pieces of rock began to fall from above. Some people tied pillows to their heads to protect themselves. Later, larger rocks began to fall. Many people fled the city, but some stayed behind. In my opinion, those who stayed should have known they were in great danger.

A foul odor filled the city. Deadly gases seeped through the cracks in houses. People were forced to seek fresh air outside. There, though, the air was thick with dust and gases. The rocks still rained down. The people were forced back inside again.

Soon the city was covered in ashes and rock nine feet deep. Rooftops caved in, trapping those inside. On August 25 a glowing mixture of gas and molten rock from the erupting volcano flowed over Pompeii, killing everyone in its path.

The once-great city remained hidden under layers of ash until 1594. Then workers building a water channel nearby found the buried city. Since then, digging has continued. In 1860, an Italian scientist took over the project. We should all be grateful for his careful work. The most interesting results are plaster casts of the bodies of humans and animals. These casts show the frightened victims of Vesuvius frozen in time nearly 2,000 years ago.

Checking Comprehension

1. Why did the people in Pompeii remain in the city when Vesuvius erupted? [Drawing Conclusions/Inferential]

   The volcano had been active before without erupting. The people didn't think they were

   in danger.

2. Summarize what happened in Pompeii on August 24 and 25, A.D. 79. [Summarizing/Inferential]

   Mt. Vesuvius erupted, shooting smoke into the sky. Falling ash and rock covered the city in

   a layer nine feet deep. Many people escaped, but the people left in Pompeii were buried in

   a flow of gas and molten rock from the volcano.

Practicing Comprehension Skills

Fill in the circle next to the correct answer.

3. Which of the following is a statement of fact?

   ○ We should all be grateful for his work.

   ○ The excavation of Pompeii is quite remarkable, in my opinion.

   ○ The plaster casts are extremely interesting.

   ● A volcano destroyed Pompeii in A.D. 79.

4. How could you verify the statement of fact in item 3?

   Possible answer: by looking up the fact in an encyclopedia

5. Which of the following is a statement of opinion?

   ○ Mount Vesuvius erupted in A.D. 79, burying the city of Pompeii.

   ○ Workers found the buried city in 1594.

   ● In my opinion, the people of Pompeii should have known they were in great danger.

   ○ Since then, digging has continued.

6. How can you tell the statement in item 5 is a statement of opinion?

   The writer uses the clue words *In my opinion.* The statement tells about beliefs and can't

   be proven to be true or false.

7. Find a statement of opinion in the passage that does <u>not</u> use clue words and write it on the line provided. Explain how you can tell it is a statement of opinion.

   <u>Possible answer: "The most interesting results are plaster casts of the bodies of humans</u>

   <u>and animals." This tells about ideas and beliefs. Whether or not the plaster casts are the</u>

   <u>most interesting results can't be proven true or false.</u>

Practicing Vocabulary

Choose the word from the box that best completes each sentence. Write the word on the line.

| erupting |
| molten |
| precautions |
| prolonged |
| rooftops |
| terrified |
| wealthy |

8. The archaeologists took careful <u>precautions</u> to make sure that no bones were disturbed.

9. A <u>wealthy</u> businesswoman gave the money to help explore the ancient site.

10. With its fur standing on end, the fearful cat was clearly

    <u>terrified</u> by the disaster.

11. The warning signs were <u>prolonged</u> over a period of days.

12. The heat from the volcano turned the rocks into a

    <u>molten</u> flow.

13. Rocks falling on the houses went through the <u>rooftops</u> .

14. First smoke, then rocks shot from the top of the

    <u>erupting</u> volcano.

MAKING THE Reading AND Writing CONNECTION

Writing an Editorial
Write an editorial article that expresses your ideas about a school issue such as the lunchroom or homework. Begin your editorial with a statement of opinion. Include statements of fact to support your opinion. Write on a separate sheet of paper.

Making Judgments

When you read, you develop feelings and thoughts about characters, events, and ideas. Often, you are drawing conclusions and **making judgments.** When you make a judgment, you use what you have read and your own experiences and values.

Sometimes an author makes a judgment and presents it to the reader. When you come across a judgment as you read, think about the writer's reasons for making that judgment. Ask yourself if the judgment is supported with facts or examples. A judgment that is supported with facts or examples is called a **valid judgment.**

Read the article. Use your own experience and details in the article to make your own judgment about Mother Teresa and her work.

In 1910 in what is now the country of Macedonia, a girl named Agnes Gonxha Bojaxhiu was born. As she grew up, young Agnes wanted to help people. She decided to be a nun and took the name of Teresa. While still a teenager, she went to Calcutta, India. In India, Mother Teresa saw so much hunger and illness that she decided to devote her life to helping the poor and the sick. She started schools for homeless children and shelters for sick people. She also founded the Missionaries of Charity. They run orphanages, homeless shelters, clinics, and soup kitchens all over the globe. Mother Teresa won the Nobel Peace Prize in 1979. When she died in 1997, the world mourned.

Which of the following is a valid judgment that you can make after reading the article? Fill in the circle next to the correct answer.

○ The Missionaries of Charity only help people in India.

○ Mother Teresa was never recognized for any of the work she did.

● Mother Teresa was a generous person who helped many others.

○ Volunteering makes you feel sad.

What facts or details in the article support the judgment you selected?

Possible answer: Mother Teresa started schools for homeless

children and shelters for the sick. She founded a group that helps

other people all over the world.

Tip

Before making a judgment, think about what you read and your own experiences. Decide whether the author has given accurate information and has supported judgments with facts and examples.

Read the article. As you read, identify judgments the author makes. Ask yourself whether you agree with those judgments.

Kid Power

All over America, kids are making a difference. Through volunteering, they've found exciting ways to broaden their lives. They make the world a better place for others as well. There are many different ways to lend a hand.

Some young people choose to help others. One Pennsylvania student joined a group that helped people with disabilities. She learned about laws that say everyone should be able to enter public places easily. The student knew that some business owners in her town had overlooked the needs of people in wheelchairs. They could not get up the steps of all the restaurants and stores in her town. She reminded the owners about laws for people with disabilities. In the end they built ramps that made the buildings accessible to people in wheelchairs.

Many young people work directly with the people they help. Members of some youth groups assist at food pantries. Some towns have programs in which older students help younger children learn to play musical instruments. One Massachusetts teen enjoyed spending time with her grandfather. She realized that other elderly people might be lonely. The girl asked friends to visit local seniors. Her friends enjoyed the visits as much as the seniors did. While some adults label young people as selfish, these efforts show that kids do care.

The environment is a favorite cause of young people. They send a strong message: "don't pollute!" When New Jersey youths formed Kids Against Pollution, they started a wave of action. More than 1,000 chapters soon had members from elementary school through high school. Their letters convinced fast-food chains to use paper products rather than plastic foam.

Young people in Maine helped the environment in a different way. A student saw a film about dolphins that were being caught in nets and killed during tuna fishing. This young person got students in high school science classes to send letters of protest to a company that sold canned tuna. The company began buying fish caught in ways that did not harm dolphins.

All around you, young people are cleaning up trash and building trails to make their communities more beautiful. Members of YES (Youth for Environmental Sanity) have visited schools in 42 different states. They perform plays with this message: "If we don't save the earth for ourselves, nobody's going to save it for us!"

There are volunteer jobs to suit all interests. Teachers and librarians can direct you to them. If you lend a hand, be safe. Never take a job that seems risky for someone your age. Ask for help when you need it. Find a group with an adult who can help you make suitable plans. Also, remember to show up once you offer to volunteer, even if you're only working one afternoon a month. Get your friends to join you. The more of you there are, the greater the kid power!

Checking Comprehension

1. Can kids really make a difference when it comes to helping to protect the environment? Explain your answer. [Cause and Effect/Critical]

    Yes. In New Jersey a group called Kids Against Pollution got fast-food chains to use paper

    products rather than foam. In Maine a group of students in science classes got a food

    company to buy tuna caught in ways that did not harm dolphins.

2. Do you think "Kid Power" is a good title for the article? Explain your answer. [Main Idea/Inferential]

    Possible answer: Yes. The article is about the differences that kids can make when they

    volunteer. They make the world a better place for others in many different ways.

Practicing Comprehension Skills

Complete the boxes below. Make your judgment based on details in the article and on your own experiences and values. Support the judgment with three facts or details from the article or your own experiences.

Judgment	Support
3. What kind of judgment can you make about volunteering? Possible answer: Kids can make a difference through volunteer work.	4. Possible answer: Students who wrote letters saved the lives of many dolphins. 5. Possible answer: Senior citizens enjoyed being visited by teenagers. 6. I've volunteered and I was able to see what I did really helped people/helped protect the environment.

On the lines before the following judgments, write a **Y** if you think the judgment is a valid one based on information in the article. Write an **N** if you think the judgment is not valid.

7. _____N_____ Kids can't make much of a difference in the world.

8. _____Y_____ Young people are often interested in helping to protect the earth.

9. _____Y_____ There are many ways that kids can volunteer.

10. _____N_____ Kids never work together when they do volunteer work.

11. The author makes the following judgment in the article: "While some adults label young people as selfish, these efforts show that kids do care." Do you think it is valid? Explain your answer on the lines.

    Answers will vary. Some students will say it is a valid judgment, because the author gives

    many examples of caring young people. Others will say it is not a valid judgment, because
    not all young people volunteer.

Practicing Vocabulary

Choose the word from the box that best fills each blank.

12.   My youth group leader, Mrs. Miller, sure gets around in her wheelchair! Mrs. Miller believes that everyone can _____broaden_____ their interests by _____volunteering_____. Our group of 20 students meets once a month. We work on projects that are _____suitable_____ for helping our community, like making sure local businesses don't _____pollute_____ the river. For our first project, we found a problem that a store in our town had _____overlooked_____. We asked the owner of the local ice-cream store to make the entrance _____accessible_____ to people in wheelchairs. Now we hold our _____afternoon_____ meetings there!

| accessible |
| afternoon |
| broaden |
| overlooked |
| pollute |
| suitable |
| volunteering |

Writing a Character Sketch
On another sheet of paper, describe someone you know who volunteers or gives to others in some way. Tell how you feel about that person. Support your judgment with facts and details.

Point of View

Before an author writes a story, he or she must decide from whose **point of view** the story will be told. Will it be told from the point of view of one character, or will a narrator who describes all of the characters tell the story? The point of view determines the information you learn about the characters and events in a story. A story can be told from the **first-person point of view** or the **third-person point of view.**

Point of View	
First-Person Point of View	**Third-Person Point of View**
The author uses pronouns such as *I, me, my,* and *we.* The narrator, or speaker, is a character in the story. When telling a story from the first-person point of view, the "I" narrator, or first person, tells only his or her thoughts. The narrator cannot enter the minds of other characters. He or she can only tell what others are doing, not what they are thinking.	The author uses pronouns such as *he, she,* and *they.* The narrator is not a character in the story but has the ability to see into any or all of the characters' thoughts. A third-person narrator can tell the reader what all the characters are thinking and feeling, or may reveal only one character's thoughts and feelings.

Read this story about a yo-yo collection. Look for clues that tell you the narrator's point of view.

When my grandfather first suggested that I start collecting yo-yos, it sounded like a lot of work. I never knew it would be so interesting!

I now have eighteen yo-yos stored in a box in my room. My grandfather gave me my favorite yo-yo. It's candy apple red and was made in 1948. Grandpa taught me some great tricks, and I learned more from a book. Grandpa also encouraged my sister to start a shell collection. Shells are all right, I guess, but you sure can't make a shell do tricks!

Who is the narrator, or speaker, in the story?

The narrator is a boy who collects yo-yos.

Is the story told from the first-person point of view or third-person point of view? How can you tell?

The story is told from the first-person point of view. The author uses the pronouns *I* and *my,*

and the narrator is a character in the story.

Now read this version of the same story. Think about who is telling the story.

Grandpa watched Kaya and Len drawing circles in the sand with sticks. His grandchildren looked bored and unhappy.

"They need something fun to do," Grandpa thought. "I know!" He went into the house and pulled two things off a shelf in his room. Then he went back down to the beach.

"You should each start a collection," he suggested. "Len, I'll give you my prize 1948 yo-yo. Kaya, here is a shell I picked up on a trip to a faraway island."

At first, Kaya and Len weren't thrilled with the idea. Each one thought to themselves that Grandpa's idea sounded more like work than fun. However, both of them had to admit that Grandpa's advice was often right! That's when their collections started.

Within a month, Len was a yo-yo champ. He learned to do tricks such as "Around the World" and "Rock the Baby."

Kaya spent many hours at the shore finding new shells. She decorated boxes to hold them. Soon, she could name every shell she had.

Kaya was happy. Secretly, she thought her collection was much nicer than her brother's. Len was happy, too. Privately, he thought his collection was a lot more fun than his sister's. Grandpa was happiest of all. His idea was a success!

Fill in the circle next to the word or words that complete each statement.

This version of the story is told by

○ Len   ○ Kaya   ○ Grandpa   ● an outside narrator

The second story differs from the first because in the second version

○ the reader learns about collecting yo-yos and shells.

● the narrator tells what more than one character is thinking and feeling.

○ the story is told only from Grandpa's point of view.

○ the narrator is a character in the story.

Is the story told from first-person point of view or third-person point of view?

third-person point of view

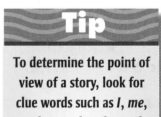

Tip

To determine the point of view of a story, look for clue words such as *I*, *me*, and *my* or *he*, *she*, and *they*. Ask yourself, "Who is doing the talking? Whose thoughts and feelings does the narrator reveal?"

Read the following story about a yo-yo contest. Look for clues that tell the point of view.

Walking the Dog

A voice blared over the speaker. "All those in Class A Beginners report to the stage." Maddy Shaw took her place with the other kids. She heard her brother Kenny's voice in the crowd.

"No way!" Kenny could not believe his eyes. "Look, Philip! It's Maddy!"

Maddy felt her face turning hot. She didn't want to appear overeager in front of her big brother and his friend. They had been doing yo-yo tricks for years, and she was just a beginner.

Maddy tried to stay calm. When it was her turn, she whipped the yo-yo straight down with her palm facing up. It went down until it rested just off the ground. She lowered it lightly to the floor. Once the yo-yo touched the floor, it "walked" out in front of her. With a slight jerk on the string, she brought the yo-yo back up into her palm. All in all, she thought her performance had been satisfying.

"Nice move!" Philip thought as they applauded. "A 'Walk the Dog.'" He nudged Kenny and said, "Where'd she learn that?"

Kenny scratched his head. He'd just been wondering the same thing. "I don't know," he said. "She's watched us doing tricks forever, and she never expressed any interest in getting a yo-yo. I didn't even think she had one!"

The boys caught up with Maddy after the contest was over. She was wearing the silver cap of the second-place winner.

"OK, Maddy," said Kenny. "Come on. Let me see it."

Maddy took her hand out of her jacket and opened her palm. "I found it in Gran's garage. Gran said I could have it," she told them. Kenny and Philip stared at the yo-yo. Its blue plastic face was smudged and scratched.

"How did you pull off such an excellent trick with such an old yo-yo?" asked Philip.

"What I want to know is, when did you practice?" Kenny asked. "I didn't even know you had a yo-yo."

Maddy looked from one boy to the other. "Aren't they going a little overboard?" she thought, wondering if they were teasing her. They seemed to be serious, however.

"I practiced over and over at Gran's house," she said. "Philip, I found some good hints about the trick on a Web site. I'll show it to you sometime."

"Thanks," said Philip. He was impressed.

As the boys walked away, Kenny realized that he had forgotten to congratulate his sister. He turned around and called to her.

"Hey, Maddy!" Maddy waited for one of his teasing remarks. "Nice hat," he said with a grin.

Checking Comprehension

[Drawing Conclusions/Inferential]

1. Why were Kenny and Philip surprised that Maddy could do a yo-yo trick?

   The boys did not know that Maddy had a yo-yo or knew how to do any yo-yo tricks.

   _____

2. Why do you think Maddy might have wanted to learn to do a yo-yo trick? [Character/Inferential]

   Maddy found the yo-yo and wanted to learn how to use it. She might have enjoyed

   surprising her brother.

Practicing Comprehension Skills

Fill in the blanks to answer each question.

3. Who is the narrator of "Walking the Dog"?

   The narrator is someone who is not a character in the story.

4. Whose thoughts and feelings does the narrator describe?

   Kenny's, Maddy's, and Philip's

5. Is the story written from the first-person point of view or the
   third-person point view? Explain your answer.

   The story is written from the third-person point of view. The narrator is someone

   outside the story who can see into all the characters' thoughts. The narrator uses

   pronouns such as *he, she,* and *they.*

6. Rewrite the first paragraph of "Walking the Dog" so that it is told from
   Maddy's first-person point of view. Remember to use pronouns such as
   I and *my.*

   A voice blared over the speaker. "All those in Class A Beginners report to the stage." I

   took my place with the other kids. I heard my brother Kenny's voice in the crowd.

   _____

Read the following story about another kind of contest.
Think about who is telling the story.

The Ping Pong® Tournament

OK! I'm ready for the big game. Let me tell you, I'm more than a little nervous. There's a sensation like butterflies deep in the pit of my handle. I've never been in a tournament before, but I think I'm ready. Both sides of my face are clean and my frame has been sanded and polished. I even have a new grip made of 100% leather!

Here we go. OK, Jerome, it's our serve.

Whack! Ah, that was a solid, sturdy smack in the face!

Whack! There's no doubt that one will be a challenge. It grazed the boundary line, precisely where I aimed it!

Are you ready to finish them off? Hold on tightly, Jerome, because here comes that little white ball. It's just you and me, kid—a player and his paddle. Let's give them all we've got!

Whack! Yes! Our point!

Write your answer to each question.

7. Who is the narrator of the story?

The narrator is a Ping-Pong paddle.

8. What is unusual about the narrator?

It is an object rather than a human.

9. Whose thoughts and feelings does the narrator describe?

The paddle describes its own thoughts and feelings.

10. What pronouns does the narrator use?

I, my, we, and our

11. Is the story told from a first-person point of view or a third-person point of view?

First-person point of view

Read each sentence below. Tell whether the sentence is written from a first-person or third-person point of view. Underline the clue words that help you determine the point of view. Then rewrite the sentence so that it is told from the *other* point of view.

12. I've been playing Ping-Pong since I was seven years old, and I'm ready for this tournament.

    Point of view: _____ first-person _____

    Your sentence: Possible answer: He's been playing Ping-Pong since he was seven years old,

    and he's ready for this tournament.

13. Sarah gripped her Ping-Pong paddle tightly as she faced her opponent.

    Point of view: _____ third-person _____

    Your sentence: Possible answer: I gripped my Ping-Pong paddle tightly as I faced my opponent.

Practicing Vocabulary

Complete each analogy with a word from the box.

14. *clap* is to *cheer* as *applaud* is to _____ congratulate _____

15. *cliff* is to *over the edge* as *boat* is to _____ overboard _____

16. *exciting* is to *thrilling* as *pleasing* is to _____ satisfying _____

17. *spoke* is to *said* as *stated* is to _____ expressed _____

18. *pushed* is to *pulled* as *whispered* is to _____ blared _____

19. *winner* is to *loser* as *spotless* is to _____ smudged _____

20. *relaxed* is to *calm* as *too enthusiastic* is to _____ overeager _____

blared
congratulate
expressed
overboard
overeager
satisfying
smudged

Writing a Story
How would "Walking the Dog" be different if it were told by Kenny or Philip? On a separate sheet of paper, write the story from either character's first-person point of view.

Identifying Text Structure

Knowing how the text is organized when you read a story or article will help you become a better reader. **Text structure** is the way a piece of writing is organized. Authors choose the text structure that best helps them to say what they want to say.

Fiction stories tell about imaginary people and events. They are usually told in chronological, or time, order. **Nonfiction** tells about real people and events. Nonfiction can be organized in different ways. The chart below shows different ways that a piece of writing can be organized.

Chronological Order	This form of text structure organizes a piece of writing by the order in which events happen in time. Many fiction stories and some nonfiction texts are organized this way. Clue words that signal chronological order usually refer to time. They include **first, next, eventually**, and **later.** The use of dates also signals a chronological text structure.
Main Idea and Supporting Details	Nonfiction writing is often organized by main idea and supporting details. In this form of text structure, the writer states his or her most important idea about a topic. Then he or she gives supporting details that tell more about the main idea.
Cause and Effect	Nonfiction pieces are sometimes organized with a cause-and-effect structure. The writer tells about something that happened (the effect) and tells why it happened (the cause). Look for clue words such as **because, as a result,** and **therefore** to show cause and effect.
Problem and Solution	Nonfiction texts sometimes organize ideas by stating a problem and then suggesting solutions. For example, an editorial might open with a description of a problem and then offer some possible solutions.
Compare and Contrast	Some nonfiction texts show how two subjects are alike, different, or both alike and different. Look for clue words such as **both, in the same way, similar,** and **but, however, unlike,** and **on the other hand.**

Read the following article about John F. Kennedy, the 35th President of the United States. As you read, think about how the information is organized.

To those who elected him, John F. Kennedy stood for youth and new ideas. His inaugural speech in 1961 was an expression of these things.

He talked about how a torch had been "passed to a new generation of Americans … born in this century." Kennedy himself was the first President sworn in during the twentieth century who had actually been born in that century. His ideas included ending poverty and war. His speech called on Americans to help make those dreams happen. He said, "Ask not what your country can do for you … ask what you can do for your country."

Is this passage fiction or nonfiction? How do you know?

The passage is nonfiction. It tells about real people and events.

What text structure does the author use in this passage? How can you tell?

The text structure is main idea and supporting details. The main idea is given in the first

paragraph. It states that President Kennedy stood for youth and new ideas. The author

supports the idea by providing quotes from Kennedy's inaugural speech.

Read the letter from a Peace Corps volunteer. Think about how the letter is organized.

Dear Kris,

I'm so excited—I'm going to be a Peace Corps volunteer! I've always wanted to join, because the program was started by my hero, President John F. Kennedy. First, I got the application forms in January. It took me about a month to fill out all the forms. I sent them in, and then in the first week of March, I had an interview. I told the recruiter how much I loved teaching and volunteering. I guess I convinced him, because eventually I was nominated for an assignment!

What text structure does the author use in this passage? How can you tell?

The author uses chronological order. He or she uses dates and

words like *first* and *eventually*.

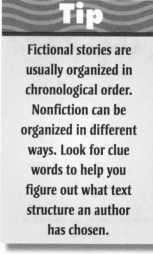

Tip

Fictional stories are usually organized in chronological order. Nonfiction can be organized in different ways. Look for clue words to help you figure out what text structure an author has chosen.

Read the article about two famous presidents. As you read, think about how the information is organized and presented.

Lincoln and Kennedy: Mystery or Coincidence?

Ask people to list the United States presidents. Most people will remember to name Abraham Lincoln and John F. Kennedy. The subject of these two bold leaders and the similarities between their lives and deaths is endlessly fascinating.

Many comparisons between Kennedy and Lincoln have been made over the years. For example, Lincoln's sons and Kennedy's brothers were named Robert and Edward. Lincoln was elected to Congress in 1846. Kennedy's election to Congress was in 1946. Both men married stylish, dark-haired women who were as comfortable speaking French as English. Lincoln was elected President in 1860. Kennedy was elected President in 1960. Both presidents were killed on a Friday before a holiday. Lincoln's senseless assassination occurred in Box 7 at Ford's Theater. Kennedy was attacked in a Ford car, the seventh in a motorcade. Lincoln was followed by President Andrew Johnson, who was born in 1808. Kennedy was followed by President Lyndon Johnson, who was born in 1908.

Most any of these similarities can be explained as a simple coincidence. For example, Lincoln and Kennedy were both important men. It is not unusual that they would marry well-educated women, and the chance of these women having dark hair is one in three. The men had a one-in-seven chance of dying on a Friday. Presidential elections are held every four years, explaining why the timing is exactly 100 years apart. Finally, it is no great surprise that both Kennedy and Lincoln were followed in office by men named Johnson. That last name was as common in Lincoln's and Kennedy's time as it is today. Actually, a person would be likely to find similarities and coincidences between many different pairs of historical figures.

Just as there are similarities between presidents Kennedy and Lincoln, there are also differences. Both led rich and varied lives, but there are contrasts in their backgrounds and terms in office. Lincoln grew up in poverty. Kennedy's family was rich and privileged. Lincoln was from the Midwest. Kennedy was from New England. Lincoln was reelected to a second term. Kennedy, however, died before he finished his first term.

Interest in Lincoln and Kennedy has never subsided. Their lives seem unfinished. That is one reason why so many people look for ways to connect them. No matter how interesting it is to look for patterns between people and events, though, there's no proof that these "connections" are anything more than chance.

STRATEGY: Identifying Text Structure 73

Checking Comprehension

1. What is the main idea of this passage?   [Main Idea/Inferential]

   There are many coincidences in the lives of U.S. presidents Lincoln and Kennedy.

2. Why are people fascinated by the idea of connections between [Making Judgments/Critical]
   Kennedy and Lincoln?

   Possible answer: They were both famous presidents who were assassinated, and their lives

   seem unfinished.

Practicing Comprehension Skills

Fill in the circle for the best answer to each question.

3. Which text structure does "Lincoln and Kennedy: Mystery or
   Coincidence?" use?

   ○ main idea and supporting details   ○ problem and solution

   ○ chronological order   ● compare and contrast

4. Which clue words in the passage help you identify the text structure?

   ● similarities, comparisons, contrasts,   ○ example, explained, coincidences
      however

   ○ years, 1846, Friday, four years   ○ unusual, chance, timing, varied

5. What might have been the author's purpose in choosing this text
   structure for "Lincoln and Kennedy: Mystery or Coincidence?"

   Possible answer: The compare and contrast text structure lets the author show how the

   presidents were both alike and different.

6. On the lines below, list three of the similarities and three of the
   differences the author found between Lincoln and Kennedy.

   Similarities: Possible answers: years elected, day of death, details of assassinations, name
   and date of birth of next President

   Differences: Possible answers: their backgrounds, their birth places, their time in office

Read the following passage. Think about how the text is structured.

Lincoln's Beard

It's hard to picture President Abraham Lincoln without his long, full beard. However, when he was running for president in 1860, Lincoln was beardless. Then he received a letter from an 11-year-old girl named Grace Bedell.

Grace's letter said that she wanted Lincoln to be elected. She told him that some of her four brothers were likely to vote for him. "If you let your whiskers grow," she said, "I will try and get the rest of them to vote for you." She thought a beard would suit Lincoln's thin face.

As a result of Grace's letter, Lincoln did indeed grow a beard—and he was elected President. On his way to the White House, he stopped to see Grace and tell her he was glad he took her good advice.

Fill in the circle next to the best answer.

7. Which text structure is used in the passage?

- ○ main idea and supporting details
- ● cause and effect
- ○ chronological order
- ○ comparison and contrast

8. List any clue words that helped you decide the text structure.

as a result _____

Read this passage about Jacqueline Kennedy, the wife of President Kennedy. Notice how the author has organized the information.

Jacqueline Lee Bouvier first visited the White House as a twelve-year-old tourist. Jackie, as she was called, already was interested in history. She was sorry to find very few decorations from the White House's past.

Jackie married Senator John F. Kennedy, who was elected President in 1960. The stylish first lady now lived in the White House, but she still thought it was dreary and uninteresting. Her solution to the problem was to turn the White House into a museum of American history. She tracked down furniture that had belonged to past presidents and put the pieces on display. Then she conducted a tour of the White House—on television! Thanks to Mrs. Kennedy, the White House is a national treasure today.

9. Which text structure is used in the passage?

○ main idea and supporting details   ○ comparison and contrast

○ chronological order   ● problem and solution

10. List clue words that helped you decide the text structure.

solution, problem

Practicing Vocabulary

Choose a word from the box that best replaces the underlined word or words. Write the word on the line to the left.

privileged   11. The Kennedy children led lives that were full of special opportunities.

subsided   12. Over the years John F. Kennedy's popularity has not lessened.

coincidence   13. The fact that both Kennedy and Lincoln studied law is no chance occurrence.

senseless   14. The book about Lincoln seemed meaningless because no historical background was provided.

varied   15. Lincoln and Kennedy had many widely different interests and talents.

subject   16. The topic of Kennedy's presidency is still studied.

poverty   17. Lincoln experienced the condition of being poor as a child.

> coincidence
> poverty
> privileged
> senseless
> subject
> subsided
> varied

Making the Reading and Writing Connection

Writing Nonfiction

Think of a nonfiction subject that interests you. Then think of a text structure that you could use to write about the subject. You could pick cause and effect, main idea and details, chronological order, problem and solution, or compare and contrast. On a separate sheet of paper, write a nonfiction passage about your subject using the text structure you chose.

Understanding Author's Viewpoint

An **author's viewpoint** is how the author feels about a subject. You can tell how authors look at the subject they are writing about by the language they use and the facts they offer. Authors can choose to take a viewpoint that is either balanced or unbalanced. In **balanced writing,** the author tells two sides of a story or issue. The good and bad points are presented. Everyone's views are given, including people who are for the subject and those who are against it.

In **unbalanced** or **biased writing,** the author presents only one side of an issue. He or she uses "loaded" words. These are words meant to bring out strong feelings for or against the subject. To decide whether an author's writing is balanced or biased, read carefully. Look at the author's opinions and choice of words. Decide whether the author has given facts to support the opinions he or she expresses.

Read this letter to the editor of a newspaper. Think about whether the writer presents a balanced view or just one side of the issue.

To the Editor:

I'm sure I'm not the only student at Milton School who is unhappy with the new year-round schedule. There are several problems. First, it's too hot in the classrooms. Second, many of us have brothers and sisters at other schools. They are having fun at the beach, pool, or camp while we study. This isn't fair. Finally, most parents work. It is hard for everyone to take a vacation together when brothers and sisters have different school schedules.

Give us back time to be kids. We need to have some fun!
Sincerely,
Carl Delgado

Does Carl's letter tell one side of the issue of the year-round school schedule, or does he present both sides?

Carl's letter gives one side of the issue.

Does Carl's letter show balanced writing or biased writing? Explain.

Biased writing. He tells only the bad points about the schedule and

uses "loaded" words such as "unhappy" and "isn't fair."

To decide the author's viewpoint, ask yourself: "Does the author tell one or both sides of an issue? Do the author's words show strong feelings for or against the subject? Are the author's opinions supported by facts?"

On Your Own

Read the following script for a television program. Think about the viewpoints that are presented. Ask yourself whether the writer presents a balanced view or a biased view.

News and Views on Year-Round School

Cast of *Today's Show*
Tim Wilson, host
Gladys Torres, principal
Willis Jones and Katie Bell, students

TIM WILSON: American students may be in for a change . . . or maybe not! I'm Tim Wilson, your host on *News and Views* for today. We are at Carver Elementary School. The thermometer reads 90 degrees today and local pools are crowded. Carver students, though, are in classrooms. This school is one of the thousands that have gone to a year-round program. That may sound like a lot of schools, but in fact, only a small percentage of all school districts have made the change. Meanwhile, others are watching the effect of year-round schooling on students' grades and attendance. The results may convince schools to make the change themselves. Let's hear from Carver's principal, Gladys Torres.

GLADYS TORRES: For two years, Carver has conducted a test of year-round schooling. Now the district may adopt the plan for all its schools. Here's how it works. Carver is open 12 months a year. Students participate in classes for nine-week sessions. Those are followed by a three-week break. Groups attend school on different schedules. That way, the building is constantly occupied and classes are small. Absences are down and test scores are up. I predict that year-round schooling will catch on as

the new idea for the entire country!

TIM WILSON: Thank you, Ms. Torres. Willis Jones, you're a student at Carver. What do you think about year-round schooling?

WILLIS JONES: When I first heard about year-round school, I wasn't so sure about the idea. I thought, "Who has the right to dictate that I have to study all year? Give me a break!" I soon realized I do get a break, and more than one. Three weeks is plenty of time to relax. On the old schedule, we were off for the whole summer. I used to forget much of what I'd learned, but now I don't have time to forget or get bored. I say, let's give the year-round schedule a chance.

TIM WILSON: Very interesting, Willis. Now let's hear from another student, Katie Bell.

KATIE BELL: I think year-round school is a bad idea. I could be mowing lawns and earning money right now. I could be riding my bike and having fun. Where we live, warm weather lasts only a few months, and I have to miss it. I think summer school should be a choice, not a requirement! I do not believe students with this weird schedule are any smarter than those with a normal schedule.

TIM WILSON: Thank you, Katie. There you have it, viewers. As more schools consider year-round school, we ask: "Are Americans ready to give up the traditional family summer?" Some say yes, some say no. That's all from *News and Views.*

Checking Comprehension

[Comparing and Contrasting/Inferential]

1. What is the difference between the new schedule at Carver Elementary School and the traditional schedule of many schools?

   <u>Carver is open 12 months of the year, with shorter student sessions and several short</u>

   <u>vacations. Traditional schools run from September through June, with a break for the summer.</u>

2. After reading the selection, what do you think about a year-round schedule? Why? [Making Judgments/Critical]

   <u>Answers will vary. Students who favor year-round school are likely to say classes would be</u>

   <u>smaller, and they would not get bored or forget things over the long summer. Those who favor</u>

   <u>a traditional schedule might say that they enjoy summer vacation and activities, or that their</u>

   <u>families would have problems adjusting their work schedules.</u>

Practicing Comprehension Skills

Fill in the circle before the answer that best completes the sentence.

3. In this script for a *News and Views* show, the writer

   ○ chose to present only arguments in favor of year-round school.

   ● chose to present both sides of the year-round school issue.

   ○ chose to present only arguments against year-round school.

   ○ did not understand the idea of year-round school.

4. The script for this *News and Views* program

   ● presents the issue and lets viewers make up their own minds.

   ○ presents only facts and no opinions.

   ○ tries to get viewers to think a certain way.

   ○ presents only opinions and no facts.

5. Did the person who wrote this script for *News and Views* show balanced writing or biased writing?

   <u>balanced writing</u>

STRATEGY: Understanding Author's Viewpoint   **79**

6. Which people on the TV show clearly favor year-round school, and why?

Gladys Torres and Willis Jones. Gladys Torres says absences are down and test scores are up.

Willis Jones says he doesn't have time to forget what he learned or to get bored.

7. Who is clearly against year-around school? Give examples of "loaded" words used by this person.

Katie Bell; bad, weird

8. Which person on *News and Views* does not show strong feelings about the subject of year-round schools? Explain your answer.

Tim Wilson, the host. He introduces and sums up the topic without giving an opinion

about it.

Practicing Vocabulary

Choose the word from the box that best matches each clue.
Write the word on the line.

absences	**9.** times that someone is not present	
dictate	**10.** to command or order	
districts	**11.** areas under the same control	
predict	**12.** to forecast	
conducted	**13.** led	
adopt	**14.** to choose	
participate	**15.** to take part in	

> absences
> adopt
> conducted
> dictate
> districts
> participate
> predict

Writing an Editorial
Think of a topic that has to do with your last school vacation. It might be a place you visited or an activity or sport you were involved in. Decide how you feel about your topic and whether you want to show a balanced or biased viewpoint toward it. On a separate piece of paper, write an editorial article about your topic. Use language and facts that show your viewpoint.

Making Generalizations

Sometimes when you read, you'll find a number of examples or facts that have something in common. For instance, if you are reading an article about birds, the author might talk about the things that all birds have in common, giving many examples. You can make a broad statement that includes all these examples, such as "All birds have feathers." This is called a **generalization.** Most generalizations use clue words, such as *most, all, always, sometimes, in general, often,* and *never.*

As you read, look for facts and details to support a generalization. If there are enough facts to support it, the generalization is **valid,** or accurate. If there are not enough facts, the generalization is **faulty,** or not accurate. The generalization "All birds have feathers" is accurate because it can be supported by facts. However, the generalization "All birds can fly" is not accurate because there are birds such as penguins that cannot fly.

Read the paragraph about barnstormers. Look for generalizations.

In the early 1900s, most people loved to see a plane fly. Across the country air shows were held. Certain fliers, called barnstormers, drew huge crowds. Each team had its own special acts. They circled and spun. They even flew upside down. While one pilot steered, another performed. A barnstormer might walk out on the plane's wing or hang from its tail. Hanging from a rope under the plane was a popular trick. Some barnstormers were injured doing these tricks, and some died. A few became rich.

Based on the article, what is a generalization you can make about barnstormers?

Possible answer: Barnstormers thrilled crowds. They were daring.

_____

What details in the paragraph support your generalization?

Students may say that barnstormers attracted huge audiences.

They might also cite the stunts that barnstormers performed.

Tip

A generalization is a broad statement or rule that applies to many examples. Generalizations often use clue words such as *most, usually, few,* or *all.* Facts can help you decide if a generalization is valid or faulty.

Read the article about Bessie Coleman, a barnstorming pilot. Look for the author's generalizations and think about generalizations you could make.

Bessie Coleman, Pilot

In Texas in 1901, Bessie Coleman picked cotton. She was a nine-year-old working beside her mother. Their fingers bled. Their backs ached. Many African American children like Bessie worked in the cotton fields. Their educational opportunities were often limited by unfair laws.

Bessie Coleman didn't want to pick cotton all her life. She dreamed of doing something different and special. When she was older, Bessie went to college for a while. There she heard about a woman pilot. Suddenly Bessie Coleman knew what she wanted to do!

When her family ran out of money, Bessie had to leave college. She returned home and worked at several jobs. For three years she saved her money. During that time, her dream of flying kept her going.

By 1915, Bessie Coleman had saved enough money. She was ready to make her dream come true. After moving to Chicago, Bessie began to visit airfields. She asked pilots to teach her to fly. In those days, however, few people thought African Americans should be pilots. No one was willing to teach Bessie to fly.

In the *Chicago Defender*, a weekly newspaper, Bessie read about a black man in France who was learning to fly. That article inspired her. If she had to go to France to achieve her goal, she would do it. One way or another, she would fly!

Bessie Coleman studied French and saved more money. In November of 1920, she sailed for France. There, she began taking flying lessons. By then the French were using planes to carry mail and cargo. On June 15, 1921, Bessie got her license to fly. She was the first female African American pilot in the world!

When she returned to the United States, Bessie was famous. The press called her "Brave Bessie" and "Queen Bess." She dazzled crowds at air shows. She had to fly borrowed planes since she couldn't afford one of her own.

In January 1923, Bessie did buy a plane of her own. The cheap plane had engine problems. A month later, she flew in a show in Los Angeles. At 300 feet, her motor stalled. Bessie crashed, breaking a leg and some ribs. Afterward, she sent her fans a telegram. It said, "As soon as I can walk, I'm going to fly!"

Two years later she was again participating in shows. In Texas, supporters helped her buy a "new" plane. Actually, it was older than her last one and needed a lot of repairs.

Bessie's last tour was in Florida. Before the show, another pilot took Bessie's plane up to view the show grounds. Bessie sat in the passenger seat. Suddenly, the plane dropped downward. Because there were no seat belts, Bessie was thrown out of the plane. Both she and the pilot were killed.

The memory of Bessie Coleman's heroism stays alive. Every year, on the date of her death, pilots fly over her grave and drop flowers.

Checking Comprehension

Write the answer to each question on the lines.

1. What challenges did Bessie Coleman face in the air?   [Main Idea/Inferential]

   <u>She faced the normal risks of flying and being a barnstormer. In addition, her old and</u>

   <u>inexpensive planes made flying dangerous.</u>

2. What challenges did Bessie Coleman face on the ground? What did she
   do about them?   [Summarizing/Inferential]

   <u>She faced poverty and prejudice, but she didn't let those things stop her. She saved her money</u>

   <u>and went to France to take flying lessons when she couldn't take them in the U.S.</u>

Practicing Comprehension Skills

Think of a generalization you can make about Bessie Coleman based
on the article. Write it in the box labeled **Generalization.** In the boxes
labeled **Fact or Detail,** write three facts or details from the biography
that support your generalization and make it valid.

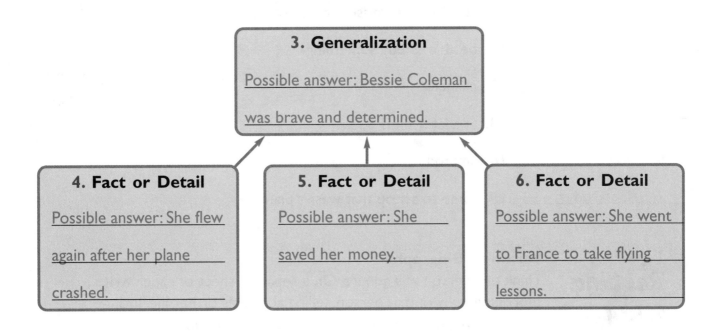

3. Generalization

Possible answer: Bessie Coleman was brave and determined.

4. Fact or Detail

Possible answer: She flew again after her plane crashed.

5. Fact or Detail

Possible answer: She saved her money.

6. Fact or Detail

Possible answer: She went to France to take flying lessons.

7. Read the following generalization. Circle the clue word. Then tell whether the generalization is faulty or valid and why.

The planes used in early air shows were (sometimes) unsafe.

Possible answer: The generalization is valid. The clue word is sometimes. The article mentions

a plane with no seat belts. Also, some planes were old and had motor problems.

Fill in the circle before the correct answer.

8. Which generalization is faulty, according to details in the article?

○ Accidents often happened at the early air shows.

○ Most Americans admired the early pilots.

○ Sometimes reaching a special goal takes a long time.

● In the 1920s, airplanes were used only for fun.

Practicing Vocabulary

Choose the word from the box that best matches each definition. Write the word on the line.

afford
afterward
dazzled
downward
license
opportunities
stalled

_____downward_____ 9. toward a lower spot

_____license_____ 10. an official permission to do something

_____afford_____ 11. be able to buy something

_____opportunities_____ 12. chances

_____afterward_____ 13. at a later time

_____dazzled_____ 14. amazed

_____stalled_____ 15. came to a stop that wasn't planned

Writing a Biography
Think of a person you admire. On a separate sheet of paper, write a short biography of that person, telling about his or her life. Include one or more generalizations. Be sure to support your generalizations with facts.

LESSON 18

Outlining

Making an **outline** can help you understand and organize the main points of what you read. An outline is quick to write and easy to read. Outlines are made up of short **headings** that list the most important information in a piece of writing.

The main points of the article will be the **main topics** in the outline. Write them next to Roman numerals I, II, III, and so on. Next, decide on the important points about the main topics and write them as **subtopics**. Subtopics are written next to capital letters A, B, C, and so on. Finally, find examples or facts that tell more about the subtopics and write them as **details**. Details are written next to numerals 1, 2, 3, and so on.

Read the article. Notice how the information is listed in the outline, and fill in the blank spaces with any missing topics, subtopics, and details.

Tip

Before you begin making an outline, you must decide whether all the headings will be written as sentences, phrases, or key words.

The Guitar

The first stringed instrument was probably a bow and arrow. When plucked, a bowstring makes a humming tone. At some point an ancient hunter added a second string to the bow. That way the bow made two different tones.

The modern guitar, which developed from that simple instrument, has several parts. Most modern guitars have six strings that run across a round sound hole and up a long neck. The neck has small cross bridges, called *frets*. Pressing a string down between the frets makes the sound shorter or longer. That changes the pitch of the string, so many notes can be played with only six strings.

(Title)   The Guitar

(Main Topic) **I.** Bow and arrow probably was first stringed instrument

(Subtopic)   A. Bowstring makes a humming sound

(Subtopic)   B. Hunter added second string

(Main Topic) II. Modern guitar has several parts

(Subtopic)   A. Most have six strings

(Subtopic)   B. They have round sound hole

(Subtopic)   C. They have long neck with frets

(Detail)   1. Pressing string changes sound

(Detail)   2. Strings can play many notes

Electrifying the Guitar

In the 1920s and 1930s, big dance bands were all the rage. Horns blared. That was a problem for the guitar players. They played classical, or acoustic, guitars. The other instruments drowned out the sound of the acoustic guitars. What could be done? A teenage guitar player named Les Paul created one solution. At a dance in 1929, he stuck a phonograph needle into his guitar. Then he wired the needle to a radio speaker and a car battery. The speaker made the sound of his guitar playing louder. This contraption may have been the first electric guitar.

During the 1930s, Les Paul and other musicians worked hard to electrify guitars. These first guitars looked like acoustic guitars but had one major difference. The electric guitars had pickups under the strings. These were tiny devices. Their job was to "pick up" the sounds of the strings. The pickups changed the sounds into electric signals. Wires carried the signals from the pickups to an amplifier, a device that made the sound louder. With pickups and an amplifier, a guitar could play as loud as any horn.

Loud volume didn't solve all the problems for the early electric guitars, however. The guitars sometimes played *too* loud. Often they acquired screeches or hums. Early electric guitars ruined many songs. Players couldn't rely on the pickups. Engineers designed better pickups, and the sound got better. Still, musicians weren't happy. Another problem with electric guitars was their shape. Like acoustic guitars, they had large, hollow bodies. The space under the strings was necessary to amplify the sound of an acoustic guitar. In an electric guitar, however, the space was unnecessary. It also got in the way of the work of the pickups.

Would a guitar with a solid body sound better? Les Paul thought so. The so-called "Electric Guitar Wizard" experimented with new guitar designs in the 1940s. He called one guitar the Log because it was built from a solid piece of wood. At about the same time, another guitar expert named Leo Fender went to work. He designed a famous solid-body electric guitar called the Telecaster. These new guitars had a better, purer sound. They were also smaller and easier to hold than acoustic models. They came in eye-catching shapes.

Once the guitar "went electric," music changed forever. Country and western singers played electric guitars right away. So did blues and jazz musicians. In the 1950s, musicians began to experiment with a new sound. Before long the electric guitar was the center of a new musical fad called . . . rock and roll.

Checking Comprehension

1. Compare electric and acoustic guitars. How do they differ? [Comparing and Contrasting/Inferential]

   Acoustic guitars need a hollow body to amplify the sound of the strings. Electric guitars have

   solid bodies. They use pickups and amplifiers to increase the sound.

2. Based on information in the article, why do you think the solid-body
   electric guitars became so popular with musicians? [Cause and Effect/Inferential]

   Possible answers: Solid-body guitars were louder and easier to hold than acoustic guitars. They

   also came in eye-catching shapes.

Practicing Comprehension Skills

3. Complete the outline of the article by writing the missing main topics,
   subtopics, and details. Include the missing Roman numerals, capital
   letters, and numerals.

Electrifying the Guitar

I. Need for a louder guitar

   A. Big dance bands popular

   B. Other instruments drowned out sound

   C. Les Paul, 1929, first electric guitar

II. Pickups on electric guitars

   A. Small devices under guitar strings

   B. Changed sounds into electric signals

   C. Wires carried signals

III. Problems with early electric guitars

   A. Problems with sound

     1. Pickups not reliable

     2. Better pickups invented

   B. Problems with shape

     1. Hollow body unnecessary

     2. Interfered with pickups

IV. Solid-body guitar invented

   A. Les Paul, 1940s, the Log

   B. Leo Fender, 1940s, Telecaster

   C. Advantages of new style

     1. Better, purer sound

     2. Smaller, easier to hold

     3. New, eye-catching shapes

V. Electric guitars popular by 1950s

   A. Country/western, blues, and jazz musicians

   B. Helped create rock and roll

4. How is the subject of each paragraph represented on the outline?

Each paragraph is represented by a main topic on the outline.

5. Which of the following details does not belong in the outline?

○ The fact that electric guitars helped to create rock and roll

● The fact that Les Paul's nickname was the "Electric Guitar Wizard"

○ The fact that the hollow body shape of the guitar interfered with pickups

○ The fact that better pickups were invented to solve sound problems

Practicing Vocabulary

6. Choose the word from the box that best completes each sentence in the paragraph. Write the word on the line.

acoustic
acquired
amplify
contraption
electrify
fad
guitar

Les Paul needed a louder _____guitar_____. As a teenager he played

an ordinary classical, or _____acoustic_____, guitar. Les Paul wanted to

_____amplify_____ the sound so people could hear him play in a dance

band. He decided to _____electrify_____ the guitar by sticking an old

phonograph needle into it. His _____contraption_____ also made use of a

car battery and a radio speaker. His work helped to make the worldwide

_____fad_____ called rock and roll possible. If you had

_____acquired_____ an original Les Paul guitar, it would be very valuable today!

Writing an Outline
On a separate sheet of paper, write one or two paragraphs about your favorite type of music or musical instrument. You may want to read about it in an encyclopedia or on the Internet. Include some interesting facts and history. Then exchange papers with a partner. Make an outline of the information each person shared through his or her writing.

Persuasive Devices and Propaganda

Sometimes a writer's purpose is to convince you to do something or to think a certain way. A writer's efforts to persuade you are sometimes called **propaganda.** Because advertisers always try to persuade, you'll find propaganda in most of the ads you see and hear.

In order to recognize propaganda, ask yourself what the author's purpose for writing might be. See if the statements are backed up with facts and details. Then you can decide whether you agree or disagree with the ideas.

The following chart describes three kinds of propaganda used to persuade readers.

DEVICE	DEFINITION	EXAMPLE
bandwagon	This device suggests that if so many people are doing something, it must be the right thing to do.	*Join the thousands of smart shoppers who make their first stop the Save-Rite Market!*
testimonial	This device uses well-known people to recommend an idea or a product.	*Olympic long jumper Rock Ridges says, "Every jump takes a burst of energy. I get mine from a breakfast of Muscle Mush."*
loaded words	Loaded words are words that call up strongly negative or positive feelings. They try to slant a reader's view of a product, person, or idea.	*Are you suffering with a miserable cold? Feel better fast with a steaming cup of soothing, delicious Health Nog.*

Read the statements below. Fill in the circle before the name of the propaganda device that each statement uses. On the blank lines, write clue words that helped you identify the device.

Each day, millions of happy Americans are brightening their smiles with Glisten Toothpaste. Wouldn't you like a whiter smile, too?

● bandwagon   ○ testimonial   ○ loaded words

Clue words: <u>millions of happy Americans</u>

A vote for Millie Masters for mayor is a vote for honesty, honor, and experience.

○ bandwagon   ○ testimonial   ● loaded words

Clue words: <u>honesty, honor, experience</u>

The following passage describes a television commercial for a person who is running for governor. Look for persuasive devices in the commercial.

As the ad begins, the viewer hears a group of people singing. The tune is the beginning of "Take Me Out to the Ball Game." The words are, "Let's all vote for Joy Reynolds. She'll bat for you and for me."

Candidate Joy Reynolds and baseball star Roy Farrow shake hands. They are both smiling. Roy turns to the camera and says, "At the plate, I need a good eye and quick hands. In the governor's office, you need honesty and experience. Joy Reynolds has both of those. She hits a home run on my ballot. Let's all join the right team with a vote for Reynolds. She cares about all of us."

Write the answers on the lines provided.

What makes this commercial a testimonial?

A star athlete endorses the candidate.

In the commercial, find two loaded words or phrases.

Possible answers: honesty, experience, cares

Find two words, phrases, or ideas in the commercial that use the bandwagon technique.

Possible answers: a group of people is singing "Let's

all vote for Joy Reynolds"; join the right team, all of us

On the lines provided, write the name of the propaganda device used in each of these statements.

Joy Reynolds has the energy, ambition, and enthusiasm needed to govern the state.

loaded words

Local television talk show host Chip Chase says, "I'm casting my vote for Joy!"

testimonial

Tip

To recognize propaganda, ask yourself, "What is the author's purpose for writing? Are the statements backed up with facts and details, or do they contain types of propaganda such as the bandwagon technique, testimonials, or loaded words?"

Read the following speech. As you read, think about the speaker's reasons for giving the speech. Look for persuasive devices.

☑ Vote for Beth Chang!

Hi, folks! You know me, Joseph Wall. You know what I stand for. I've been student council president for the last year. Now I'm standing here to ask you to vote for my friend Beth Chang in the next election!

Let me tell you about Beth. She's a real go-getter. I worked closely with her when the student council organized our successful food drive last winter. As a homeroom representative, Beth did more than her share of work. She convinced local businesses to put out food collection bins. She was responsible for collecting more food than any other volunteer. When Beth sets out to reach a goal, nothing can stop her. She's also someone who really cares about our school, just like you and me. She knows this election is not a popularity contest. She will work night and day for our school.

Beth is honest and energetic. She's helped the chess team become city champs. She has marched in parades with the school band. She has helped younger students as a peer tutor. She's the best president you could have! With Beth as student president, our school will be a better place for everyone.

Truth and fairness are what Beth Chang stands for. She'll be open-minded and will listen to everyone's concerns. She'll try to make the school lunches more interesting and flavorful. She'll improve the recess activities and the after-school programs. A student president has to give

100% to the job. Trust me—I've been there and I know. If you tell Beth something is important, she will work for it!

Zack Pappas, star center of the school basketball team, says Beth has spirit! Mr. Brodsky, our music teacher, says Beth is a marvelous leader. Fellow student Jodi Katz says, "Beth is the most loyal friend I've ever had!" You have their words for it as well as mine—Beth is the one for the job!

On election day, join me and Beth's many supporters in casting ballots for Chang. Remember her motto: "Just add an *e* to *Chang*, and you get *CHANGE*!" *Change* means a better school for us all! Thank you very much.

Checking Comprehension

1. Why do you think Joseph wants Beth to be elected? [Main Idea/Inferential]

   Possible answers: He says that Beth is his friend. He has worked with her and is impressed

   by her. He's been the student president, and he knows the qualities needed for the job.

2. If you were in the crowd listening to the speech, would you be tempted
   to vote for Beth Chang? Why or why not? [Making Judgments/Critical]

   Possible answers: Some students may say that they would not be convinced by a good

   friend's appeals. Others may say that Joseph was very convincing and may cite reasons

   such as Beth's past performance on student council.

Practicing Comprehension Skills

Reread "Vote for Chang!" Look for examples of *bandwagon, testimonial,* and
loaded words. Write one example of each in the chart below.

PERSUASIVE DEVICE	EXAMPLE
3. bandwagon	"On election day, join me and Beth's many supporters in casting ballots for Chang."
4. testimonial	Students may say the whole speech is a testimonial from the current student body president. Joseph also says "Trust me—I've been there and I know." Or they might pick out examples: "Zack Pappas, star center of the school basketball team, says Beth has spirit!"
5. loaded words	"Beth is honest and energetic" or "Truth and fairness are what Beth Chang stands for."

Read the following "Beth Chang for President" poster. Look for persuasive devices as you study it.

BETH CHANG FOR STUDENT PRESIDENT

Chang + e = Change!

Change = delicious, more nutritious lunches

Change = a longer recess with more exciting, fun-filled activities

Change = more computers in an updated, modern computer lab

Join students who know what's best for the school.

Vote for Chang!

Beth Chang is backed by student president Joseph Wall
and student athlete Zack Pappas.

---

6. What persuasive device is mainly used in this part of the poster?

   Change = delicious, more nutritious lunches

   Change = a longer recess with more exciting, fun-filled activities

   Change = more computers in an updated, modern computer lab

   loaded words

7. What persuasive device does this sentence use?

   Join students who know what's best for the school.

   bandwagon

8. What persuasive device is used in the last sentence of the ad?

   testimonial

Give your own examples of statements that a speaker could make to support Beth Chang's campaign. Use the following persuasive devices.

9. Bandwagon: <u>Possible answer: Let's all vote for Beth—She's a winner!</u>

10. Testimonial: <u>Possible answer: The chess team's advisor, Mrs. Cooper, says, "Vote for Beth!"</u>

11. Loaded words: <u>Possible answer: Beth is a superior candidate with the best skills.</u>

Practicing Vocabulary

Fill in the circle next to the word or phrase that means about the same as the underlined word.

| energetic |
| fairness |
| flavorful |
| peer |
| popularity |
| representative |
| successful |

12. This new ice cream is very <u>flavorful</u>.
    ○ colorful   ● delicious   ○ boring   ○ cold

13. The judge showed <u>fairness</u> by listening to all sides.
    ● honesty   ○ humility   ○ greed   ○ intelligence

14. The candidate was elected after a <u>successful</u> campaign.
    ○ losing   ○ boring   ● winning   ○ unfair

15. Because he was a <u>peer</u>, students listened to their president's advice.
    ○ onlooker   ● equal   ○ enemy   ○ athlete

16. We chose Anna to be our <u>representative</u> on the student council.
    ● chosen speaker   ○ junior   ○ trainer   ○ good friend

17. Some games enjoy <u>popularity</u> among both children and adults.
    ● wide acceptance   ○ loudness   ○ density   ○ great concentration

18. She was an <u>energetic</u> helper, never seeming tired or bored.
    ○ terrible   ● lively   ○ tired   ○ convincing

Making a Poster
Imagine that a friend of yours is running for an office. On another sheet of paper, make a campaign poster for your friend that uses the bandwagon, testimonial, and loaded words devices.

LESSON 20

Literary Elements: Character

Characters are the people or animals in stories. As a story unfolds, you learn more and more about these characters. Reading is more enjoyable if you pay attention to the characters and what they are like.

Sometimes the author tells you directly what a character is like. Usually, however, you need to think about what the character says or does. Often, another character in the story will give you information about a character's traits. Watch what other characters in a story say about a character and how they act toward the person. Words and actions can tell you a lot. Using your own knowledge of people can also help you reach decisions about the characters you meet in a story.

Read this story about an escaped slave named Selah who led other slaves to freedom. As you read, look for words and phrases that reveal Selah's character.

"We can't go on. They'll catch us for sure." The scared slave looked around wildly to the others for support.

"You stay where you are!" Selah ordered. "If you go back, the slave hunters will surely find you. Then you'll tell on me and the other people in the Underground Railroad. What will happen then? Listen, I've brought hundreds of slaves out and I've never been caught. I will never be a slave again, you can be sure of that. So be brave, and let's get moving!"

The man relaxed, and the others murmured in agreement with Selah's words. Minutes later they were again following Selah to freedom.

1. What character traits does Selah possess?

   Possible answers: courage, determination, leadership

2. How does the author reveal Selah's character traits?

   We learn about Selah from her own words and from how the

   escaping slaves react to her.

Tip

To learn about a character, look for clues about what the character says, thinks, and does. Also look to see what other characters say about the character, and how they treat the person.

As you read the following story about a family involved in the Underground Railroad, look for clues that tell you what each character is like.

Onions to the Rescue

by Betsy Sterman

For weeks the house was filled with whispers. Jake did his own chores and Louisa's, too, while she worked with Mama on the special quilt. He watched Papa build a hidden room beneath the floorboards. They were readying a station on the Underground Railroad.

Jake knew the Railroad was a secret way to help runaway slaves escape to freedom. People called themselves "conductors" and their homes "stations." Jake thought, "Everyone's doing something important except me."

Louisa was especially annoying. "I'm a conductor," she bragged.

Jake clenched his fists. "Only because of me," he replied angrily. He hated doing his older sister's chores. How could chopping stew onions help runaway slaves? Jake knew he was small for eleven, but there must be something else he could do.

Finally the quilt and the room were finished. Mama hung the quilt over the porch railing so its code could be recognized. Small black squares set in colorful blocks signaled a safe haven. A large center block held a group of stars pointing north. If runaways needed shelter, they could find it here. If they chose to pass by to the next station, the quilt told them which way to go.

At sunrise a few days later, a runaway stumbled out of the cornfield. "Dogs!" he gasped as he fell over the doorstep. "Got my scent!"

Mama and Papa hurried the slave into the hidden room, but Louisa froze. "They'll come straight here!" she said. "They'll find him!"

In the distance Jake heard bloodhounds barking. Once they had a person's scent, nothing but another strong smell could put them off the trail. He dashed into the kitchen and grabbed a sharp knife. *Chop!* Half an onion in each hand, he scrubbed at the porch floor and the steps, then swiped at the grass as he ran toward the woods.

Jake rubbed at tree bark, going as deep into the woods as he dared. Then he tossed the onion stumps into the underbrush and ran back. He was in the doorway when the dogs burst out of the cornfield. Two slave hunters followed.

"In this house!" one shouted.

"No, in the woods!" the other cried, watching as the dogs ran in circles and skittered off toward the trees.

Jake watched and listened. "Dogs lost the scent," he heard one of the men say. "Let's get out of here."

When they were gone, Jake took a deep breath. The runaway was safe. When they sent him on his way, Jake would give him a cut onion.

"Not to eat," Jake would say. "To rub on your shoes and throw dogs off your trail." Then he'd smile at Louisa and say, "I'm a conductor, too."

Checking Comprehension

1. Describe the time and place in which "Onions to the Rescue" occurs.   [Setting/Inferential]

   "Onions to the Rescue!" takes place during the time in the 1800s when families helped

   runaway slaves through the Underground Railroad. The family lives in a house with a cornfield

   near the woods.

2. What part do onions play in the story? [Main Idea/Critical]

   At first, onions are used for food, and Jake does not like chopping them. Later, they are used to

   confuse the slave hunters' dogs and keep them away from the house.

Practicing Comprehension Skills

Write your answers on the lines.

3. What character traits does Mama have? Give evidence to support your
   answer.

   Possible answer: Mama is brave, hardworking, creative, and careful. She is willing to hide runaway

   slaves in her home. She makes a special quilt that has a secret code to let runaways know that the

   home is a safe place to stop. She quickly hides the slave in the secret room so he won't be seen.

4. How is Jake different from Louisa in an emergency?

   Possible answer: Students may say that Jake is more quick-thinking and decisive, since

   he quickly finds a way to throw the dogs off the scent. Louisa, on the other hand, froze

   in the emergency.

Fill in the circle next to all the answers that are correct.

5. How does the reader learn about Jake's character?
   - ○ by what other characters have to say about him
   - ○ by what he says and does
   - ○ by the way his sister acts toward him
   - ○ by what the narrator says about him

Fill in the chart with words describing Jake. Support your answers with evidence from the story.

Jake's Character Traits	Evidence from Story
6. hardworking	did his chores and Louisa's chores
7. trustworthy, courageous	knew his family would be hiding a runaway slave
8. clever	rubbed an onion all around to get rid of the slave's scent
9. proud	hates doing Louisa's chores, wants to be a conductor too

Practicing Vocabulary

Choose the word from the box that best replaces the underlined word or phrase. Write the word on the line.

clenched
haven
readying
recognized
runaway
swiped
underground

haven   **10.** The family prepared its home as a <u>place of safety</u>.

runaway   **11.** They led the <u>escaping person</u> to the hidden room.

underground   **12.** Hiding runaways was an <u>extremely secret</u> activity.

clenched   **13.** Jake <u>tightly rolled</u> his fingers into a ball.

swiped   **14.** He <u>quickly rubbed</u> the onion over many surfaces.

recognized   **15.** The quilt had markings the runaways <u>understood because they had seen them before</u>.

readying   **16.** The family was <u>preparing</u> the room for a visitor.

Writing a Character Sketch
On a separate sheet of paper, write one or two paragraphs describing the appearance and personality of a character you remember from a favorite story. Think about how to describe the character's traits.

Literary Elements: Plot

Every story has important events at the beginning, in the middle, and at the end. These events, which almost always center around a problem or goal, are called the **plot**.

Part of the Plot	Description
Background	information you need to know about the setting and characters
Goal or problem	a struggle between two forces, whether between two or more characters or within an individual
Rising action	the events that build to the climax
Climax	the "high point," where the characters face the conflict directly
Outcome or resolution	where the action winds down and the conflict ends

Most plots follow time order. Sometimes, however, authors interrupt the time order to tell more about a character or the plot. A **flashback** tells about something important that happened before the story began. Often authors use phrases such as *I remember when* to alert readers to a change in time. **Foreshadowing,** on the other hand, hints at what will happen later in the plot. It builds excitement or suspense for the reader.

As you read the following story, look for the plot elements.

Paul and José rode their horses to a fork in the trail. "Let's take Hills Trail," said José, turning right.

"No," said Paul, turning left. "My uncle was bitten by a snake there. I'm taking Creek Trail." In his mind, Paul recalled that terrible day. He had raced to a nearby ranch for help.

"OK, see you later," José called. The boys lost sight of each other. José was worrying about snakes. Paul was wondering just where Creek Trail ended. Suddenly the two trails met. "Wow, am I glad to see you!" both boys yelled.

What problem did the story characters face?

Possible answer: Paul and José wanted to go different ways on the trail.

Write a sentence from the story that illustrates flashback.

"In his mind, Paul recalled …"

> **Tip**
>
> To keep track of the plot, identify its most important parts. They include the background, goal or problem, rising action, climax, and outcome.

On Your Own

Read the story about a horse named Bay. Look for the elements of plot, including flashback and foreshadowing.

Keeping Bay

"We're going to have to get rid of Bay this year," Meg's dad said. "That horse can't work another winter."

It was October, and snow was falling lightly over their part of Montana. Meg knew the ranch needed strong, steady horses to bring the sheep back from pasture. Still, she could hardly take in the enormity of her father's words.

"I know Bay's old," Meg told her dad, "but he's my horse. Won't you let me keep him? I'd feed him. He won't be a problem."

"We use horses for labor," her dad said. "We don't keep them as pets."

Meg understood. She thought about Casey, a dog she had once loved. He became lost when he chased a wandering sheep and never came home. Meg had been sad for weeks. She knew that on a ranch, animals come and go. You couldn't grow attached to them. Bay was different, though. The horse had a personality all his own.

She went to the stable and stroked the old brown horse's head. As Bay nuzzled her hand, Meg tried to imagine what the ranch would be like without her favorite horse.

The snow was falling faster, and dark gray clouds were settling over the peaks. Meg had an idea. She saddled Bay, put her foot in the stirrup, and swung up. "Let's go!" she cried, and nudged him with her heels.

They galloped over the meadow, onto a steep and narrow trail, and up a wooded slope. "We'll round up the sheep now, before the snow gets too thick," Meg said. "We'll show Dad how well you can work."

The sheep stood in a high pasture, bleating at the storm clouds. Meg heard a lone bleat from above. She looked for the lost sheep but couldn't see it. "It must be stuck in the brush above the rock wall," she thought.

She got off her horse and began to ascend the steep wall. She was almost at the top when the heel of her boot slipped into a crack. She lost her balance and fell onto a ledge. She tried to stand, but her foot hurt too much.

Then Bay got into position under the ledge. He was telling Meg to crawl onto his back!

Painfully, Meg got her feet into the stirrups. Slowly and carefully, Bay carried her down the snowy trail.

On the way down, they met Dad riding his gray mare. "What happened?" he asked anxiously.

"Bay saved me." Meg told him what happened.

Dad's voice shook when he said, "I wouldn't get rid of that horse for anything."

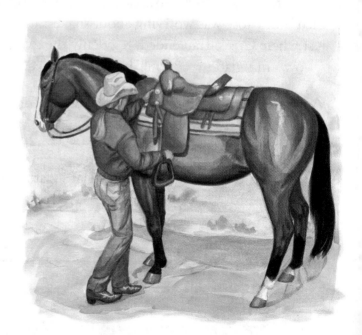

Checking Comprehension

1. Why does Dad change his mind about Bay? [Main Idea/Inferential]

   <u>Bay proved he was important by rescuing Meg after she fell and hurt her foot.</u>

2. What do you think Meg learned from her experience? [Theme/Critical]

   <u>Possible answers: Meg learned that her horse was smart, that she was brave, that her father</u>

   <u>was more tenderhearted than he seemed, or that she shouldn't take foolish risks.</u>

Practicing Comprehension Skills

Fill in this story map for "Keeping Bay." Use complete sentences.

3. **Background:** <u>Meg and her dad live on a sheep ranch in Montana. It is October.</u>

4. **Problem:** <u>Dad tells Meg they will have to get rid of her horse, Bay,</u>
   <u>because the horse is too old to work.</u>

5. **Rising Action:** <u>Meg rides Bay up the mountain trail to round up the sheep,</u>
   <u>but she falls and hurts her foot.</u>

6. **Climax:** <u>Bay saves Meg by getting into position for her to crawl onto his back</u>
   <u>and carrying her down the trail.</u>

7. **Outcome:** <u>Dad learns what happened and says he will never give Bay away.</u>

8. Find an example of flashback in "Keeping Bay." How does this affect the sequence of events in the story? Why would the author use a flashback there?

Possible answer: The scene where Meg thought about Casey, a dog she had once loved, is a

flashback. It interrupts the time order to let readers know how Meg feels about animals.

9. Find a sentence that shows foreshadowing. What does it tell you?

"The snow was falling faster, and dark gray clouds were settling over the peaks." The bad

weather hints that a character or animal may get caught in the storm.

Practicing Vocabulary

10. Choose the word from the box that best completes each sentence in the paragraph. Write the word on the line.

Meg watched the sheep and lambs eating the thick grass in the upper

_____pasture_____. Suddenly Meg saw three coyotes moving

toward a lamb. The lamb was one Meg had raised by hand, and she

was struck by the _____enormity_____ of the situation. "If a

coyote catches the lamb, all my _____labor_____ will have been

for nothing," she thought. Quickly, she climbed onto Bay and they

_____galloped_____ up the hill. With her heels, Meg

_____nudged_____ Bay to go faster. When the coyotes saw

Meg and Bay, they scrambled to _____ascend_____ the slope

toward safety. As Meg patted Bay, the horse whickered as if he were

laughing. "Thanks, boy," she said. "You have quite a _personality_!"

ascend
enormity
galloped
labor
nudged
pasture
personality

Planning a Short Story
On another sheet of paper, plan a short story about an animal helping a person, or about a person helping an animal. Be sure your story has all the elements of plot: background (characters and setting), problem or goal, rising action, climax, and outcome. Use a story map to organize your story.

Literary Elements: Setting

The **setting of a story** is where and when the events take place. Sometimes an author tells you the setting directly, such as "a town in Missouri 150 years ago." At other times, the author gives you details to help you figure out the setting on your own. For example, the story might mention cactus plants, hot sun, and endless sand. Then you know the story is set in a desert. The setting sometimes, though not always, has an effect on what the characters do or even how the story turns out. It can also help to create a **mood**, or feeling. The mood of a story can be lighthearted, sad, dreamlike, or eerie, for instance. As you read, ask yourself if the story would be different if it had a different setting.

Read the story about a hiking adventure. As you read, think about how the setting affects the characters.

On a bright, chilly morning, the Viera family set out to hike the lower trails of Goat Peak. Partway up one forest trail, Tina stopped in a sunny spot to rest. High in the sky, she saw the airy trail left by a jet. Then her gaze fell on the mountaintop, rising above the trees to meet the blue sky. As she looked at the peak, she imagined the mountain's rough granite under her hands. She could feel the cold, hard rock face against her cheek. In her imagination, she pulled herself up toward the snow-capped summit.

"Are you with us?" teased Dad, passing Tina on the trail.

Tina capped her water bottle. "I'm way ahead of you," she laughed.

What is the setting of the story? What clues help you figure out when and where the story takes place?

It takes place on a cold, clear day on a forest trail at the foot of a snow-

covered mountain, Goat Peak. The trail left by a jet and the water bottle

are clues that the time is around the present.

Tip

As you read a story, think about when and where it takes place. Ask yourself, "Does the setting affect the characters' actions? Does it affect the way the story turns out?"

Read the following story about a special summer school. Look for words and phrases that help you figure out the story's setting.

Kayaking School

Andy squirmed down in his sleeping bag and stared at the walls of the tent. After the day he had had, he wished he were home in his own bed. Marco, Andy's tentmate, had said "Good night" and had quickly fallen asleep. Andy was also tired. He was too upset to sleep, though. He looked out of the tent opening. Shadowy figures still drifted back and forth by the flickering fire. The row of kayaks looked like shiny seals resting in the moonlight. Beyond them the surface of the lake shimmered, glassy and smooth. How peaceful it all looked now. How unpleasant it had been just a few hours before. Andy tried to get comfortable, but his body ached too much. Slowly his mind replayed the events of the day.

That morning, as the sky turned from pink to blue over the mountains, the area had been alive with campers and guides. It was his first day at kayak camp, and the counselors reviewed the basics of water safety and first aid. Then they had divided the group into teams. Team leaders passed around an instruction booklet and a notebook for keeping a journal.

After that the day was a watery blur. Andy tried to count how many times he had tipped over in the chilly water, but he lost track. No matter how hard he had tried, he didn't seem to get any better at kayaking. Now every muscle of his body hurt. At sun-up, they would expect him to get back in that kayak. Andy shuddered. Would he be able to last out the week?

Andy must have dozed off. When he woke up later, the predawn light was gray and foggy. Wind whispered through the branches and rippled over the lake. Andy could hear the water lapping against the shore. Marco was up on his knees, looking through the tent flap. When Andy stirred, Marco poked his shoulder and pointed. Andy used a strand of rope to tie the opening back more firmly, then looked toward the misty shore. At the lake a moose was bending to drink.

"Wow," whispered Andy. "This is better than watching a nature show!"

"I'm surprised the moose came so close to the camp," Marco said softly. "It must have followed the track that comes out of the woods."

The boys watched the moose as it moved along the shore. It didn't make a sound.

Andy laughed. "My dad said I was going to summer school. I didn't dream that he meant a week of kayaking school."

Marco laughed, too. "Yeah. It sure is different. Maybe sleeping on the ground, paddling until your arms fall off, and getting dunked in an icy lake 300 times isn't so bad."

"Right," thought Andy, suddenly hopeful about what the day would bring.

Checking Comprehension

1. Why does Andy have trouble sleeping?   [Character/Inferential]

   He is upset by the day he had at camp. His body aches,

   and he is worried.

2. Do you think Andy will grow to like kayaking school?   [Making Predictions/Inferential]

   Answers will vary. Students might say that Andy will probably like kayaking school

   once he gives it a chance.

Practicing Comprehension Skills

Reread "Kayaking School." Answer the questions about the story.

3. What is the setting of "Kayaking School"?

   It is summer at a campground by a lake. There are woods by the shoreline.

   The story takes place in the present.

4. What details tell you about changes in the time of day?

   At night, moonlight shines on the water. When Andy remembers that morning,

   the sky was changing from pink to blue. The predawn morning is gray and misty.

5. How would the story be different if it took place by the ocean?

   Possible answer: An ocean setting would have waves, a beach, and seashells.

   The boys might see sea creatures or gulls instead of a moose.

6. What problems or difficulties does the setting cause for Andy at first? Explain.

   Possible answer: Andy isn't sure he can make it through kayaking school.

   He has tipped over into the freezing water many times, and his muscles hurt.

STRATEGY: Literary Elements: Sett

7. How does the setting affect the outcome of the story?

Possible answer: The beautiful setting makes Andy feel more upbeat.

Andy seems determined to stay at kayaking school despite the challenges.

Fill in the circle before the correct answer.

8. How did the setting affect the mood of the story?

○ The setting had no effect on the story's mood.

● The appearance of a moose in the foggy morning created a sense of awe.

○ The blue daytime sky created a joyous mood.

○ Andy was afraid of storms by the lake.

Practicing Vocabulary

Choose the word from the box that best completes each sentence. Write the word on the line.

| blur |
| kayak |
| replayed |
| shadowy |
| shimmered |
| strand |
| surface |

9. At night the trees make _____shadowy_____ shapes on the sides of the tent.

10. The evening news _____replayed_____ the film of the dramatic lake rescue.

11. The lake gleamed and _____shimmered_____ in the moonlight.

12. The _____surface_____ of the water was as smooth as blue glass.

13. I tucked a _____strand_____ of hair under my cap.

14. Usually, just one person paddles a _____kayak_____.

15. In the fog the island became a _____blur_____ and was hard to see.

Writing a Story
On a separate sheet of paper, write a short story about a visit made by you or a character you invent to a special place you know about or would like to go. Make sure that you describe the setting with details. Show how the setting has an effect on the way your character acts.

Literary Elements: Theme

The characters in the stories you read make decisions, and they learn from their mistakes and their successes. If someone asks you what a story is about, you think about what the characters have learned and about the "big idea" the writer is trying to show. The underlying meaning, or big idea, of a story is the **theme**. The theme might be a familiar idea such as "If you want something done right, do it yourself." Other themes are about ideas the author has such as "We're lucky that some of our wishes *don't* come true!"

Sometimes a writer will tell you the theme by stating it directly. Other times, you must use evidence from the story to figure out the theme on your own.

Read this story about figure skating. As you read, think about its theme or underlying meaning.

Carl closed his eyes. In his mind he went over each part of the jump. He tried to feel his body make the midair turn. He had been practicing the axel, over and over. Coach Marion would be surprised to see that he'd finally mastered the jump.

"OK, Carl, let's try that axel," shouted Coach Marion.

Carl took a deep breath.

"Take it nice and easy!" Coach Marion's voice echoed across the rink.

Carl skated backward.

"Don't rush the takeoff!" yelled the coach.

Carl switched directions, gliding forward on the outside edge of the blade. He lifted himself up, turned himself around in the air, and then made an almost perfect landing.

For once, Coach Marion was speechless!

What is the theme of this story?

Possible answers: Practice and concentration pay off. It takes hard

work to master a new skill.

What evidence from the story helped you figure out the theme?

Carl goes over the jump in his mind. The author says he has

practiced the jump many times.

Tip

Remember that a story's theme isn't always stated directly. Sometimes you must figure out the theme yourself. Think about what "big idea" the writer is trying to show.

Read the following story about an ice skating party. Notice how the characters' actions relate to the story's theme.

MAKE NEW FRIENDS...

by Norma Johnston

"What do you want to do for your birthday this year?" Betsy's mother asked her one morning.

"How about a skating party?" Betsy asked. She was just learning how to figure skate.

"That sounds like fun," her mother said. "Whom do you want to invite?"

"I'll think about it," Betsy promised and ran outside just as Trevor, the new kid next door, came down his steps. As usual, Trevor had a book bag slung over his shoulder, in contrast to Betsy's friends' usual backpacks. He was a grade ahead of Betsy, so Betsy didn't know him very well.

At lunchtime she told her friends Tasha, Lauryn, and Jill about the skating party. "Who else will you invite?" Tasha asked.

"I was thinking about Brian, Will, Mark, and Doug," Betsy said. They were old friends who had attended school with the girls since kindergarten.

When her father asked Betsy about her guest list at dinner, Betsy recited the names of her seven friends.

"And Trevor, of course," her mother added.

"Mom!" Betsy said. "He's in sixth grade. He doesn't know any of my friends. He won't even want to come—"

"How do you know?" her mother inquired. "Give him a chance, Betsy. Remember,

'Make new friends, but keep the old.' " Betsy knew from the glint in her mother's eye that further discussion would be futile.

On Betsy's birthday her father drove the girls to the rink. The boys were already there, warming up on the ice. Betsy spotted Trevor tying his skates across the rink. She watched as he tried a few experimental strokes. Then he pushed off across the ice. He executed a glide and an effortless axel jump. Then he swooped to a stop. "Happy Birthday, Betsy!" he said.

"Hey, Trevor, where'd you learn to skate like that? Do you play hockey?" Brian asked.

Trevor grinned. "I grew up in northern Minnesota, and I've been skating and playing hockey all my life. I practice here just about every day. I also like figure skating."

"So that's why he carries a book bag, rather than a backpack—for his skates!" Betsy thought.

"Trevor, can you show me some jumps?" Lauryn asked.

"Sure," Trevor said, "Betsy, do you want to watch, too? I can give you some tips."

Betsy skated to the center of the ice after Trevor. "I'm glad I gave him a chance," she thought. "'Make new friends, but keep the old'—sometimes Mom really *does* know best!"

Checking Comprehension

1. Why doesn't Betsy want to invite Trevor to her party?   [Drawing Conclusions/Inferential]

   She doesn't know him well, and she doesn't think he will fit in.

2. How do you think Trevor feels about being invited?   [Character/Critical]

   He is probably glad to be included. He enjoys skating and is probably interested in meeting

   new people.

Practicing Comprehension Skills

Reread "Make New Friends . . ." Then answer the questions.

3. Is the theme of the story stated or unstated? stated

4. What is the theme of the story? Write it on the line, then restate it in
   your own words.

   "Make new friends, but keep the old." It's good to have old friends, but it's also important

   to make new friends.

5. How might Betsy behave differently in the future because of what she
   has learned?

   Possible answers: Betsy might be more open and friendly to newcomers. She will

   remember that making new friends can be fun.

Fill in the circle next to the correct answer.

6. Why does Betsy's mom want Trevor to be invited?
   ○ She knows Trevor can skate.   ● She wants Betsy to make a new friend.
   ○ She knows Trevor will like Brian and Lauryn.   ○ She wants Betsy to skate better.

7. Explain your answer to question 7 on the lines provided.

   Possible answer: Her mother tells Betsy to give Trevor a chance. She reminds Betsy that it's

   good to make new friends, but keep the old ones.

8. "Mom knows best" sounds as if it *could* be a theme. Why isn't it the best theme for this story?

  ○ The story is about ice skating, not relationships.

  ● The best theme for the story should say something about friendship, because that is the "big idea" of the whole story.

  ○ This theme is directly stated, and writers never state a story's theme directly.

  ○ Betsy's father is part of the birthday planning, too.

9. Which of these lines from the story supports the theme by showing what a character has learned?

  ○ "Do you play hockey?" Brian asked.

  ○ "Who else will you invite?" Tasha asked.

  ● "I'm glad I gave him a chance," she thought.

  ○ "Happy birthday, Betsy!" he said.

Practicing Vocabulary

Choose a word from the box to complete each analogy. Write the word on the line.

| attended |
| effortless |
| experimental |
| friends' |
| futile |
| mother's |
| recited |

10. *father's* is to *his* as ___mother's___ is to *hers*

11. *useful* is to *useless* as *helpful* is to ___futile___

12. *difficult* is to *hard* as ___effortless___ is to *easy*

13. *relationships* is to *families'* as *friendships* is to ___friends'___

14. *missed* is to *absent* as ___attended___ is to *present*

15. *stared* is to *eyes* as ___recited___ is to *voice*

16. *usual* is to *familiar* as ___experimental___ is to *new*

MAKING THE Reading AND Writing CONNECTION

Writing a Realistic Story
On a separate sheet of paper, write a realistic story that shows a big idea you have learned about friendship. Trade stories with a partner. Then try to identify the theme in your partner's story. Think about the evidence in the story that supports the theme.

Synonyms

Read these sentences and think about the underlined words.

Johnny Appleseed was a <u>nomad</u>. With a tin pot on his head, this <u>wanderer</u> traveled the land planting apple seeds.

The word *wanderer* is a synonym for *nomad*. A **synonym** is a word that has the same or nearly the same meaning as another word. Authors choose synonyms that show the exact meaning, mood, or tone that they want a piece of writing to have. Synonyms change the strength, seriousness, or other characteristics of the things being described. They also help an author to avoid repeating words. In the sentences above, both *nomad* and *wanderer* tell us that Johnny Appleseed was a great traveler. However, *nomad* carries the meaning of a traveler without a home. *Wanderer* tells us that Johnny Appleseed covered many miles in his travels.

Read the following tall tale about Angela Appleseed. Look for synonyms the author uses.

Many legends tell of Johnny Appleseed. He traveled around America planting apple trees. Few people know about his great-grandniece Angela. She was given Johnny's caring spirit and interest in the earth. In Angela's time there were plenty of orchards, but she faced another kind of challenge.

Litter had always been a problem in the parks around her city. Angela set to work. The industrious twelve-year-old carried a leather satchel, the very bag that had been her uncle's. Where he had planted seeds, the hardworking girl labored to collect litter. She was so diligent that even today, visitors in a tidy park nod and say, "Angela Appleseed has passed this way."

Find the word *satchel* in the tale. Then find a synonym in the nearby words and sentences and write it on the line.

<u>bag</u>

What are two synonyms for *hardworking* in the tale?

<u>industrious and diligent</u>

Tip

Remember that a *synonym* is another word with the same meaning. When you read, think about how synonyms change the mood, meaning, or tone of the piece of writing.

Read the legend from the San people of Namibia in southwestern Africa. As you read, look for synonyms.

How the Zebra Got Its Stripes
A Tale From Namibia

Long ago, when the earth was young, the weather was always hot and dry. Water could be found in only a few places. Being in such scarce supply, water was very precious indeed. One of these rare watering holes in a great desert was guarded by a large baboon. This selfish baboon protected the watering hole and never let anyone come near it, claiming himself to be its king. He kept a fire burning next to it so that he could watch his water day and night.

One day the baboon saw a beast with a coat of white fur traveling toward the watering hole. This animal was the zebra, who did not have any stripes in those days. The zebra had been wandering through the desert for a long time, searching for a pool of water just like the one the baboon guarded. "Aha!" thought the zebra. "After looking for so long, I have found water at last."

As the zebra came to the water to drink, the baboon shouted, "Go away! I am king of this watering hole!"

The tired zebra didn't understand the overbearing baboon's words. "I will just drink a little water," he thought as he moved closer. The nearer he came, the angrier the baboon grew. He confronted the zebra, ready to fight.

Zebra's bafflement increased. He said to the baboon, "I am weary and parched from thirst. This water does not belong to you, you silly monkey.

All animals should be allowed to drink from it. Let me have some!"

This only angered the baboon more. He shouted back, "This is my water! I am the king of this place, and if you want to drink, you must fight me."

The zebra had no desire to fight, but he was terribly thirsty. He sprang at the baboon, and they rolled back and forth for a long time. Neither animal could defeat the other. Finally, the zebra kicked the baboon with his hind legs. "That's your payment for selfishness!" he yelled.

The baboon flew up in the air. He soared over the sand and landed on some hard rocks. He tried to get up again, but he was too sore.

The zebra had lost his balance from kicking so hard. He stumbled to the edge of the baboon's fire. Hot sticks flew up and singed his beautiful white coat with dark stripes.

Startled, the zebra began to run. He kept running until he reached the plains, and he stays there to this day. In time he grew to like his marks, which distinguished him from other animals. As for the baboon, he remains among the rocks, still shrieking at every stranger he sees.

Checking Comprehension

1. Why did the baboon guard the water hole so closely?   [Plot/Inferential]

   Water was very scarce, and the baboon was selfish about sharing it.

2. Do you think the baboon learned from his experience? Explain your answer. [Making Judgments/Critical]

   Most students will say no. The story tells us that the baboon is still

   angry when he sees a stranger.

Practicing Comprehension Skills

3. Find two synonyms for *scarce* in the first paragraph and write them on the line.

   precious and rare

Find each of the following words in the tale. Then find a synonym in nearby words and sentences. Write the synonym on the line.

4. nearer   closer

5. parched   thirsty

6. searching   looking

7. flew   soared

8. stays   remains

Think of more synonyms for these story words. At the end of the spokes, write other synonyms for the word in the center circle. You can use a dictionary or thesaurus to find the synonyms.

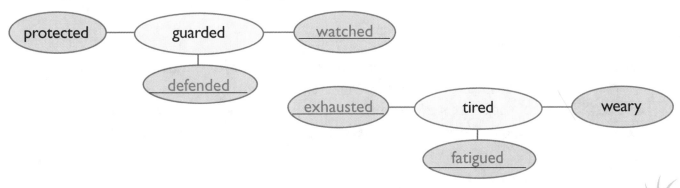

Find another pair of synonyms in the story. Write them on the line.

Possible answers: wandering, traveling; beast, animal; shouted, yelled

In each of these sentences, a word has been repeated. Think of a synonym that would be a good substitute for the underlined word. Write the synonym on the line.

13. Myths that tell why animals look or act a certain way are my favorite <u>myths</u>.

    Possible answers: legends, stories, tales

14. The baboon thought he was king of the watering hole, and he <u>thought</u> nobody else should come near it.

    Possible answers: believed, felt

Practicing Vocabulary

Choose the word from the box that is a synonym for each listed word below. Write the word on the line.

confronted	15. faced	bafflement
shrieking	16. screaming	confronted
singed	17. burned	distinguished
bafflement	18. puzzlement	overbearing
overbearing	19. arrogant	payment
payment	20. reward	shrieking
distinguished	21. separated	singed

Writing a Myth
The San people of Namibia pointed to the myth of how the zebra got its stripes to explain this animal's unusual markings. On another sheet of paper, create a myth that explains why an animal looks or behaves a certain way. Then trade papers with a partner. Replace five words in your partner's myth with synonyms.

Antonyms

Authors often use antonyms to point out contrasts between ideas, characters, and settings. **Antonyms** are words that have opposite meanings. The words *happy* and *sad*, for instance, are antonyms. So are *begin* and *end*. The prefixes *un-*, *in-*, and *im-* can change words into their antonyms. For example, *usual* and *unusual*, *secure* and *insecure*, and *mature* and *immature* are all antonyms.

In the stories and articles that you read, pay attention to antonyms the author uses. They can help you understand how characters, ideas, or other things are different.

As you read the article, look for antonyms. Notice how they show contrasts.

Abigail Adams will always be remembered for her advice to her husband, President John Adams, who served from 1797 to 1801. She told him, when planning national laws, to "Remember the ladies." Today we think of Abigail Adams as an early fighter for women's rights.

Abigail Adams never went to school, yet she was not uneducated. By reading, she became well informed. Her spelling was weak, but the letters she wrote were powerful.

In paintings, Abigail's husband appears short and heavy. He has a plain face. Abigail is tall and slender. Her looks are striking. John and Abigail were unlike in appearance, but the views they held were similar. For more than 50 years, Abigail advised her husband on important issues.

Look back at the article. Find the antonym for each word listed below. Write the antonym on the line.

weak _____powerful_____

uneducated _____informed_____

slender _____heavy_____

unlike _____similar_____

Find an additional pair of antonyms in the article.

Possible answers: short/tall; plain/striking

Tip

Look for antonyms when an author compares two people, events, or things. Antonyms can show you how the things being compared are different.

As you read the article about the White House, look for antonyms.

The President's House

In 1791, George Washington picked the site of our nation's capital—Washington, D.C. He also chose the spot where the President's house would be built. The "Father of Our Country" never saw the completed building, though. When he died in 1799, the walls and roof were just about finished. President John Adams and his wife, Abigail, were the first to live there.

The Adamses arrived in Washington, D.C., in November of 1800. Stunned by what they saw, they tried to remain calm. Mud and rubble covered the grounds of their new home. A bridge of planks led from the roadway to the front door. All around the mansion stood the workers' shacks. Washington was a village of some 40 houses, not the big city we know today.

At least the President's house was finished on the outside. Inside, everything was incomplete. Many of the walls had not been plastered. The central staircase was unfinished. The floors were rough boards. There was no indoor bathroom. The furniture was inadequate, too. There wasn't nearly enough, and in the huge rooms the furniture looked like dollhouse furniture.

Congress thought it had spent enough on the mansion. Abigail felt that much had been left undone. She complained that there were no lamps or mirrors. Compared with her cozy home in Boston, Massachusetts, this was cold and damp, and the firewood supply was insufficient to keep her 13 fireplaces burning and her rooms warm. To dry laundry, the first lady had to string up a clothesline in the huge East Room.

In private, Abigail Adams complained about the living arrangements. In public, however, she praised the location of the house. After all, the huge building was the center of a new city springing up in the wilderness. With a sparkling new coat of white paint, "the white house" shone like a gem even against the drabbest surroundings. Built on a rise, it had sweeping views of hills, forests, and the Potomac River. Indeed, it seemed to hover above the earth rather than being sunk, as it actually was, into the side of a hill.

Abigail Adams was a smart woman. She realized that the White House—as it was now being called—would have a great future. She knew that her present living conditions would soon change for the better. "This house," she wrote to a relative, "is built for ages to come."

Checking Comprehension

1. How do you think the White House got its name? [Cause and Effect/Inferential]

   <u>After it was painted white, people started calling it that.</u>

   _____

2. Why do you think that Abigail Adams did not complain about the mansion in public? [Drawing Conclusions/Inferential]

   <u>Possible answers: She did not want to appear ungrateful. She wanted to emphasize what was</u>

   <u>good about the new house and city.</u>

Practicing Comprehension Skills

Read the word in the central circle. Fill in each surrounding circle with an antonym from the story.

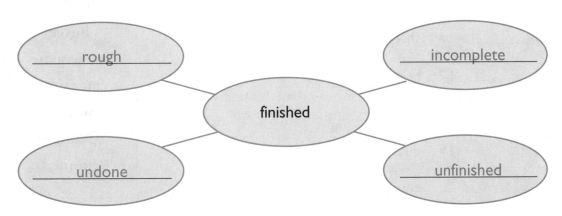

Fill in the circle next to the antonym of the underlined word.

7. The White House was a <u>mansion</u>, not a _____.
   ○ gem   ○ plank   ○ village   ● shack

8. The President's House was <u>damp</u>, not _____.
   ○ huge   ● dry   ○ insufficient   ○ unfinished

9. Washington, D.C., was a <u>city</u>, not a _____.
   ● village   ○ cozy   ○ damp   ○ whitewash

Complete each sentence by providing an antonym for the italicized word.

10. Never a *cowardly* person, Abigail Adams very <u>possible answer: bravely</u> advised her husband on women's rights.

11. The *present* Washington, D.C., is very different from that of the <u>possible answer: past</u> .

Turn each word into an antonym by adding *in-*, *im-*, or *un-*.

12. perfect <u>imperfect</u>

13. popular <u>unpopular</u>

14. capable <u>incapable</u>

15. sufficient <u>insufficient</u>

Practicing Vocabulary

Choose a word from the box that is an antonym for each word below. Write the word on the line.

<u>mansion</u>	**16.** shack
<u>drabbest</u>	**17.** brightest
<u>stunned</u>	**18.** bored
<u>sparkling</u>	**19.** dull
<u>inadequate</u>	**20.** enough
<u>public</u>	**21.** private
<u>hover</u>	**22.** fall

drabbest
hover
inadequate
mansion
public
sparkling
stunned

Writing a Personal Essay
On another sheet of paper, write a personal essay. Describe how a person, place, or thing in your life was different from what you expected. Use antonyms to show differences.

Understanding Homonyms

Sometimes when you read, you'll come across words you know in a different context. These words can be homonyms, homographs, or homophones.

	Definition	Example
Homonyms	words with the same pronunciation and spelling, but different meanings.	**foot** (body part) **foot** (12-inch measure)
Homographs	words that are spelled alike, but pronounced differently	**wind** the clock the **wind** is blowing
Homophones	words with the same pronunciation but different spellings and meanings	**to, too, two**

To understand homonyms, homographs, and homophones, pay attention to:

- **spelling.** The homophones **male** and **mail** sound alike, but mean different things.
- **parts of speech.** As a noun, the word **track** means "a path." As a verb, **track** means "to follow."
- **context.** You tie a **bow** around a present. You make a **bow** after a performance.

Read the story about a track meet.

Cari and Sue had to stand around and wait for the rest of the track team.
"I think the others went to rest by the concession stand," Cari said.
"There they are!" Sue cried. "Pam, what did you buy?"
Pam said, "I wanted to present matching blue shoelaces to the team."
Wearing the shoelaces, the team won their meet.
"Our hard work and your present paid off," Sue said to Pam.

For these homonyms, write two different meanings used in the story.

stand, stand: <u>to be on your feet; a booth that sells things</u>

Are the words *there* and *their* homonyms, homographs, or homophones? How do you know?

<u>Homophones.</u>

<u>They sound the same, but have different spellings and meanings.</u>

Find a homograph in the passage and write it on the line:

<u>present</u>

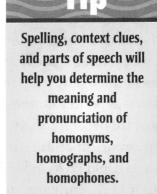

Tip

Spelling, context clues, and parts of speech will help you determine the meaning and pronunciation of homonyms, homographs, and homophones.

Read the article about sneakers. Look for homonyms, homophones, and homographs, and note how they are used.

A Sneak Peek at Sneakers

These days it is easy to get lost when you shop for sneakers, or "gym" shoes. People aren't content buying simple styles. They want shoes in every shade, and for every sport and speed. Over the years, styles have been developed for every activity. In fact, the content of shoe stores changes with each passing fad. Now there are special styles for everyone. A kick boxer and a sailboat racer can each buy sneakers suited to his or her sport.

Shoe makers make new styles and update old ones. They hope that consumers will buy their latest model. Yet some of the most popular gym shoes of all time have been best-sellers for almost one hundred years.

It took Charles Goodyear a long time to perfect his way of making rubber. At last, in 1839, he came up with a rubber that would not turn hard and brittle in subfreezing conditions and would not get sticky and gooey when the temperature rose to 100° in the shade. The firm rubber was perfect for the sole of cloth shoes, and sales of rubber-soled shoes took off. By the turn of the twentieth century, dozens of styles of sneakers could be found in every shoe shop.

One of the early manufacturers, the United States Rubber Company, developed a line of rubber-soled cloth shoes called *Keds*®. Their most popular styles were especially designed for women. Over the years, Keds has kept this traditional style. The company has also added new designs to keep its products current.

In 1917, another firm, *Converse*®, came out with its all-purpose cloth and rubber basketball shoe called the *All Star*®. A basketball star named Chuck Taylor liked these new shoes. He started wearing them. Soon, he became one of Converse's salespeople. In 1923, Chuck's name was added to the logo on the All Star. The popular shoes became known worldwide as *Cons*® or *Chucks*®. They are the "sole" of the company. The All Star's design is that of a simple, high-top basketball shoe. Its design has remained basically unchanged. That's because it suits many people's tastes and needs.

Recent technology has created fads such as pump-up sneakers and lighted shoes. Some of the fads, like the pumps, have been long-lasting. The light-up shoes, on the other hand, suffered from technical problems. The fad is only popular now with children. The next time you shop for gym shoes, check out the styles. You might be looking at a passing fad—or a model that will last for a long, long time.

Checking Comprehension

1. What is the main idea of "A Sneak Peek at Sneakers"? [Main Idea/Inferential]

   Possible answer: People have worn sneakers, or "gym" shoes, for over 100 years. There is a

   style for every purpose and taste.

   [Drawing Conclusions/Critical]
2. Why was Goodyear's invention important for the success of sneakers?

   Possible answer: The rubber sole of a sneaker has to stay the same in any temperature.

   Goodyear invented a rubber that wasn't affected by heat and cold.

Practicing Comprehension Skills

Reread "A Sneak Peek at Sneakers." Look carefully at how these homonyms are used in the article. Write two meanings for each homonym in the chart.

Homonym	Meaning 1	Meaning 2
3. last	in the end	endure
4. shade	color	not in the sunshine
5. firm	stiff	company

6. Find two words in "A Sneak Peek at Sneakers" that can be homonyms, though only one meaning appears in the article. Write them on the line.

   Possible answers: suits, line, model, rose

Fill in the circle before the correct answer.

7. The word *sole* is a homophone for

   ○ sold   ○ soil   ● soul   ○ cell

8. The word *by* is a homophone for

   ● buy   ○ bind   ○ bite   ○ buoy

9. Complete the sentence with the correct homophone: Manufacturers come up with _____ styles each year.

   ○ knew   ● new   ○ many   ○ now

10. On the line, explain what happens when you change the pronunciation of these homographs:

con-TENT; CON-tent   per-FECT; PER-fect

The meaning of the word changes.

11. The homograph *content* is used twice in the first paragraph of the passage. Write each sentence and its meaning.

"People aren't content buying simple styles." The word content means "satisfied." "In fact, the content of shoe stores changes with each passing fad." The word content means "the things found inside."

12. The homograph *perfect* is used twice in the passage. Write the meaning and part of speech of the homograph for each of these uses.

Perfect is used to mean "to make perfect." It is a verb. Perfect also means "without flaw." It is an adjective.

Practicing Vocabulary

13. Choose a word from the box that best completes each sentence in the paragraph. Write the word on the line.

Manufacturers produce sneakers that they hope people will want to buy. Their _salespeople_ sell their line to shoe stores. Sneakers come in many designs and _styles_. Some _traditional_ designs have been around for almost a century. _Consumers_ buy these sneakers for themselves and for their _children_. Some buyers want sneaker _products_ with the latest features.

children
consumers
manufacturers
products
salespeople
styles
traditional

Writing a Narrative
On a separate sheet of paper, write a personal narrative about an exciting moment you had while wearing sneakers. Tell the story from your sneakers' point of view. Use at least one pair of homonyms, one pair of homographs, and one pair of homophones.

Using Figurative Language

Writers often use words that help you picture what is being described. To do this, writers may use **figurative language.** These are expressions that give words a meaning beyond their usual, everyday definitions. Similes, metaphors, idioms, and personification are four types of figurative language that writers often use.

- A **simile** compares two things using the word *like* or *as*.

  The stars twinkled like candles in the sky.

- A **metaphor** compares two things by saying one is the other. It does not use *like* or *as*.

  The opening of the cave was a giant mouth.

- An **idiom** is a phrase whose meaning cannot be understood from the usual meaning of the words.

  Last night, it rained cats and dogs.

- **Personification** gives human characteristics to animals or objects.

  The sky wept buckets all day long.

Look for examples of figurative language as you read about this one-room schoolhouse and its teacher.

When Emma entered the schoolhouse, the room was as cold as ice. Emma had come early to build a fire before the children arrived. The thick pipe was a tree trunk, rising from the iron stove. Emma stared at the desks, six rows of silent soldiers. The school held 52 students, but she didn't expect nearly that many. Farm families often depended on their children to help at this time of year. Finally, boys and girls began to arrive. As they saw Emma, their murmurs died down. They seemed to take a crumb of comfort from her welcoming smile.

Tip

As you read stories and articles, look for figurative language. Use the words to form a picture in your mind of what is being described.

Find an example of each of the following types of figurative language in the passage. Write it on the line.

1. Simile: <u>"the room was as cold as ice"</u>

2. Metaphor: <u>"the thick pipe was a tree trunk"</u>

3. Idiom: <u>"they seemed to take a crumb of comfort"</u>

4. Personification: <u>"the desks, six rows of silent soldiers"</u>

On Your Own — Read the following story. Notice where the author has used figurative language. Use the expressions to form pictures in your mind.

My Greatest Teachers

by Joseph Bruchac

School isn't easy. It doesn't matter if you're a shrimp with thick glasses, as I was, or a sports giant. There are times when you wish you were grown up and graduated. If you're lucky, in the midst of that sea of uncertainty, you will find teachers who draw out the best in you. Let me tell you about two of mine.

The first was Mrs. Monthony. When I first saw her, I fell in love with her. Her hair was as red as autumn leaves. Her face was warm as the glow of a campfire. I was the smallest kid in second grade, always chattering nonstop like a bluejay.

Mrs. Monthony opened her heart to me. When I held up my trusty pencil box in show-and-tell to describe how moving a certain panel would reveal a secret compartment, I looked at her hopefully. Would she be yawning in boredom like my classmates? Instead, she nodded her head and smiled. My voice slowed down, my nervousness was gone.

I saw Mrs. Monthony recently. Her hair had burned gray as ashes, but her eyes still sparkled like the first stars in the sky. "Hello, my precocious second grader," she said. "Remember that pencil box?"

The second memorable teacher was Charles Swick. His house was just up the road from my grandparents' general store, and I often took the Swicks their groceries. What I liked best about delivering to Mr. Swick, apart from the attractions of walls lined with bookshelves and the open books everywhere, was his voice. It was as clear and resonant as a copper bell. I looked forward to the day when I would walk into Mr. Swick's tenth-grade English class. When it came, it as even better than I expected. In our mental race, Mr. Swick was always waiting for me at the finish line.

"Mr. Bruchac," he would say, leaning over his desk like an owl looking down from a tree, "give us the benefit of your infinite wisdom on this poem." Then, no matter what I said, he would look at me with a sly smile and point out something I'd never thought of before. He truly thought on his feet—except that you never saw Mr. Swick standing without the aid of his crutches. He'd had polio as a child, wore heavy braces, and could barely move his legs. His subtle courage taught us as much as his wide knowledge.

To this day, whenever I speak well in public, I think how Mr. Swick would have approved. The measure of a person is never in his height, but in the heart.

Checking Comprehension

1. What judgment does the author make about the teachers he describes? [Making Judgments/Critical]

   They were excellent teachers who brought out the best in their students.

2. What is one way Mrs. Monthony and Mr. Swick were alike? What is one way they were different? [Comparing and Contrasting/Inferential]

   Possible similarities: Both were caring teachers. Possible differences: Mrs. Monthony was more

   kindly and nurturing. She gave the author confidence. Mr. Swick was more challenging and
   inspired the author to work hard.

Practicing Comprehension Skills

Reread the second paragraph of the selection. Complete the similes.
Then explain what each one means.

3. Mrs. Monthony's hair was as _____red_____ as _____autumn leaves_____.

   The teacher's hair color is being compared to the red color of fall leaves.

4. Mrs. Monthony's face was as _____warm_____ as __the glow of a campfire__.

   Her face was warm and welcoming, like a campfire.

5. The author was always _____chattering_____ like a _____bluejay_____.

   He spoke rapidly and noisily, like a bluejay.

Fill in a circle to complete each statement.

6. When the author says he was a "shrimp with thick glasses" in school,

   ○ he is using an idiom meaning he was good in sports.

   ● he is using a metaphor to show how small and nearsighted he was.

   ○ he is using a simile comparing a shrimp to being nearsighted.

   ○ he is using personification showing he was a sports giant.

7. The author compared Mr. Swick's clear, resonant voice to

   ○ a hooting owl.   ○ a public speaker's.   ○ his grandfather's.   ● a copper bell.

Identify the type of figurative language in each of the following sentences.
Then explain what each expression means.

8. He truly thought on his feet.

   Idiom. Possible answer: He came up with good answers on the spur of the moment.

9. He was in the midst of a sea of uncertainty.

   Metaphor. Possible answer: He was so unsure of himself that he felt he was drowning in doubts.

10. I held up my trusty pencil box.

    Personification. Possible answer: He felt his pencil box was something he could rely on.

11. Her eyes still sparkled like the first stars in the sky.

    Simile. Possible answer: Her eyes were as bright as stars.

Practicing Vocabulary

Write the word from the box that belongs in each group.

| attractions |
| benefit |
| hopefully |
| infinite |
| resonant |
| reveal |
| uncertainty |

12. endless, unlimited, _____infinite_____

13. booming, resounding, _____resonant_____

14. doubt, indecision, _____uncertainty_____

15. expectantly, wishfully, _____hopefully_____

16. show, disclose, _____reveal_____

17. assistance, help, _____benefit_____

18. charms, fascinations, _____attractions_____

Writing a Character Sketch

On another sheet of paper, write a character sketch of a teacher who "draws out the best" in students. Use figurative language as you describe your teacher's physical appearance and personality. Support your comments with an example of something the teacher said or did.

Connotation and Denotation

When you read a story or article, you often see words that have more than one meaning. There is the meaning that you find in a dictionary. That is called the **denotation.** Some words also have a **connotation.** The connotation of a word includes the different feelings and images that a word suggests to you. For example, the words *skinny* and *lean* both mean "thin." *Skinny,* though, often means "thin *and* weak." It calls up negative feelings and has a **negative connotation.** *Lean,* on the other hand, suggests fitness. "Lean" calls up positive feelings and has a **positive connotation.**

Authors choose words carefully accordingly to their connotations. As you read, pay attention to how writers use connotations of words to create moods or images.

Read the letter about a camping trip. As you read, think about the connotations of the words.

Dear Joan,

    Thank you for inviting me on the campout. Except for the downpour during our trudge through the woods, it was wonderful. I was very glad to have a huge blaze on Saturday night! My favorite part of the trip was fishing. I can't believe I caught such a gigantic fish, or that we ate it!

                Love, Toni

Find a word in the letter that has nearly the same meaning as each of the following words. Then tell if that new word has a positive or negative connotation to you.

	Word	Positive or Negative Connotation
campfire	blaze	positive
rain	downpour	negative
hike	trudge	negative
big	gigantic	positive

Tip

Remember that the *connotation* is how you feel when you read a word. As you read, think about the connotations of the words the author has chosen. Ask yourself, "Does this word have a positive or negative connotation?"

Read the story about a special dance. Notice how the connotations of words can create a mood for the story.

The Fabulous 50's Sock Hop Committee

At lunch the Fabulous 50's Sock Hop committee met in the cafeteria. Coach West was the adviser.

"OK," said Jessie. "Let's get moving. I hope that the research team has done its work. Tom, do you have something to report?"

"I sure do," said Tom. "I found out how to make our dance really authentic. I spent hours digging through volumes of ancient history."

"Is that true?" asked Ben.

"Ben!" Carly laughed. "Don't be so gullible. I bet Tom looked on the World Wide Web. That's what I did, and it took me about two seconds flat."

"Actually, I asked my uncle Peter," said Tom. "It really did take ages. We had to sort through every box in the garage to disentangle his old records and movie magazines."

"What did you find?" Jessie asked.

"We found Fifties records and pictures of kids in bobby socks, poodle skirts, ponytails, and ducktails," said Tom. "Wait until you see the wild hairstyles. We will also need to find an old record player."

"I have one of those museum pieces," said Coach West. "It will be a snap to set up. I'll be the disk jockey."

"Perfect," said Jessie. "Carly, what were you planning for decorations?"

Carly said, "I thought we could make jukeboxes out of cardboard boxes to decorate the gym and hang make-believe records from the ceiling. In one corner we can set up a drive-in restaurant where the refreshments will be served."

"Great!" Art said. "Let's ask our parents to cruise around on roller skates, balancing soft drinks on trays, just like in olden times."

"I love that idea," said Jessie. "Art, how are you doing with the publicity?"

"I discharged those duties with my usual speed," said Art. He pulled a stack of flyers out of his backpack. "Ben and I are going to put these up all over the school."

"Do you have enough?" Jessie asked, picking up the stack. "Oh, yes, I see there are plenty. These look terrific! From being a shambles, our event is really coming together."

On the night of the sock hop, everyone was in good spirits. "Carly, the dog on your skirt is adorable," said Jessie.

Ben said, "Tom, your hair looks slippery."

"The word is *slick*," said Tom. "I'm going to wear it like this forever. It suits me."

"Do you think this music is dull?" Carly asked anxiously. "Coach West doesn't think so. He knows every word to every song!"

"Look at my mom, will you? She's having a blast!" said Art. "Did you see her scoot by?"

"Yeah! I was transfixed!" said Tom. "Who knew she could roller-skate like that?"

Checking Comprehension

1. What did the committee members do to make the sock hop authentic? [Summarizing/Inferential]

    They researched the 1950s to find out about clothes, hairstyles, and music.

    _____

2. Would you say that the committee was disorganized or well organized?
    Explain your answer. [Making Judgments/Inferential]

    The committee was well organized. Everyone pitched in to complete all of the jobs that

    needed to be done.

Practicing Comprehension Skills

For each of the following words, find a word or phrase from the story with
nearly the same denotation but a different connotation. Tell whether the
connotation is positive or negative.

	Story Words	Positive or Negative Connotation
3. enough	plenty	positive
4. trusting	gullible	negative
5. disorganized	in shambles	negative
6. slippery	slick	positive
7. antique	museum piece	negative

Compare these pairs of words with similar denotations. Tell how the
connotations are different.

8. *old* and *ancient:* Possible answer: *Old* means from some time in the past. *Ancient* means from a

    very long time ago.

9. *attractive* and *adorable:* Possible answer: *Attractive* means pleasing to look at. *Adorable* means

    very cute and sweet.

10. *find* and *discover:* Possible answer: *Find* means to come upon something you've been looking for. *Discover* means to find something new.

Complete the sentences by circling the word with the more positive connotation.

11. The students had an (**extraordinary**, unusual) time.

12. I found the music to be on the (**quiet**, dull) side.

13. I was glad to see that the committee put out the (food, **refreshments**).

Practicing Vocabulary

Write a word from the box to complete each sentence.

discharged	
disentangle	
gullible	
publicity	
shambles	
transfixed	
volumes	

14. Tom returned the heavy history _____volumes_____ to the library.

15. Ben tried to _____disentangle_____ two ropes that were twisted together.

16. Carly was _____gullible_____ enough to believe the tall tale.

17. The flyers around school were all the _____publicity_____ the committee needed.

18. Art _____discharged_____ all his jobs without complaining.

19. The kids were _____transfixed_____ by the sight of Coach West dancing.

20. In the end the committee showed that they could organize a _____shambles_____ into a hit.

Making the Reading and Writing Connection

Writing a Friendly Letter
On a separate sheet of paper, write a letter to a friend describing an event that you attended, such as a dance, a party, or a fair. Think about the words you could use to show how you feel about the event. Use words with positive and negative connotations to create a vivid picture.

LESSON 29

Using Maps

A **map** is a drawing of a place that helps you to find locations. Different features on a map make the map easier to use. A map **key** explains the special symbols, or pictures, on the map. A **scale** shows how distances on the map compare with real-life distances in miles or kilometers. A **compass rose** shows the direction arrows for north, south, east, and west.

Different kinds of maps have different purposes, so they show different things. Types of maps include road maps, political maps, and maps that show physical features. There are also maps with special purposes, such as to show rainfall or crops. When a map accompanies something you are reading, look at the map title, the captions, and the symbols. Then you will see how the map can help you understand the information.

As you read the passage, look at the map to help you understand what you read.

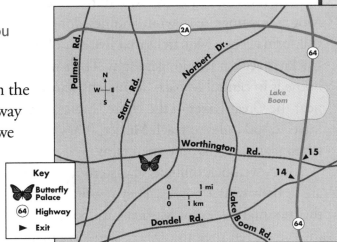

Ramon's mother wondered whether they had taken the correct turn for Butterfly Palace after getting off Highway 64. "We're on Worthington Road," she said, "but are we going east or west?"

Ramon studied the map. "Well, we just passed Norbert Drive, so we're going west. There should be a sign coming up on the left . . . there it is!"

If Ramon's mom continued driving instead of turning off for Butterfly Palace, what is the next intersection she would come to?

The intersection of Worthington Rd. and Starr Rd.

Suppose that you started out at the intersection of Route 2A and Palmer Road. How would you get to Butterfly Palace?

Go south on Palmer and then east on Worthington; or go east on

2A, south on Starr, and then east on Worthington.

When you read a map, study the key. The key lists special symbols, or pictures, and tells what each one stands for.

On Your Own Read the article about an amazing journey. Look at the map to see why it is amazing.

 Migrating Monarchs

In early fall, before the winter cold sets in, delicate black and orange monarch butterflies leave the milkweed fields and patches where they hatched. As they fly to their warm winter homes, they fill the sky with their colorful midair displays.

The monarchs that live west of the Rocky Mountains migrate to winter homes along the California coast. Monarchs that live east of the Rockies face a much longer flight. Their winter home is in central Mexico. Monarchs starting near the Great Lakes in the United States may travel 2,500 miles to reach Mexico. They cross lakes, plains, rivers, and mountains.

By November, millions of eastern monarchs are in their winter homes. They nest in forests in the mountains west of Mexico City. Some of them have returned to the very same tree that their "great-grandparents" were in years before. The new generation of monarchs settles in the trees in such large numbers that the trees seem made of butterflies. They are such a popular attraction for tourists that visitors are advised to visit midweek to avoid crowds.

By winter's end the monarchs head back to their summer homes. The females lay eggs on plants along the way. The life cycles of the monarchs are almost complete. Some will reach their places of birth before they die. Others will die along the way. Even if they don't make it back, their "children" will continue the journey back to the starting point. There the cycle begins again.

No one knows how these fascinating insects find their way across long distances to their places of birth or winter homes. Maybe they have a built-in compass, as some scientists suspect. Maybe they just know how to follow the sun. Only time and research will tell.

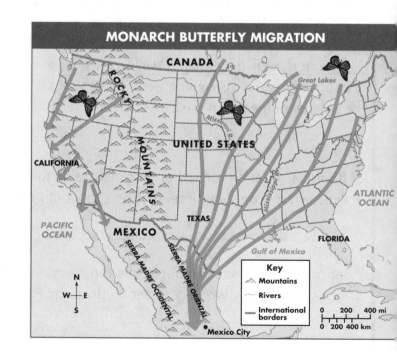

MONARCH BUTTERFLY MIGRATION

Key
Mountains
Rivers
International borders

Checking Comprehension

1. Why do eastern monarchs fly to Mexico each year? [Cause and Effect/Inferential]

   Possible answer: The winters where they live are too cold, so they spend the winter in

   Mexico, where it is warmer.

2. Why does the monarchs' migration amaze people? [Drawing Conclusions/Critical]

   Possible answer: They fly very long distances, and nobody understands how they know where

   to go.

Practicing Study Skills

Fill in the circle next to the correct answer. Use both the article and the map.

3. Which of the following will be crossed by a monarch that begins its migration
   near the Great Lakes?

   ○ the Rocky Mountains   ○ the Atlantic Ocean

   ● the Mississippi River   ○ the Pacific Ocean

4. What U.S. state do most of the eastern monarchs fly over?

   ● Texas   ○ Maine   ○ California   ○ Colorado

Write **True** or **False** after each statement. If a statement is false, rewrite the
statement so that the underlined part is true.

5. Some monarchs fly over water in the Gulf of Mexico.

   True

6. Western monarchs migrate to the mountains near Mexico City.

   False. Western monarchs migrate to the California coast.

7. A monarch that hatches near the Great Lakes travels directly north to
   its winter site.

   False. A monarch that hatches near the Great Lakes travels southwest to its winter site.

8. Female monarchs lay eggs while traveling <u>north or northeast</u>.

   <u>True</u>

9. Look at the migration map. How do you know where the United States ends and Mexico begins?

   <u>Possible answer: The key shows that a heavy gray line indicates an international boundary.</u>

10. What physical feature such as a mountain range, a river, or an ocean divides the migrating route of the western monarchs and the eastern monarchs?

    <u>The Rocky Mountains</u>

Practicing Vocabulary

11. Choose the word from the box that best completes each sentence in the paragraph. Write the word on the line.

cycle
delicate
fascinating
midair
midweek
migrate
tourists

My family's trip to Mexico included a <u>fascinating</u> visit to the butterfly site near the village of El Rosario. We went at <u>midweek</u>, when there were fewer <u>tourists</u> around. Seeing so many beautiful and <u>delicate</u> monarch butterflies resting in the trees was worth the trip! My father told me how the eastern monarchs <u>migrate</u> thousands of miles to reach Mexico. Nobody knows exactly how they navigate as they fly in <u>midair</u>. Every fall the amazing <u>cycle</u> of migration begins again as a new generation of monarchs flies to Mexico.

MAKING THE Reading AND Writing CONNECTION

Writing Directions
On another sheet of paper, write directions from one place in your town to another, but do not name your destination. Draw a map to go with your directions. Trade papers with a partner and try to guess the destination by following each other's directions.

Understanding Charts and Tables

When you read newspaper stories, magazine articles, and other sources of information, you often come across charts and tables. A **chart** presents information visually in the form of words, numbers, or both words and numbers. A **table** is a special kind of chart that organizes information. Tables are set up with details arranged in rows and columns. Rows run from left to right. Columns run from top to bottom.

To use a table, first look at the title. The title tells you the topic of the table. Then read the headings for the rows and columns. Refer to the headings as you read across the rows and down the columns to understand and compare the data.

Read the pet-day announcement and the table.

Powell Park Pet Day

June 15 is Pet Day at Powell Park for neighbors of all ages and their feathered and furry friends. The pet parade assembles at the picnic shelter at 10:00 A.M. Owners and pets may wear costumes.

Competitions for cats, dogs, birds, and rodents follow the parade. Local veterinarians will award prizes for best appearance and best trick. See the schedule for details.

POWELL PARK PET COMPETITION		
Pets	**Best Appearance**	**Best Trick**
Cats	12:00 P.M.	12:45 P.M.
Dogs	1:00 P.M.	1:30 P.M.
Birds	2:00 P.M.	2:30 P.M.
Rodents	3:45 P.M.	4:15 P.M.

Use the announcement and table to answer the following questions.

1. When will a pet owner show a dog trained to do a trick?

   ○ 12:45 P.M.   ○ 3:45 P.M.   ○ 12:15 P.M.   ● 1:30 P.M.

2. What pet should come to the judges' stand at 12:00?

   ○ a talking parrot   ○ a dog trained to sit and heel on command

   ● a beautiful, silky cat   ○ a hamster with blue eyes

Tip

When you are reading a table, pay attention to the headings for the rows and columns. They help you to understand and compare the information in the table.

STRATEGY: Understanding Charts and Tables 135

As you read, look for information in the two tables to help you understand the story.

A Day at the Races

It's race day. The racers are in position. They are fit and eager. I won't be racing today. I've seen plenty of races in my younger days. I watch from the side now, but I still feel that old excitement.

Let me tell you who I am. I'm Beachcomber. I'm named after a brave messenger that served in World War II. The original Beachcomber was among 32 homing pigeons that won service medals in the war. They carried important messages for British troops.

Let's return to race day. The pigeon owners have transported their birds and their race clocks to the starting point. It is nearly time to let their homers go. My owner, Larry, has his hopes placed on a feisty bird named Phoebe. I remember when Phoebe went into training. The first time Larry took her several miles from his loft and let her go, she was only a few months old. Phoebe headed home like a pro.

When Larry entered his birds in the county fair, Phoebe took a blue ribbon. Larry hung her scorecard up in our loft. Phoebe got high marks in every category.

WESTBROOK COUNTY FAIR RACING PIGEON STANDARDS
Pigeon name: *Phoebe* Owner: *Larry McMurphy*

Categories Judged	Maximum Points	Points Awarded
Head, Eye, Expression	10	9.8
Balance and Size	30	29.4
Bone Structure	15	14.8
Back and Tail	15	14.7
Wings and Feathers	30	24.3
Total	100	93

As soon as Larry lets his birds go, he will head home. There his wife is waiting to note the arrival of Larry's first bird on their time clock. Not all the birds live precisely the same distance away from the release point, of course. The winner will be the bird with the highest average speed. No one will know the winner until the judges check the clocks.

I know Phoebe is nervous. She is racing against a veteran racer called Samson. I'm here to give Phoebe support.

This is it. The owners are letting their birds go! "Go, Phoebe! Head for home!" Let's keep our claws (or fingers) crossed for her. We will know who wins when we read the final results.

GRASS VALLEY PIGEON FANCIERS RACE RESULTS

Homing Pigeon*	Distance	Departure	Arrival	Flight Time	Average Speed
Blue Angel	250 miles	7:00 A.M.	1:15 P.M.	6 hr 15 min	40 mph
Pedro	245 miles	7:00 A.M.	12:00 P.M.	5 hr	49 mph
Phoebe	250 miles	7:00 A.M.	12:00 P.M.	5 hr	50 mph
Samson	260 miles	7:00 A.M.	12:30 P.M.	5 hr 30 min	47.3 mph
Sundance	255 miles	7:00 A.M.	12:15 P.M.	5 hr 15 min	48.6 mph

*Top racers listed alphabetically.

Checking Comprehension

1. What are three things you can tell about the narrator of this story? [Character/Inferential]

   Possible answers: The narrator is Beachcomber, a racing pigeon. He once flew races, but

   now is too old to race. He is named after a World War II messenger pigeon. He belongs to
   Larry McMurphy.   [Drawing Conclusions/Inferential]

2. What qualities mentioned in the story make Phoebe a prize homing pigeon?

   Phoebe won a prize for her appearance. She has excellent homing instincts.

Practicing Study Skills

Refer to the story and the tables to fill in the circle before the right answer
or answers.

3. The contest at the Westbrook County Fair judged racing pigeons on
   which of these qualities?

   ● balance and size   ● back and tail   ● bone structure   ○ intelligence

4. Which pigeon had the longest journey in the Grass Valley race?

   ○ Phoebe   ○ Blue Angel   ○ Pedro   ● Samson

5. Which birds are listed in the race results table?

   ○ all the pigeons in the race   ○ all of Larry McMurphy's pigeons

   ● the five top racers   ○ the pigeons that were favored to win

Write the answer on the line.

6. Who was the slowest pigeon of the five top finishers in the Grass Valley Pigeon
   Fanciers race? How can you tell?

   Blue Angel was the slowest. She had the lowest average speed.

7. Pedro and Phoebe both finished the race in 5 hours. How could you
   figure out which bird was faster without calculating the speeds?

   Since they finished in the same amount of time, you can compare the distances they traveled.

   The one who traveled the longest in the same amount of time went faster.

Use the table to compare the racing pigeons. Fill in the blanks to complete each sentence. Use names and data from the table and words of comparison such as *slower, faster,* and *fastest.*

9. Phoebe, who flew at an average speed of _____50_____ mph, was the _____fastest_____ pigeon in the race.

10. Sundance, who flew a distance of _____255_____ miles at an average speed of _____48.6_____ mph, was _____slower_____ than Phoebe but _____faster_____ than Blue Angel.

11. Phoebe was at home in her loft at _____12:00 P.M._____, half an hour before _____Samson_____ arrived home.

Practicing Vocabulary

Choose the word from the box that best matches each definition. Write the word on the line.

category
feisty
loft
precisely
support
transported
veteran

_____veteran_____ 12. one who has had much experience

_____transported_____ 13. carried from one place to another

_____loft_____ 14. an upper room or area

_____category_____ 15. division of a main group

_____feisty_____ 16. lively and energetic

_____precisely_____ 17. exactly

_____support_____ 18. the act of holding someone or something up

Writing a News Story
On another sheet of paper, write a news report of a real or imaginary sports event such as a game, race, or meet. You can refer to the sports section of a newspaper if you need ideas. Make a table that will help readers keep track of the players and their achievements in the event.

Using Graphs

A **graph** gives you information in the form of a picture. Three types of graphs are bar graphs, line graphs, and circle graphs. **Bar graphs** use vertical or horizontal bars to show groups of data. With a bar graph, it's easy to compare pieces of information. **Line graphs** connect data points with straight lines. Line graphs make it easy to see how information, such as temperature, changes over time. **Circle graphs** are useful for showing how parts of the data compare with the whole. Circle graphs are sometimes called pie graphs because they are divided into pie-shaped sections. The data is usually labeled. It is represented as percents or fractions.

As you read newspapers, magazines, and your textbooks, pay attention to the graphs you see. They will help you make comparisons quickly.

Read the story about a fifth-grader who wants to represent his class in the student council. Study the circle graph he made for his classmates.

Favorite Lunches

Meatball Subs 4%
Corn Dogs 4%
Sloppy Joes 12%
Burritos 16%
Chicken nuggets 24%
Pizza 40%

Monday was speech day for the students running for the student council. Marc decided to make a presentation that would really stand out. He questioned his classmates about an issue they cared about. Then he put the information together in a circle graph.

On Monday, Marc told his classmates, "I've asked each of you to tell me about changes you'd like to see at school. Many of you said that the lunch menu needs to be changed. I took a poll of your favorite lunches. This is the graph I made of the results. As class representative, I promise you that I will work to see that pizza and chicken nuggets are on the menu more often!"

Use the circle graph to answer the questions.

Why did Marc's campaign focus on pizza and chicken nuggets?

More than half of the students voted for pizza or chicken nuggets.

If he gets the votes of all those students, he'll win the election.

What percent of students chose burritos as their favorite lunch?

16%

Tip

When you read a circle graph, pay attention to the labels on the pie-shaped sections and the sizes of the sections. They will help you compare data.

Read the story about a fifth-grade class. Notice that the circle graph gives you information that is not in the story.

Fifth-Grade Free Time

"Good morning, class!" Mrs. Lee said. "Today we'll begin our fifth-grade class book. We'll be working with all the other fifth-grade classes to make a book that tells all about you as a group. It will include some photos of memorable things we did together, such as the class trip. We'll also include some data that we'll collect.

"Our first assignment," Mrs. Lee continued, "is to survey all of the fifth graders about their favorite free-time activities. We'll collect the data, then organize it and display it in a graph. Let's start by doing some brainstorming to come up with activities we'll ask about in our survey. What are your ideas?"

Kyle's hand shot up. When Mrs. Lee called on him, he blurted out, "Soccer!"

"What about basketball?" Brittany suggested.

"Baseball, too!" Juan said.

Mrs. Lee wrote the ideas on the board.

Angela raised her hand. "My favorite activity is reading," she said.

"I'm glad to hear it, Angela," Mrs. Lee said with a smile. "Who else has an idea?"

"I like to watch television," Larry remarked as other students nodded in agreement. Patrick said he liked to play with his pet snake. Mallory enjoyed getting together with her friends.

"Mrs. Lee," Taylor asked, "does collecting posters count?"

Favorite Free-Time Activities

Watching Television 6%
Other 4%
Collecting 8%
Reading 16%
Getting Together with Friends 16%
Playing Sports 50%

Mrs. Lee replied, "It certainly does." A hum of voices rose as students discussed other things they collected. Stuffed animals, stamps, and trading cards were popular collectibles.

"I hate to interrupt this interesting discussion, but we have a problem," Mrs. Lee said. "We'll have a terribly long list if we write each collection separately. What one name could we give this activity so we can include it in our survey?"

Marshall raised his hand. "Collecting," he suggested.

Soon the list was complete—but it was very long. The class discussed the merits of individual activities such as babysitting, which only one person enjoyed. They combined babysitting and other suggested activities enjoyed by only a single person under the label "Other."

The class got their list of activities ready. Then they prepared ballots for all the fifth graders to complete. When the ballots came back, Mrs. Lee's class put the data into a circle graph.

"What do you think?" Mrs. Lee asked as the class checked out the finished graph. "Is it a good picture of you?"

"No," said Patrick. "My snake ended up under 'other'!"

The class laughed. Most of them thought the graph did represent them accurately. Taylor said it best. "Mrs. Lee, it's better than a snapshot!"

Checking Comprehension

1. Why does Mrs. Lee want the students to discuss their favorite activities?   [Plot/Inferential]

   Possible answer: They are going to prepare a graph for the fifth-grade class book, and she

   wants her students to name their favorite free-time activities for a survey of fifth graders.

2. Why wasn't Patrick happy with the results of the survey? [Drawing Conclusions/Critical]

   Patrick was disappointed that his favorite free-time activity, playing with his pet snake, was

   represented on the survey as part of "other" activities.

Practicing Study Skills

Fill in the circle next to the correct answer.

3. Which free-time activity was most popular among the fifth-graders
   surveyed?
   - ● playing sports
   - ○ reading
   - ○ watching television
   - ○ getting together with friends

4. What percent of students listed collecting as their favorite free-time
   activity?
   - ● 8 %
   - ○ 40 %
   - ○ 6 %
   - ○ 100 %

Write the answer on the lines.

5. Does the circle graph tell how many students were surveyed? Explain.

   No, the circle graph does not tell the number of students for each activity. It only

   gives percentages.

6. Which two activities did the fifth-graders enjoy equally?

   Reading and getting together with friends

7. What percent of students listed watching television as their favorite
   free-time activity? 6%

8. What percent of students enjoyed activities that didn't fit into the
   major categories? 4%

9. What do the percentages add up to? What does this figure represent?

The percentages add up to 100%. This represents the total number of students who answered the survey.

Fill in the circle next to the answer that best completes the sentences.

10. Playing sports was as popular as:

○ reading and getting together with friends combined.

○ collecting, watching television, and "other" activities combined.

● the five remaining activities combined.

○ reading and collecting combined.

Practicing Vocabulary

Choose the word from the box that best completes each analogy. Write the word on the line.

blurted
brainstorming
collectibles
individual
interrupt
memorable
merits

11. *go* is to *stop* as *continue* is to _____interrupt_____

12. *values* is to *qualities* as *worth* is to _____merits_____

13. *apple* is to *fruit* as *stamps* is to _____collectibles_____

14. *idea* is to *thinking* as *inspiration* is to _____brainstorming_____

15. *sad* is to *happy* as *forgettable* is to _____memorable_____

16. *many* is to *one* as *group* is to _____individual_____

17. *told* is to *shouted* as *said* is to _____blurted_____

Writing a Descriptive Paragraph
On a separate sheet of paper, write a paragraph describing your favorite free-time activity. Then compare your favorite activity with that of your classmates. Working in a group or with a partner, make a circle graph that lists the class's favorite activities. Group activities together as Mrs. Lee's class did.

Using a Dictionary

A **dictionary** can help you find out what a word means, how to spell and pronounce it, and how to use the word. The words listed in a dictionary are called **entry words.** They appear in alphabetical order. **Guide words** at the top of the page tell you the first and last words that appear on the page. Following the entry word is the **pronunciation,** or way to say the word. You can use the syllable breaks in the entry word along with the pronunciation key to help you pronounce the word. Usually the word's **part of speech,** such as *noun* or *verb,* appears. You will also find one or more **definitions** and sometimes **example sentences** that show how the word is used.

Read this dictionary entry for the word *residence.*

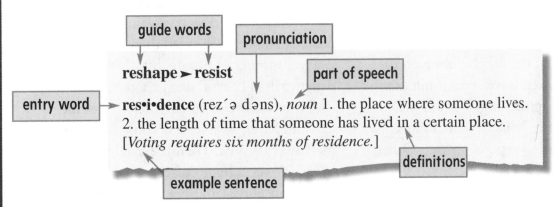

guide words

pronunciation

part of speech

entry word

reshape ➤ resist

res•i•dence (rez´ə dəns), *noun* 1. the place where someone lives. 2. the length of time that someone has lived in a certain place. [*Voting requires six months of residence.*]

definitions

example sentence

Use the dictionary entry for the word *residence* to answer these questions.

1. Which definition of *residence* is used in this sentence? "Buckingham Palace is the official residence of the queen of England when she is in London."

   Definition 1: the place where someone lives.

2. Would the word *restless* appear on the same dictionary page as *residence?* Explain your answer.

   No, because *restless* comes after *resist,* the last word on

   the page.

Tip

A dictionary helps you to understand the meaning, spelling, pronunciation, and part of speech of a word. Pay attention to entry words and guide words and the word's pronunciation, definition, and part of speech.

On Your Own

Read the article about a family's tour of a royal residence that was also one of England's most famous prisons.

TOURING THE TOWER

Kevin's heart beat a little faster as his family drove over the Tower Bridge toward the famous Tower of London. Kevin, his sister Jessie, and his parents were in London for a vacation. They were crossing the Thames River. Kevin knew that the bridge would open up only if a large ship needed to pass under it. The likelihood of the bridge dumping them in the river was exceedingly small. Still, he was glad when they were back on land.

Jessie had read all about the historic Tower of London. She knew that the first building on the site was the White Tower. It had been built as a fort in 1078 by the English king William the Conqueror. Later, King Richard I had a moat dug around the tower to keep people out. Other kings added smaller towers. They created a neighborhood surrounded by a high stone wall. All the towers together are called the Tower of London.

After parking, the family walked over a bridge that once crossed the moat. Kevin hurried into the interior area to get a closer look at the Beefeaters, or guards. They were wearing blue uniforms and big hats and carrying spears called pikes. Kevin pointed out one of the famed ravens that lived in the Tower. Legend has it that if the ravens ever left, the Tower would fall down.

Next on the tour was the Bell Tower. Jessie told them that long ago it had been a prison. "One prisoner was Princess Elizabeth," she explained. "She was locked up by her half sister, Princess Mary, to keep Elizabeth from becoming queen. In time, Elizabeth I did become queen—and she locked her enemies in the Tower, too!"

Jessie was surprised by the Queen's House. The other buildings were made of stone or brick, but the Queen's House was wooden. A guide told them it was the only wooden structure still standing after the Great Fire of London in 1666. The Tower's stone walls kept the flames from reaching it.

Then the family crossed the grassy area called the Tower Green. A sign explained that several people had been beheaded there, including Anne Boleyn, mother of Elizabeth I. Both mother and daughter had been Tower prisoners.

Next was the Traitor's Gate. It faces the Thames River, so prisoners could be brought to the Tower by boat. Then Jessie led them to the White Tower, a huge palace where kings and queens once lived and made laws. This was also where they would entertain.

As they walked back to their car, Kevin pointed out that they had not seen everything there was to see. "We will return!" he promised the great stone towers.

Checking Comprehension

Write the answer to each question on the lines.

1. Explain why the name "Tower of London" actually describes more than one tower. [Summarizing/Inferential]

   <u>William the Conqueror built one large tower meant to be a fort. When other kings built</u>

   <u>smaller towers, the entire group of towers was still called the Tower of London.</u>

2. Every year, two to three million visitors visit the Tower of London. Why do you think the Tower attracts so many visitors? [Drawing Conclusions/Critical]

   <u>Possible answer: People are fascinated by the history of the royalty who lived there and were</u>

   <u>imprisoned there.</u>

Practicing Study Skills

Read the following dictionary entry. Then answer the questions.

> **strong ► studio**
>
> **struc•ture** (struk´chər) *noun* **1.** something that is built, such as a house or bridge. **2.** the arrangement of parts that make up a thing. [*What is the structure of that sentence?*] **3.** a thing made from parts arranged in a particular way. [*A car engine is a complex structure.*] **4.** the way something is built. [*The structure of the tower is strong.*] *verb* to make into a structure. [*How did you structure that model airplane?*]

3. What part or parts of speech can *structure* have? Explain your answer.

   <u>*Structure* is both a noun and a verb. Definitions 1 through 4 follow the part of speech *noun*.</u>

   <u>The last definition follows the part of speech *verb*.</u>

4. Find *structure* in the article. Which definition was used?

   <u>Definition #1 as a noun</u>

On the line provided, identify the definition of *structure* that is used in the sentence. Include the part of speech in your answer.

5. I'm going to *structure* this science project so that it won't fall apart.

the definition for *structure* as a verb

Look back at the entry words on page 145. Fill in the circles before all the words that answer the question.

6. Which of the following words might appear on the same dictionary page as *structure*?

   ○ star   ○ striped   ● struggle   ● strum

Practicing Vocabulary

Choose the word from the box that best replaces the underlined word or words in each sentence. Write the word on the line.

conqueror
entertain
exceedingly
historic
likelihood
neighborhood
prisoners

entertain
7. The clown did tricks to <u>hold the attention of</u> the children.

exceedingly
8. My piece of cake was <u>extremely</u> small.

neighborhood
9. Do you live in this <u>part of town</u>?

likelihood
10. What is the <u>chance</u> of seeing your brother here?

prisoners
11. The <u>captives</u> were locked in the tower.

historic
12. This is a <u>famous old</u> monument.

conqueror
13. The <u>invader who gained the rule</u> of England had a large army.

Writing a Dictionary Page
On another sheet of paper, create a dictionary page using five of the vocabulary words from "Touring the Tower." Include guide words, entry words, syllable breaks, parts of speech labels, definitions, and sample sentences. Use a dictionary to help you.

Using an Encyclopedia

One reference book you may use often is the **encyclopedia.** This book or set of books contains articles about different topics. Each volume has a number and one or more letters on the spine. To find an article or **entry,** use the volume with the letter that begins your subject name. To use an on-line or CD-ROM encyclopedia, type the name of the subject into a search box.

To look up a subject in a print encyclopedia, use the **guide words** at the top of the page. Guide words name the first and last entries on the left-hand and right-hand page. Long articles often have **section headings.** They are subtopics of the main article. At the end of many articles, you will find **cross-references.** In a print encyclopedia, these are indicated by the words *See* or *See also.* In an on-line or CD-ROM encyclopedia, they are shown as links. Cross-references direct you to other articles about the subject.

Read this brief part of an encyclopedia article. Notice the section heading and the listing of cross-references.

guide words ─ **Olympic Games**

entry word ─ **Olympic Games** are an international athletic competition held every two years in a different country, in which athletes from around the world compete in different sports. History records that the Olympic Games started in Greece around 776 B.C. The games ended in A.D. 394.

section heading ─ **The Modern Olympics**

cross-references ─ French educator Pierre de Coubertin (1863–1937) revived the Olympic Games. In 1896, thirteen countries competed in Greece in the first modern games. Since then, the games have been held throughout the world. *See also* **de Coubertin, Pierre; Winter Olympic Games.**

Write your answers to the questions on the lines.

Which cross-reference is to a person?

<u>de Coubertin, Pierre</u>

How does the section "The Modern Olympics" relate to the main article?

<u>This section is a subtopic of the main article.</u>

Tip

Use the special features of an encyclopedia to learn more about a topic. In a long article, section headings help you find the facts you want. Cross-references point to other topics that you might want to research.

On Your Own

Read this encyclopedia article about the Special Olympics. Pay attention to the section headings and cross-references.

Special Olympics is an international program of athletic training and competition for people with mental retardation.

History

Eunice Kennedy Shriver, a sister of President John F. Kennedy, founded the Special Olympics after working with mentally handicapped people. The Special Olympics held its first games in Chicago, Illinois, in 1968. These games were based on the oath, "Let me win. But if I cannot win, let me be brave in the attempt." Athletes from Canada and France joined Americans in the first games.

Special Olympics Today

Today, Special Olympics programs can be found in 150 countries. In the United States alone, 25,000 communities take part in these programs. Special Olympics is modeled after the Olympic Games, but the competitions are held year-round. Over 20 events are held. They include gymnastics, bicycling, skiing, soccer, track and field, aquatics, and bowling. Not every sport in the Olympic games is played in Special Olympics. For instance, there is no triathlon, the Olympic event that includes swimming, bicycling, and running.

Special Olympics One "Special Olympian"

Loretta Claiborne is an outstanding example of a "Special Olympian." Claiborne was born in York, Pennsylvania, in 1953. In spite of being physically and mentally challenged, she excelled at running.

Claiborne first took part in Special Olympics in 1970. Since then, she has completed more than 25 marathons. The marathon, a 26-mile race, puts many demands on athletes. In 1988 she was named Special Olympics Female Athlete of the Year. In 1996, Loretta Claiborne received the Arthur Ashe Award for Courage. "I would like to break the trophy into a million pieces," Claiborne said, "in order to share the award with the one million Special Olympics athletes around the world." *See also* **Shriver, Eunice Kennedy; Mental Retardation; Olympic Games.**

Loretta Claiborne

Checking Comprehension

1. Why was the Special Olympics program created? [Cause and Effect/Inferential]

   Special Olympics was created to provide a chance for mentally handicapped people to take

   part in sports.

2. In what ways do you think Special Olympics helps the athletes who
   take part? [Drawing Conclusions/Critical]

   Possible answer: The athletes get training, exercise, and the chance to compete. They get to

   meet new people from all over the world.

Practicing Study Skills

3. List the section headings that are given in the article.

   History, Special Olympics Today, and One "Special Olympian"

4. List the cross-references that are given in the article.

   Shriver, Eunice Kennedy; Mental Retardation; Olympic Games

Fill in the circle next to the correct answer.

5. Which section heading would you look under to find out what some of
   the events in Special Olympics are?
   ○ Olympic Games   ● Special Olympics Today   ○ History   ○ One "Special Olympian"

6. Which of these tells you where to look in the article to find out when
   the first Special Olympics were held?
   ● a section heading   ○ the title of the article   ○ a cross-reference   ○ under *See also*

Write your answer on the line.

7. Under which section heading would you find out about Loretta Claiborne?

   One "Special Olympian"

8. What cross-reference would tell you about the founder of Special Olympics?

   Shriver, Eunice Kennedy

Fill in the blank with the name of the cross-reference that answers the question.

9. What cross-reference can you look up to find out more about resources for mentally challenged people?

Mental Retardation

10. What cross-reference can you look up to find out more about Olympic events?

Olympic Games

Practicing Vocabulary

Choose the word from the box that best completes each sentence. Write it on the line.

bicycling
excelled
handicapped
marathon
oath
physically
triathlon

11. Mentally _____handicapped_____ people enjoy the challenge of the Special Olympics.

12. A 26-mile run is called a _____marathon_____ .

13. An Olympic event that involves three different sports is called a _____triathlon_____ .

14. The woman who won the race was very _____physically_____ fit.

15. In their _____oath_____ , participants promise to compete bravely.

16. Swimming, _____bicycling_____ , and running make up the three sports in a triathlon.

17. The runner won the race because she _____excelled_____ at the sport.

Writing a Summary

Choose a sport to research in a print encyclopedia or an on-line or CD-ROM encyclopedia. Read the article. Use section headings to help you take notes. Use cross-references to find and read additional information on the sport. On a separate sheet of paper, write a summary of the information you learned.

Using a Library Card Catalog/ the Internet

Every library has a system that organizes materials, such as books and magazines, so that you can find what you need. You probably have used a **card catalog** before. Some libraries have a print card catalog. This is a set of drawers containing cards listing library books. There are three sets of alphabetized cards: author, title, and subject cards.

Author cards give you the author's name first. **Title** cards give you the book's title first. **Subject** cards list each nonfiction book by its subject. They give you the subject of the book first. They also list **cross-references** to other subjects you might want to look up. The word *See* in a cross-reference means you must go to other cards to find out about the subject. *See also* means you might find out more about the subject from books listed under the other subject cards.

SUBJECT CARD	AUTHOR CARD	TITLE CARD
929.1 GENEALOGY P365 Pressman, Lillian. How to Shake the Family Tree; tips and strategies for investigating your family history. Drawings by Kate Rios. New York, Windsong Books, 1999 451 p. illus. See also: family history	929.1 P365 Pressman, Lillian. How to Shake the Family Tree; tips and strategies for investigating your family history. Drawings by Kate Rios. New York, Windsong Books, 1999 451 p. illus.	929.1 How to Shake the Family Tree P365 Pressman, Lillian. How to Shake the Family Tree; tips and strategies for investigating your family history. Drawings by Kate Rios. New York, Windsong Books, 1999 451 p. illus.

Use information on the subject, author, and title cards to answer these questions.

1. If you wanted to find another book by Lillian Pressman, under what words would you look? Which set of cards would you use in a print card catalog?

   Pressman, Lillian; author cards

2. Look at the subject card. What do the words *See also: family history* mean?

   The words are a cross-reference. They mean that you might also want to look

   under "family history" for more information.

In many libraries the catalog is on a computer. First, you decide if you want to search for a book by the author's name, the subject of the book, or a title. Then you type in your selection and look at your choices.

Whether you use a print or computer card catalog, you will always need to know a **call number** for all nonfiction books. This number is made up of numbers and letters. It appears in the upper left-hand corner of each print catalog card or within the computer entry.

Library call numbers are part of the **Dewey Decimal System.** This system classifies nonfiction books in groups shown on the chart. A similar chart will be available in the library.

Dewey Decimal System	
000–099	General Reference Works
100–199	Philosophy
200–299	Religion and Mythology
300–399	Social Sciences
400–499	Language
500–599	Pure Science
600–699	Technology
700–799	The Arts
800–899	Literature
900–999	General Geography and History

It's easy to get from the card catalog to the book you want. If the book is fiction, the card or computer database will show an **F** or **Fic.** Books of fiction are arranged on the library shelves alphabetically by the author's name. If the book is nonfiction, you use the call number to find it on the numbered shelves. When you match up the call number you are looking for with the number on the book's spine—you've got your book!

Write *author, subject,* or *title* to tell where you would look for each book in the card catalog. Then use the Dewey Decimal System chart to tell between which two numbers the book's call number would be found.

What You Need	Where to Look	Call Number Section
book about Egypt's Nile River	subject	900–999
book called *Jazz and Blues: America's Music*	title	700–799

Some of the information you need can be found rapidly on the **Internet.** With a search engine, you can find encyclopedia and magazine articles or entire Websites about a subject. Some search engines are meant especially for students and young people.

To put a search engine to work, you describe what sort of information you need by typing in a **keyword** or keywords. The search engine finds articles and Websites that contain that word. Be specific. If your keyword is too broad, you'll end up with more listings than you need. Many of them will not be on your subject.

For example, imagine that you are writing a report on how the people of Gettysburg, Pennsylvania, viewed the Civil War battle fought there. If you typed in *Civil War,* you would get thousands of listings. You could make your search clearer by typing "*Battle of Gettysburg.*" Putting quotation marks around a phrase such as "Battle of Gettysburg" can help to refine a search. You can also find more specific information by entering more than one keyword, such as *Gettysburg* and *civilians.* Then only information with both those words will be listed.

Read the following paragraph about a girl who is interested in finding out more about her ancestors. Think about keywords you could enter in a search engine to find more information on the subject.

Sara knew her ancestors had traveled the Oregon Trail as pioneers. They left a prosperous dry goods business in Iowa in 1855 to join a wagon train west. Sara knew a little about the great-great-great-grandparents who made the brave journey. She knew, for instance, that her great-great-grandmother had been born along the trail. After she studied the Oregon Trail in school, she couldn't wait to start finding out more about what her ancestors' life on the trail was like. She sat down at her computer and logged onto the Internet.

7. Fill in the circle for the keyword or keywords that will give Sara the most specific information.

  ○ Oregon Trail

  ○ Oregon Trail history

  ● Oregon Trail pioneers

  ○ Ancestors

Tip

Cross-references in a card catalog are indicated by the words *See* or *See also.* Cross-references can help you find additional information about a related topic.

On Your Own

Read the following story about a young baseball player. Think about how he uses a library's on-line catalog to satisfy his curiosity.

J.R.'S DREAM

J. R. Williams had just played a great game of baseball. The Hornets player had hit a home run. Jackie Robinson Williams, known as J. R., hoped to become as famous as the player for whom he was named. He wanted to play as well as Jackie Robinson, the first African American to play baseball in the major leagues.

As a joke, J. R. once convinced his friends that Robinson was his great-grandfather. His parents had told him that they weren't really related to the baseball hero, but J.R. thought he noticed some similarities.

"Mom!" J. R. called. "Are we sure we aren't related to Jackie Robinson?"

Mrs. Williams smiled. "Not that I know of, J. R. We admired him, so we made you his namesake."

J. R. felt disappointed. Then he looked at his hands, and excitement surged again. He'd seen photos showing Jackie's hands grasping a bat. They looked a lot like his own!

Rather than spending Saturday at the ballfield, J. R. headed for the library. If Robinson was a relative, he'd find out! He went to the children's room. A sign on the card catalog said that it held only subject cards. The sign said to use the on-line catalog for author and title searches.

J.R. decided to start with the on-line catalog. He sat down at the computer and pressed a key to bring up the menu. For his search he selected AUTHOR and typed in *Robinson, Jackie*. "Maybe he wrote a book about himself," he thought.

"Yes!" J. R. exclaimed as his search results were returned. The library, indeed, had a copy of *Breakthrough to the Big League* by Jackie Robinson and Alfred Duckett.

Next J.R. went to the card catalog. Under the subject of *Robinson, Jackie,* J.R. found over a dozen books. "Wow!" J. R. thought while copying call numbers. At the bottom of one subject card, he spied the words: "*See also:* Robinson, Sharon. *Stealing Home: A Family Portrait by the Daughter of Jackie Robinson.*" J.R. wrote that call number down, too. He retrieved both autobiographies from the shelves.

J. R. spent the weekend in his room, only coming out for meals. On Sunday night he came downstairs just before bedtime. He stated, "I hate to disappoint you, but we are not related to Jackie Robinson."

"You don't say," said J. R.'s father. "How did you figure that out?"

"Jackie had three kids, but none came within miles of our family. Hey, did you know Robinson got a Medal of Freedom for his civil rights work?"

"I did know that," his father said. "It's one of the things that makes him such a fine hero."

"Jackie Robinson made it to the Baseball Hall of Fame," J. R. said thoughtfully. "I think I can do that too, if I try as hard as he did."

"That's a great goal," his mother said. "How about starting by getting a good night's sleep?"

"OK," J.R. said. "Then I can really make the Hall of Fame—in my dreams!"

Checking Comprehension

[Drawing Conclusions/Inferential]

1. What makes J. R. Williams suspect he is related to Jackie Robinson?

   Possible answers include: He has the same name. He sees physical similarities. He thinks he

   may have inherited Robinson's athletic abilities.

2. As you read the story, did you think that J. R. would turn out to be
   related to Robinson? Why or why not? [Predicting Outcomes/Critical]

   Most students will likely predict that J. R. was not related to Robinson. Possible reasons: He

   was a daydreamer; his mother said there was no evidence of a relationship.

Practicing Study Skills

Read each question. Fill in the circle next to the best answer.

3. Under what letter did J. R. look to find a book written by Jackie Robinson?

   ○ J for Jackie   ● R for Robinson   ○ B for Baseball   ○ W for Williams

4. Which other subject category would have led J. R. to some information
   on Robinson?

   ● Baseball, history of   ○ Genealogy

   ○ Little League   ○ America, history of

5. The *See also* reference led J. R. to what information?

   ○ a book by Alfred Duckett

   ○ a book written by Jackie Robinson

   ○ proof that he was related to Jackie Robinson

   ● a book written by Robinson's daughter

Circle the correct answer.

6. Think about how J. R. might use the Internet for his research. Circle the
   most specific keyword or keywords he could use to begin his search.

   baseball   baseball players   sports   (Jackie Robinson)

7. Look back at the chart on page 152. In what group of books would you find *Stealing Home,* call number 796.375R?

The Arts

Practicing Vocabulary

Fill in the circle next to the word or words that mean the same as the underlined word.

admired
autobiographies
grasping
menu
namesake
related
spied

8. J. R. had a picture of his hero grasping a bat.

○ throwing   ○ hitting

● holding tightly on to   ○ practicing with

9. J. R. learned that he and Jackie Robinson were not related.

○ interested in sports   ○ part of a club

○ athletic   ● part of the same family

10. Many famous people write autobiographies.

○ books written by others   ● books about their own lives

○ sports stories   ○ short notes

11. J. R. spied a book about his hero on a top shelf.

● glimpsed   ○ took   ○ missed   ○ couldn't reach

12. The computer's menu included SUBJECT, AUTHOR, and TITLE.

○ terminal   ● main list of choices   ○ subject card   ○ on/off switch

13. If you are Robert Wilson III, you must be someone's namesake.

○ twin   ● person named for another   ○ cousin   ○ ancestor

14. After doing research, J. R. admired Robinson more than ever.

● looked up to   ○ wrote about   ○ chased   ○ researched

MAKING THE
Reading
AND
Writing
CONNECTION

Writing Nonfiction
Use a library or the Internet to find information about the time or place when your grandparents grew up. On another piece of paper, write a nonfiction passage showing what you learned. Include your source or sources.

Level E Glossary

absences (ab′ səns əz) *noun* occasions of being away

accessible (ak ses′ ə bəl) *adjective* easy to reach

achievement (ə chēv′ mənt) *noun* something achieved by skill, work, or courage

acoustic (ə kōōs′ tik) *adjective* referring to a musical instrument that is not electronically amplified

acquired (ə kwīrd′) *verb* became the owner of

adapted (ə dapt′ əd) *verb* changed to fit new conditions

admired (ad mīrd′) *verb* had much respect for

adopt (ə däpt′) *verb* to take and use as one's own

afford (ə fôrd′) *verb* to have money enough to spare for

afternoon (af tər nōōn′) *noun* the time of day from noon to evening

afterward (af′ tər wərd) *adverb* at a later time

aligned (ə līnd′) *verb* arranged in a straight line or other pattern

amplify (am′ plə fī) *verb* to make larger, stronger, or louder

anchors (aŋ′ kərz) *verb* attaches firmly; fastens

annual (an′ yōō əl) *adjective* happening once a year

ascend (ə send′) *verb* to go up; move upward; climb

atmosphere (at′ məs fir) *noun* the gases around any planet

attended (ə tend′ əd) *verb* was present at

attractions (ə trak′ shənz) *noun* things that attract

autobiographies (ôt′ ō bī ä′ grə fēz or ät′ ō bī ä′ grə fēz) *noun* stories of a person's life written by that person

bafflement (baf′ əl mənt) *noun* confusion that keeps one from understanding or solving

behold (bē hōld′) *verb* look at; see

benefit (ben′ ə fət) *noun* help; advantage

bicycling (bī′ si kliŋ) *noun* the sport of riding bicycles

blared (blerd) *verb* sounded out with loud, harsh tones

blur (blʉr) *noun* something that is not clear

blurted (blʉrt′ əd) *verb* said suddenly or without thinking

brainstorming (brān′ stôr miŋ) *verb* solving problems or gathering information by thinking and discussing

broaden (brôd′ n) *verb* to make or become broad or broader

cartoonist (kär tōōn′ ist) *noun* a person who draws cartoons

category (kat′ ə gor′ ē) *noun* a division of a main subject or group; class

children (chil′ drən) *noun* young boys and girls

clawing (klô′ iŋ or klä′ iŋ) *verb* scratching, pulling, digging, or tearing with claws or as if with claws

clenched (klencht) *verb* closed or pressed tightly together

coincidence (kō in′ si dəns) *noun* the happening of two or more events that seem to be connected but are not

collectibles (kə lek′ tə bəlz) *noun* objects suitable for a collection

collision (kə lizh′ ən) *noun* the act of coming together with force; a crash

complicated (käm′ pli kāt′ əd) *adjective* hard to solve, understand, or do

conducted (kən dukt′ əd) *verb* managed; directed

confronted (kən frunt′ əd) *verb* faced; stood up against

congratulate (kən grach′ ə lāt or kən graj′ ə lāt) *verb* to express happiness to another

conqueror (kän′ kər ər) *noun* a person, group, or nation that conquers or defeats another

consumers (kən sōō′ mərz) *noun* people who buy products or services for their own use and not for resale

contemplate (kän′ təm plāt) *verb* to look at or think about for a long time

contraption (kən trap′ shən) *noun* a device or gadget

crease (krēs) *noun* a line or ridge that is made by folding

cycle (sī′ kəl) *noun* a complete set of events that keep coming back in the same order

dazzled (daz′ əld) *verb* overcame, amazed, or impressed with something brilliant or showy

decision (de sizh′ ən) *noun* the act or result of deciding

delicate (del′ ə kət) *adjective* pleasing in being fine or soft

deteriorate (di tir′ ē ə rāt′) *verb* to make or become worse

devised (dē vīzd′) *verb* planned or invented something

dictate (dik′ tāt) *verb* to command or order

disappearance (dis ə pir′ əns) *noun* the act or fact of no longer being seen or existing

discharged (dis chärjd′) *verb* fulfilled; performed

disentangle (dis′ en taŋ′ gəl) *verb* to free or become free from being tangled; untangle

distinguished (di stiŋ′ gwisht) *verb* was the difference in

districts (dis′ trikts) *noun* parts into which an area, such as a city, is divided

downward (doun′ wərd) *adverb* from a higher to a lower place or position

drabbest (drab′ əst) *adjective* the least bright or cheerful

E **effortless** (ef′ ərt ləs) *adjective* using or seeming to use very little effort

electrify (ē lek′ trə fī) *verb* to charge with electricity

elegant (el′ ə gənt) *adjective* rich-looking and attractive in a dignified or refined way

energetic (en′ ər jet′ ik) *adjective* full of energy; active

enormity (ē nôr′ mi tē) *noun* greatness; importance

entertain (ent ər tān′) *verb* to have as a guest; be a host to

erupting (ē rupt′ iŋ) *adjective* bursting forth violently

exaggerate (eg zaj′ ər āt) *verb* to make something seem larger or greater than it really is

exceedingly (ek sēd′ iŋ lē) *adverb* very; extremely

excelled (ek seld′) *verb* was better or greater than others

experimental (ek sper′ i ment′ l) *adjective* being an experiment; trial

expressed (eks prest′) *verb* put into words; stated

F **fad** (fad) *noun* a custom or style that many people become interested in for a short time

fairness (fer′ nəs) *noun* the quality of being just and honest

fascinating (fas′ i nāt′ iŋ) *adjective* holding the attention by being interesting or delightful

feisty (fī′ stē) *adjective* full of spirit and energy

flavorful (flā′ vər fəl) *adjective* tasty; delicious

frantically (fran′ tik lē) *adverb* in a way that is very excited with worry or fear

friends' (frendz) *adjective* belonging to more than one friend

futile (fyo͞ot′ l) *adjective* not capable of producing any result; useless

G **galloped** (gal′ əpt) *verb* went at the fastest gait of a horse

gnarled (närld) *adjective* having a twisted and knotty look

grasping (grasp′ iŋ) *verb* seizing firmly with the hand

guitar (gi tär′) *noun* a musical instrument, played by plucking the strings with a finger or pick

gullible (gul′ i bəl) *adjective* capable of being easily tricked

H **handicapped** (han′ dē kapt′) *adjective* having a physical or mental disability

haven (hā′ vən) *noun* a place where a person can be safe

historic (his tôr′ ik) *adjective* famous in history

hopefully (hōp′ fəl ē) *adverb* in a way that shows hope

hover (huv′ ər) *verb* to stay hanging in the air near one place

I **illusion** (i lo͞o′ zhən) *noun* something that fools the eye, the ear, or any of the other senses

inadequate (in ad′ ə kwət) *adjective* not enough or not good enough for what is needed

incline (in′ klīn) *noun* a sloping surface; a slope or slant

increasing (in krēs′ iŋ) *verb* making greater or larger

individual (in′ di vij′ o͞o əl) *adjective* existing as one separate being or thing

infinite (in′ fi nit) *adjective* having no limits; without beginning or end

infrequently (in frē′ kwent lē) *adverb* seldom; not often

interrupt (in tər upt′) *verb* to put a temporary stop to

K **kayak** (kī′ ak) *noun* a light canoe usually covered with canvas, with an opening for the person who paddles

L **labor** (lā′ bər) *noun* physical work

license (lī′ sens) *noun* a document showing that someone is permitted by law to do something

likelihood (lik′ lē ho͝od′) *noun* the fact of being likely to happen

loft (lôft) *noun* the space below the roof of a house or barn

M **mansion** (man′ shən) *noun* a very large, stately house

manufacturers (man′ yo͝o fak′ chər ərz) *noun* companies that make goods, especially in large amounts

marathon (mer′ ə thän) *noun* a race for runners covering a distance of 26 miles, 385 yards

marsupial (mär so͞o′ pē əl) *noun* an animal whose newly born young are carried by the female in a pouch

memorable (mem′ ər ə bəl) *adjective* worth remembering; not easy to forget

menu (men′ yo͞o) *noun* a list that shows the commands that a computer user can choose

merits (mer′ itz) *noun* good qualities

midair (mid′ er′) *noun* the middle of the air

midweek (mid′ wēk) *noun* the middle of the week

migrate (mī′ grāt) *verb* to move from one country or region to another when the season changes

misguided (mis gīd′ əd) *adjective* led into doing wrong

mistrust (mis trust′) *verb* to have no trust in; doubt

molten (mōl′ tən) *adjective* made liquid by heat

mother's (muth′ ərz) *adjective* of, belonging to, or having to do with a mother

motivational (mō tə vā′ shən əl) *adjective* encouraging

N **namesake** (nām′ sāk) *noun* a person who is named after another

neighborhood (nā′ bər hood) *noun* a small part or district of a city or town

nocturnal (näk tur′ nəl) *adjective* active at night

nudged (nujd) *verb* pushed or poked gently in order to get the attention of

nuisance (noo′ səns or nyoo′ səns) *noun* an act, thing, or person that causes trouble or bother

numerous (noo′ mər əs) *adjective* very many

nurture (nur′ chər) *verb* to bring up, care for, or train

O **oath** (ōth) *noun* a statement in which a person swears that he or she will speak the truth or keep a promise

offspring (ôf′ spriŋ) *noun* a person or animal's children

operated (äp′ ər āt əd) *verb* kept in action; ran; worked

opportunities (äp′ ər too′ ni tēz) *noun* times or occasions that are right for doing something; good chances

opposite (äp′ ə zit) *adjective* at the other end or side; directly facing or back to back

optical (äp′ ti kəl) *adjective* of the sense of sight; visual

original (ə rij′ i nəl) *adjective* first or earliest

overbearing (ō′ vər ber′ iŋ or ō′ vər bār′ iŋ) *adjective* inclined to dictate; forcing others to one's own will

overboard (ō′ vər bôrd) *adverb* too far because of enthusiasm

overeager (ō vər ē′ gər) *adjective* too anxious

overlooked (ō vər lookt′) *verb* failed to notice

P **panels** (pan′ əlz) *noun* flat sections or parts of something

panic (pan′ ik) *verb* to show a sudden, wild fear

participate (pär tis′ i pāt′) *verb* to take part in something with other people

pasture (pas′ chər) *noun* a piece of land where grass grows and where cattle and sheep can graze

patriotism (pā′ trē ə tiz′ əm) *noun* great love for one's country and loyalty to it

payment (pā′ mənt) *noun* the act of paying or the fact of being paid

peer (pir) *noun* a person or thing of the same rank; an equal

personality (pur′ sə nal′ i tē) *noun* all the special qualities that make a person different from other people

physically (fiz′ i klē) *adverb* of or with the body

pierced (pirst) *verb* passed into or through; penetrated

pleaded (plēd′ əd) *verb* asked in a serious way

pollute (pə loot′) *verb* to let out wastes or poisonous substances into the air, water, or land

ponder (pän′ dər) *verb* to think about carefully

popularity (päp′ yoo lər′ ə tē) *noun* the fact or condition of being well liked

postpone (pōst pōn′) *verb* to put off until later; to delay

postwar (pōst′ wôr′) *adjective* after a war

poverty (päv′ ər tē) *noun* the condition of being poor

precautions (prē kô′ shənz or prē kä′ shənz) *noun* actions taken ahead of time against danger or failure

precious (presh′ əs) *adjective* having a high price or value

precisely (prē sīs′ lē) *adverb* in an exact way; accurately

predict (prē dikt′) *verb* to tell what one thinks will happen in the future

preyed (prād) *verb* hunted other animals for food

prisoners (priz′ ən ərz) *noun* people who are kept locked up in a prison

privileged (priv′i ləjd) *adjective* having special advantages

products (präd′ ukts) *noun* things that are produced by nature or made by human beings

prolonged (prō loŋd′) *adjective* lasting a long time

promptly (prämpt′ lē) *adverb* quickly; without delay

prospect (prä′ spekt) *noun* something that is expected

protested (prō test′ id) *verb* spoke out against; objected to

public (pub′ lik) *noun* where all can see or hear; openly

publicity (pub lis′ i tē) *noun* information given or things done to bring something to public attention

R **readying** (red′ ē iŋ) *verb* preparing

reappear (rē ə pir′) *verb* to appear again

reassuringly (rē ə shoor′ iŋ lē) *adverb* in a way designed to remove someone's doubts and fears

recipe (res′ i pē) *noun* a list of ingredients and directions for making something to eat or drink

recited (rē sīt′ əd) *verb* said aloud from memory

recognized (rek′ əg nizd) *verb* identified

referees (ref ə rēz′) *noun* people who make sure that the rules are followed in certain sports and games

related (rē lāt′ əd) *adjective* of the same family or kind

renewable (rē noo′ ə bəl or rē nyoo′ ə bəl) *adjective* capable of being made new or fresh again; able to be restored

replayed (rē′ plād or rē plād′) *verb* played again

representative (rep′ rē zen′ tə tiv) *noun* a person who is chosen to act or speak for others

researchers (rē′ surch ərz or rē surch′ ərz) *noun* people who engage in study to find out about a subject

resonant (rez′ n ənt) *adjective* full; rich; vibrating

reveal (re vēl′) *verb* to show

rooftops (roof′ täps′) *noun* roofs of buildings

runaway (run′ ə wā) *noun* one who runs away

S **salespeople** (sālz′ pē pəl) *noun* people who sell goods or services

satisfying (sat′ is fi′ iŋ) *adjective* pleasing

savagely (sav′ ij le) *adverb* in a wild, untamed way

senseless (sens′ ləs) *adjective* having no meaning; foolish

shadowy (shad′ ō ē) *adjective* dark; unclear

shambles (sham′ bəlz) *noun* a place where there is great disorder and confusion

shimmered (shim′ ərd) *verb* shined with an unsteady light

shoulder (shōl′ dər) *noun* the part of the body to which an arm is connected

shrieking (shrēk′ iŋ) *verb* crying out with a loud, shrill sound

signaled (sig′ nəld) *verb* made known

silent (si′ lənt) *adjective* making no sound

singed (sinjd) *verb* burned a little on the surface

skillful (skil′ fəl) *adjective* having or showing ability that comes from training and practice

smudged (smujd) *adjective* streaked with dirt; smeared

solar (sō′ lər) *adjective* having to do with the sun

sparkling (spär′ kliŋ) *adjective* giving off flashes of light

species (spē′ shēz or spē′ sēz) *noun* a group of plants or animals that are alike in certain ways

spectators (spek′ tāt ərz) *noun* people who watch something without taking part

spied (spīd) *verb* caught sight of; saw

stalled (stôld) *verb* came to a stop without meaning to

stimulation (stim′ yoo lā′ shən) *noun* anything that causes activity or excitement

strand (strand) *noun* anything like a string or rope

strewn (stroon) *verb* covered with something scattered

stunned (stund) *verb* shocked in a great or deep way

styles (stīlz) *noun* sorts; kinds; types

subject (sub′ jekt) *noun* person or thing being discussed or examined

submit (sub mit′) *verb* to give or offer to others for them to look over or decide about

subsided (səb sīd′ əd) *verb* became less intense or active

successful (sək ses′ fəl) *adjective* turning out well

suitable (soot ′ə bəl) *adjective* right for the purpose

support (sə pôrt′) *noun* the act of holding up

surface (sur′ fəs) *noun* the outside of something

swiped (swīpt) *verb* hit with a hard, sweeping blow

T **technique** (tek nēk′) *noun* a special way of doing something

telescopes (tel′ ə skōps) *noun* devices to look through that make far-off objects seem closer and larger

terrified (ter′ i f id′) *adjective* very badly frightened

thumbnail (thum′ nāl) *noun* the nail of the thumb

tourists (toor′ ists) *noun* people who travel for pleasure

traditional (trə dish′ ə nəl) *adjective* having to do with or handed down by tradition

transfixed (trans fikst′) *verb* made or held motionless with amazement or terror

transported (trans pôrt′ əd) *verb* carried from one place to another

triathlon (trī ath′ län) *noun* an Olympic contest that includes three events

U **uncertainty** (un surt′ n tē) *noun* the condition of being doubtful or unsure

underground (un′ dər ground) *adjective* done in secret

unfold (un fōld′) *verb* to open and spread out something

unknown (un nōn′) *adjective* not explored or identified

V **valid** (val′ id) *adjective* based on facts or good reasoning; true or sound

vanished (van′ isht) *verb* stopped existing; came to an end

varied (ver′ ēd) *adjective* of different kinds

veteran (vet′ ər ən or ve′ trən) *noun* a person who has had long experience in some work or position

volumes (väl′ yoomz) *noun* books

volunteering (väl′ ən tir′ iŋ) *verb* doing or giving by choice

W **wandered** (wän′ dərd) *verb* went from place to place in an aimless way; rambled; roamed

wealthy (wel′ thē) *adjective* rich

weight (wāt) *noun* the measure of how heavy a thing is